REGULATION *in the* STATES

REGULATION *in the* STATES

Paul Teske

BROOKINGS INSTITUTION PRESS
Washington, D.C.

Copyright © 2004
THE BROOKINGS INSTITUTION
1775 Massachusetts Avenue, N.W., Washington, D.C. 20036
www.brookings.edu

Library of Congress Cataloging-in-Publication data

Teske, Paul Eric.
Regulation in the states / Paul Teske.
  p.   cm.
Includes bibliographical references and index.
ISBN 0-8157-8312-4 (cloth : alk. paper)—ISBN 0-8157-8313-2 (pbk. : alk. paper)
1. Trade regulation—United States—States. I. Title
KF1610.Z95.T37 2004   2003023967
343.73'08—dc22

9 8 7 6 5 4 3 2 1

The paper used in this publication meets minimum requirements of the American National Standard for Information Sciences—Permanence of Paper for Printed Library Materials: ANSI Z39.48-1992.

Typeset in Sabon

Composition by Stephen D. McDougal
Mechanicsville, Maryland

Contents

v

Acknowledgments

This book is a compilation and synthesis of research that I have done on state regulation over the past several years. The individual empirical chapters on specific industries or topics are all coauthored with former Stony Brook University political science doctoral students. I greatly appreciate the excellent work done by these scholars and by other scholars of state regulation around the country, upon whose work I draw frequently.

From start to finish, this project lasted many years, and there are many others I would like to thank. I received helpful comments from William Berry, Paul Brace, Dan Carpenter, William Gormley, Jennifer Hochshild, Chris Mooney, Ken Meier, Mark Steinmayer, Paul Quirk, and other, anonymous reviewers.

Mark Steinmayer of the Smith Richardson Foundation greatly assisted the completion of this work with a grant that enabled me to focus on state regulation, after various education research projects had kept this book on my "back burner." I appreciate that support. The U.S. National Science Foundation also supported the doctoral research of three of my former students who are coauthors of chapters in this book: Alka Sapat, Brian Gerber, and Colin Provost.

The political science department at Stony Brook, led by Mark Schneider, provided a supportive and collegial environment in which to work on this project, as well as superb doctoral students with whom to work.

I would also like to thank Brookings's acquisitions editor, Chris Kelaher, for showing interest in this book from the start, providing excellent advice, and following it through to completion. I appreciate the superb job Robin DuBlanc did copyediting a complicated manuscript.

REGULATION *in the* STATES

PART ONE

Introduction

R egulation of major industries at the state level has historically been important in the United States since the emergence of the industrial economy after the Civil War. In many industries state governments regulated before any such federal activity, and in a few major industries, such as insurance, states have retained sole regulatory authority. In the twentieth century, however, the general growth in federal government activity included increased regulation, giving the appearance that state regulation was being relegated to a smaller role. Further, the federal push toward deregulation in the last quarter of the twentieth century—including some explicit preemption of state regulatory authority—combined with a growing globalization wherein economic activity has increasingly been subjected to supranational regulatory authority, seemed to spell the eventual end of subnational regulation.

Surprisingly, however, since 1980 the state regulatory role has emerged as more robust than expected, solidifying and even expanding as part of a trend toward devolution of powers, in which some states have chosen not to phase out their regulatory powers but instead to counter federal deregulation and "de-enforcement" with their own "reenforcement" policies. And yet very little is known about how states actually regulate, especially the similarities and differences across industries, and what effect different state regulatory institutions have on policy outputs and industry economic outcomes.

Critics of state regulation have long been concerned about the "capture" of political decisionmaking by concentrated and powerful industries and about a collective "race to the bottom" of regulatory laxity based on the need for states to attract and retain firms for economic development, jobs, and tax purposes. On the other hand, proponents believe that states can be more efficient, flexible, and responsive regulators than can federal actors.

This book provides a foundation of research upon which to assess these competing claims. Its core is several new and sophisticated quantitative analyses of specific areas of state regulation. Prefacing these, however, are the three introductory chapters that make up part 1, which provide a cogent approach to the subject, an overview of the theoretical issues involved, and an explanation of the methodology and measurement techniques employed in the case studies. (The studies themselves are presented in a reader-friendly form, with the more technical details limited to chapter 3 and to endnotes for readers who wish to peruse that material more carefully.)

Each industry chapter is placed within a broader section related to the market failure that motivates its regulation in the first place. Each section employs a similar "template," including a brief discussion of the reason for regulation of these types of industries; a brief history of state regulation of these types of industries, including some others not tested in the quantitative studies; an explanation of the critical actors and factors within each industry; a multiple regression-type quantitative analysis of the economic, political, and bureaucratic factors that influence state regulatory policy and outcomes; and conclusions about state regulation of that industry and market failure type.

The case studies begin with the regulation of telecommunications (chapter 4) and electricity (chapter 5) in part 2. These industries have long been perceived as natural monopolies that required economic regulation of prices, entry, and service quality. In recent years, first in telecommunications, then in electricity, technological advances challenged the assumptions about natural monopolies and allowed for competition in at least some segments of these industries. The same issues were also relevant in past years for transportation regulation, but that area has largely been deregulated and federal politicians preempted any ongoing state role.

Part 3 addresses state regulation that is justified by asymmetric information. Here states play a role in monitoring business activity to protect consumers who hold limited information. This section presents studies of insurance solvency (chapter 6), savings and loan solvency (chapter 7), and hospital certificate-of-need regulation (chapter 8). While states regulate insurance with no federal regulation, regulation of the other industries has included a mix of federal and state involvement.

Part 4 examines occupational regulation, which theoretically is aimed at asymmetric information problems but in practice often has elements of economic regulation of entry. States regulate occupations with no federal role. The quantitative studies are of state regulation of lawyers (chapter 9) and medical doctors (chapter 10), two of the most prestigious and well-paid American professions.

Part 5 deals with environmental regulation, which is probably the most important form of regulation practiced in the United States today, particularly in terms of the costs that governments impose on private actors. Here states implement federal regulations, with varying degrees of discretion, depending on the type of environmental regulation. Chapter 11 is a study of states gaining EPA approval of their clean air implementation permitting plans, and chapter 12 investigates state groundwater protection regulation, an area in which states have considerable discretion about whether and how to regulate.

Finally, in part 6, all the evidence is pulled together in chapter 13 to draw conclusions about state regulatory policy. Based on these quantitative industry studies across the fifty states, it appears that capture is much less of a concern than many have feared. Instead, a range of interest groups participates in most state regulatory processes, leaving political and bureaucratic actors space to make some important decisions based on their own ideologies and analyses of problems. Some industry groups in some states do capture their regulators, but this is not the overwhelming pattern. Specifically, state legislatures and regulatory agencies are generally the most important influences over regulatory policy, operating in directions that correspond to theoretical expectations, such as Democratic legislatures being more pro-regulation or pro-consumer. While interest groups are important in regulatory battles in most industries, they only demonstrate strong capture over occupational regulation; all other areas seem fairly highly contested in a typical state.

Discussion is not, however, limited only to the results of these quantitative studies, all of which have some measurement or methodological limitations. As I read and studied the political and economic literature on state regulation, I developed ideas, opinions, and impressions that I also use to provide some new insights into other, related issues about state regulation. Throughout the book, and particularly in the conclusions, I assess: How does the regulatory relationship between federal and state governments work, and how is it changing? What influences state regulatory policy choices? What reforms have states tried and how are they working? What is the future role for state regulation in an increasingly global economy?

By understanding better how different institutions shape regulatory policy, we can evaluate executive, legislative, bureaucratic, and judicial reforms. Since most of the studies herein demonstrate legislative influence over policy, chapter 14 analyzes reforms related to legislative professionalism and oversight, including oversight before policy implementation, as practiced in some states with state administrative procedures acts and similar systems, and oversight during policy implementation, such as hearings and legislative reviews. Also examined is state executive oversight of regulation, as practiced by the New York Governor's Office of Regulatory Reform and in some other large states, agencies that are modeled partly after the regulatory arm of the federal Office of Management and Budget. The role of bureaucratic accountability structures is likewise relevant, in terms of elected or appointed commissioners, and the role of bureaucratic resources and professionalism. Given the growing judicialization of regulation, chapter 15 analyzes the role of state courts in reviewing regulation and the growing role of state attorneys general in taking a legalistic approach to regulating certain activities and industries.

Finally, in chapter 16 I provide insight into the ultimate—and probably ultimately unanswerable—question: Is state regulation good or bad? The highly subjective answer is almost surely that regulation of some industries in some states is performed very well, while in other industries or in other states, it is done quite poorly and could be greatly improved or should be eliminated entirely. Overall, since state regulation is captured less often by powerful interests than many casual observers believe, state regulators do a pretty good job when they have the resources to develop, implement, and enforce appropriate policies. Still, the processes of state regulation can be improved by attention to which approaches seem to work best.

CHAPTER ONE

State Regulatory Policy

Regulation is one of the most important areas of U.S. public policy. Though a small element in direct federal and state budget allocations—generally less than 1 percent—regulation has a significant influence on national and state economies. The states play a greater role in regulating the U.S. economy than most observers realize—their position has been critical for most of American history, but their role may be relatively more important now than ever. This is the first book to treat the subject of state regulation as a comprehensive whole.

Defined broadly, regulations are policy choices made by governments that limit the private behavior of citizens or businesses. Sometimes these regulations are general decisions that are captured in laws or statutes and thus are the direct products of legislatures and signed by governors. More often, they are more specific rules or implementation decisions that are made by bureaucratic officials, or "regulators." Most of the regulation analyzed in this book is aimed at businesses or regulates professionals in their business practices, rather than regulation that focuses more on the activities of individual citizens.

While markets are often trusted to achieve high levels of efficiency in allocating scarce resources in the United States, problems with monopolies, one-sided information in transactions, and third-party impacts when two parties trade can distort market outcomes and present a case for government regulation. When these "market failures" arise, they create at least a theoretical rationale for regulation, although it is not clear what level of government should regulate, how, or whether such regulation will be an improvement. Regulations meant to address problems with competition (monopolies and antitrust) are often called *economic regulation,* as they address the structure of competitive markets and prices within a particular industry. Regulations aimed at asymmetric information and third-party problems ("externalities") cut across many industries, are based more on the level of enforcement that takes place after enactment, and are often referred to collectively as *social regulation.*[1] The amounts and kinds of regulation in these two broad areas vary greatly, with significant implications for the role of state politics relative to the federal government.

Why Analyze State Regulation?

In assessing the scope of U.S. state regulatory activities in these market failure categories, consider several recent state actions. In the area of monopoly and competition, determined state attorneys general from nine states resisted a proposed U.S. Department of Justice settlement of the Microsoft antitrust case in 2002. The most important infrastructure industries of the twenty-first century—telecommunications and electricity—have been shaped by recent state regulatory decisions; in the early 1990s state utility regulators in New York developed a model for competitive local telecommunications interconnection that was largely incorporated into the 1996 federal Telecommunications Act for use across the nation. Half the states deregulated their electricity markets between 1996 and 2000 to reduce monopoly power, and some consumers, though not those in California, experienced enhanced competition and sometimes lower prices. In occupational regulation, New Mexico became the first state to allow psychologists to prescribe medication, which had formerly only been allowed by M.D. psychiatrists.

Asymmetric information problems are very visible in the wake of many Internet firm collapses and corporate accounting scandals. New York State attorney general Eliot Spitzer successfully sued Merrill Lynch in 2002 for $100 million over the lack of objective information provided by stock analysts, using a 1921 New York State law that predated the U.S. Securities and Exchange Commission (SEC). His action prompted further SEC,

1. The regulations discussed here are aimed primarily at businesses and professional activity. Not addressed are regulations aimed at individual behavior, such as gay rights, drunk driving regulations, smoking in public places, pornography, and so on, which some would also characterize as "social" regulations. I consider the focus on individual behavior to be the key difference.

New York Stock Exchange, and NASDAQ investigations. In another case dealing with information, seven state legislatures passed "do not call" laws against telemarketers in 2001, the popularity of which prompted the Bush administration's Federal Trade Commission (FTC) chair Timothy Muris to call for a national rule limiting telemarketing, a rule that came under controversial court review in 2003. Regarding the regulation of externalities, the California legislature passed an automobile emission law aimed at reducing greenhouse gasses (an approach Congress had rejected), which will likely force automobile manufacturers to alter the cars they sell across the United States, since California is by far their largest market. Clearly, in these recent examples (which only touch on the scope of state regulations), the states are actively addressing all important market failures.

While these kinds of state regulatory decisions are already shaping the twenty-first-century U.S. economy, this is far from a recent development. Twenty states had passed antitrust legislation before Congress passed the famous Sherman Antitrust Act in 1890. Trucking regulation began in the states in the 1910s, well before the federal government regulated through the Interstate Commerce Commission (ICC) in 1935. State corporate chartering was well established for decades before the federal government first played even a minor role in corporate governance, with the Securities Act of 1933. Texas initially won innovation awards for its 1962 decision to relax regulations over the investment choices of its savings and loans (S&Ls). Growing and unregulated intrastate airlines markets in California and Texas in the 1960s provided the data upon which advocates were able to successfully challenge federal airline price regulation in the 1970s. Florida deregulated economic regulation of its intrastate trucking industry in 1980, the same year in which the federal government deregulated interstate trucking, both great successes. In these cases the states clearly provided something of the natural experimental laboratory for policy, a role that was noted centuries ago by James Madison and later explicated further by Justice Brandeis.[2]

These activist, and often successful, state regulatory experiments are just a few of the available examples, many more of which are chronicled in this book. But one can also observe a far less positive side to state

2. In the case of *New York Ice Co.* v. *Liebman*, 285 U.S. 262, 311 (1926), Supreme Court Justice Brandeis wrote: "A single courageous state may, if its citizens choose, serve as a laboratory, and try social and economic experiments without risk to the rest of the country."

regulation. By the late 1980s nearly 50 percent of the national costs of the savings and loans crisis accrued in Texas, much of it due to risky and poor investments by state-chartered S&Ls. California, one of the first states to deregulate its electricity markets in 1996, faced a severe crisis of spiraling rates and rolling blackouts in 2000 and 2001. By 1994, fourteen years after the clearly demonstrated success of trucking deregulation, several states still regulated strictly; Texas continued to allow only six intrastate carriers to provide services, at a cost of over $1 billion to its state economy. Some twenty national firms no longer provide insurance coverage to automobile owners in New Jersey due to that state's onerous pricing and exit regulations.

These examples all demonstrate the importance of state regulation in the United States. Sometimes state regulation is extremely innovative and leads to great successes and positive changes for industry and consumers. Other times it leads to colossal failures. Perhaps most often, it leads to more subtle effects on state economies that are often overlooked by scholars and by all but the most directly involved players. Across all of these scenarios, state regulation is far less well understood than federal regulation, though it is no less important.

Despite some changes over time, in 2003 states retain their role as the only regulators of some business activities, such as corporate chartering, insurance, workers' compensation, and occupational licensing. States share some regulation with the federal government, usually along the intrastate-interstate geographic division, as in telecommunications and electricity, and with a few areas of transportation. States implement specific federal regulations and standards in areas like occupational safety and environmental regulation, where they sometimes have authority to go beyond federal standards, to try different implementation approaches to meet these standards, or to address problems not handled directly by federal legislation. States have some overlapping jurisdictions with the federal government in broad and discretionary enforcement areas like consumer regulation and regulation of advertising, and some aspects of financial regulation.

This book addresses the question: How does state regulation really work in the United States? What can we learn by looking across the entire spectrum of state regulation? Is it more of a quaint and relatively harmless anachronism from the nineteenth century, like the early New England and Granger farm state railroad regulatory boards, that ultimately will fade away in the face of international trade agreements from the WTO, NAFTA, and the EU that aim to standardize national regulatory policies? Is most state regulation really captured by a few powerful local interests that hold sway in sleepy state capitals over part-time legislators who have no resources to fight them—even if so inclined—and with few countervailing interest groups to provide much opposition? Does such captured state regulation spread across the states, as they compete for firms and jobs, in an inevitable "race to the bottom" (a phrase that Donahue [1997, p. 66] ascribes to Louis Brandeis in 1933) of regulatory laxity? Or is state regulation a booming area of devolved powers in the federalist system such as conservatives often hail as helping to finally regain the states' position as a full partner with a central government that has become an overly aggressive regulator? And why are some liberals, normally skeptical of "states' rights" claims from earlier eras, recently using and praising state regulation as filling a missing regulatory enforcement gap in the face of federal retrenchment?

In the aggregate, state regulation is all of these things—and vitally important besides. By regulating significant portions of the telecommunications, electricity, insurance, and health industries, as well as occupations and several aspects of environmental pollution, the states collectively play a critical role in the U.S. economy. Nearly 20 percent of the American economy is directly regulated by the states.[3] Within occupational licensing alone, Kleiner (2000) demonstrates that at least one state licenses more than eight hundred occupations and that 18 percent of U.S. workers are in a regulated occupation. About one-third of state agencies mainly address the kinds of regulatory issues analyzed here.[4] Another indication of its importance comes from a January 2003 review of "Ten Issues to Watch"

3. This rough estimate is derived from the NAIC (formerly SIC) codes of the American economy prepared by the Bureau of Labor Statistics. The estimate assumes that one-half of SIC codes 48 and 49 (communications and electricity) are under state regulatory jurisdiction, that all of SIC 63 and 64 (insurance carriers and agents) are under state regulation, and that legal services (81) and one-half of health services (80) are under state regulatory jurisdiction. This yields a figure of over 10 percent, whether based on sales revenues or payrolls generated. A parallel calculation using newer NAIC codes yields similar results. In addition, adding some percentage of manufacturing industries to the calculation, since their environmental pollution is regulated partly by the states, increases the percentage by up to another 10 percent of the economy. Admittedly, state regulation does not cover all aspects of these industries, but it often addresses entry, prices, and other key elements.

4. This is based on a count of agencies from New York State's website, which suggests that thirty-two of ninety-seven, or one-third of state agencies, directly or mainly address the regulatory issues covered in this review.

from *Governing: The Magazine of States and Localities* (Conradi 2003). Half of the ten key issues facing states relate directly to regulation; two (air quality and insurance) are almost completely about regulatory issues, while three others (health costs, privacy, and medical worker shortages) are closely linked to regulatory issues.

Beyond economic impact, a second reason state-level regulation is worth examining is that states have become critical venues for reforms, especially in welfare, health, transportation, and education policy. States have also become the hot places to look for the policy reformers themselves, such as governors (like Bill Clinton and George W. Bush) who demonstrate the ability to rise to a higher political office, or state attorneys general like Spitzer, about 40 percent of whom eventually run for governor. Many popular articles as well as scholarly studies comment frequently that states are the places where truly exciting policies and reforms are taking place. This is true in regulation as well, as government tries to respond to rapid changes in industry structures, including greater competition, partial deregulation, and broader demands from consumers.

Theoretical Issues

State regulation, then, has a demonstrated practical importance. Beyond this, scholars can learn more on a theoretical level from the states: while it can be harder to gather the data to analyze regulation across all fifty states, numerous writers have noted that careful studies of state regulation can help answer some important questions that are not easily addressed with national level data (for example, Baron 1995; Hahn 2000; Gerber and Teske 2000). A relatively small number of federal case studies have provided much of the data for empirical tests of different theoretical approaches to regulation (Moe 1985; Wood and Waterman 1991; Eisner, Worsham, and Ringquist 2000). But the states provide a wider range of economic and political environments against which to test theories, especially those that emphasize the importance of governmental institutions. Although the primary goal here is to inform readers about the development and substance of state regulatory policy, readers can also learn a great deal about the political economy of regulation from this evidence, particularly about how institutions shape regulation.

The states are engaged in a complicated relationship with federal regulators, often filling enforcement gaps (a trend that could be called *deenforcement*) in a period marked by both deregulation and devolution.

Industry capture and regulatory "races to the bottom" are legitimate concerns about state regulation, but contested environments in which institutional actors make independent choices actually characterize most areas of state regulation. As a consequence, we can have general confidence in most state regulators performing their job as well as their federal counterparts, but we need to understand better how states make decisions in filling this role.

In addition to assessing these trends in federalism, political scientists can use the variation in state policies as a laboratory to test broader theories of interest group and institutional influence over public policy. The studies presented here all employ quantitative evidence from recent state choices to address two opposing theoretical explanations of regulatory policy. First, advocates of the Chicago School interest group explanation argue that the political system does not necessarily respond to real problems from market failures but instead provides regulatory protection to the most powerful and involved interests (Friedman 1962; Stigler 1971). This rent-seeking or capture approach provides a concise framework for assessing regulation, and it also tends to bolster normative arguments *against* many regulatory policies since they are assumed to serve parochial private, not broad public, interests. Capture may seem to be even more applicable to state regulation than to federal regulation since a smaller number of powerful, and sometimes mobile, interests are presumed to hold sway in state capitals, and since the competition for business location and economic development can fuel a race to the bottom.

Some political scientists have questioned the overly simplistic assumptions and often undemonstrated empirical support for the capture approach, asking as well how it can explain deregulation or the "social regulation" of the past thirty years, which appear to benefit more dispersed citizens at the expense of concentrated interests (Wilson 1980; Meier 1988; but see Peltzman 1989). As an alternative, scholars who favor institutional approaches to studying regulation emphasize an autonomous role for government actors. In a weaker version of this approach, institutional actors could be influential decisionmakers simply because interest groups are fairly evenly matched in the input and pressure they provide. In a stronger version, institutional actors could be autonomous decisionmakers even in the face of strong, unbalanced interest group pressure (on institutional autonomy, see Nordlinger 1981; Carpenter 2001). In either case, choices by institutional actors could lead to attempts to solve market failures or to serve broader interests in society, such as consumers.

In an ongoing debate, Chicago School advocates respond to the institutional critique by arguing that evidence correlating state institutional actors with policy decisions is insufficient because the establishment of the institutions themselves may be epiphenomenal, or "endogenous," to the interest group strength in that state. Advocates of institutional approaches generally react by arguing that this endogeneity counterargument is an overly bold and unconvincing defense.[5]

Neither approach completely explains all of state regulation. The institutional approach fares much better, however, in most of the cases examined here, which cut across nearly all of the important areas of state regulation. This finding also suggests that, by supporting strong regulatory institutions, the states are more capable of effective and balanced regulatory policy than some skeptics believe.

History

State regulation of insurance and corporate charters predated serious discussion of any forms of regulation at the federal level. For example, in 1752 Pennsylvania granted a charter to Ben Franklin's Philadelphia Contributorship for the Insurance of Houses from Loss by Fire. After Independence Pennsylvania again led the way, in 1794 chartering the first stock insurance company, Insurance Company of North America. Massachusetts in 1807 and New York in 1822 followed by passing statutes mandating information reporting for insurance firms. This pattern made sense as most industries started out in smaller geographic regions, more appropriate to state jurisdictional power over intrastate commerce. As some industries expanded to serve national markets, it was not surprising that the federal government began to assert relatively more regulatory responsibility over them.

Although the Civil War marked the first major shift toward greater federal participation in the emerging national economy, the states continued to play a crucial regulatory role, first in developing ideas about how to regulate the railroad industry, which provided the critical infrastructure for the development of national commerce. Battles over state railroad regulation in the 1860s and 1870s were among the most controver-

5. See Teske (1990) for a detailed discussion of this debate in the context of state telecommunications regulation. Teske also demonstrates that it is sometimes possible to make some aspects of institutions endogenous in empirical models to test this assertion more directly.

sial policy debates of any kind in the United States up until that time, and experiments with state regulation of railroads led to the first federal regulatory activity and agency in 1887, the ICC. While this regulation was focused on specific issues like pricing, competition, and safety, behind these debates lay bigger and more publicly salient questions about concentration of economic power and wealth as well as fears of related concentration of political power by the owners and managers of booming industries like railroads and steel. Related to that, and tapping into the emerging Progressive movement, twenty states passed antitrust statutes that attempted to limit the power of large and concentrated industries before the federal 1890 Sherman Antitrust Act.

In the early twentieth century Progressives and their opponents fought bloody political battles over the early establishment of permanent state regulatory commissions to oversee electricity and other monopoly industries, especially in Wisconsin, New York, and Massachusetts. State-level reformers fought hard to establish public utility commissions (PUCs) with the power to regulate infrastructure monopolies in a meaningful way that might protect consumer interests, led by prominent political figures like Robert LaFollette of Wisconsin and Charles Evans Hughes of New York.

As interstate commerce expanded to create truly national markets across the United States, states lost some of their regulatory roles, and court decisions constrained the definition of intrastate commerce, particularly over the railroads. The New Deal federal response to the Great Depression of the 1930s helped to centralize national regulatory powers over many industries, to the point that Harold Laski even argued that "the epoch of federalism is over" (see Donahue 1997, p. 26). Still, in practice states retained many regulatory powers, including regulation of insurance, and added some new ones over time. Even with the incredible expansion of social regulation in the 1960s and 1970s, which largely came from federal legislative initiatives, much of the implementation of federal policies still took place at the state level.

And with the devolution trend of the past twenty years, more policymaking attention has been refocused on the states, which are often viewed as the most likely place for policies to succeed (Ehrenhalt 2002). The most prominent areas of policy devolution have been welfare, health care, some transportation funding, such as the Intermodal Surface Transportation Efficiency Act (ISTEA) legislation of 1991, and some education policy (on devolution more generally, see Hanson 1999; Nathan 1996). This resurgence in policy authority has occurred in part because state governments have established themselves as professional and capable authorities (Hedge 1998; Teaford 2002). Polls taken in the mid-1990s showed that a far larger percentage of Americans trusted their state and local governments than they did the federal government (Donahue 1997, p. 13).

In the broader perspective, such dynamic shifts in jurisdictional interaction are not surprising. Dan Bucks, director of the Multistate Tax Commission, says: "When it comes to regulation in any federal system, there's always an ebb and flow. And the ebb and flow always intensifies during times of economic change and upheaval" (quoted in Walters 2001, p. 27).

In terms of reinforcing state powers, Donahue (1997, p. 27) argues that important federal politicians have articulated three separate "New Federalism" approaches in the past quarter century; the first from President Nixon, the second from President Reagan, and the third from the 1994 Republican Congress's Contract with America. This was sometimes aimed only at shifting jurisdictional responsibilities and did not always come backed with federal fiscal support; in regulatory policy after 1970, Congress passed forty-seven laws that imposed regulatory responsibilities on the states, including twelve in the area of environmental protection alone.

Still, the proper balance of federalism has become a very hot topic in recent years. Between devolution and a continued push toward greater state rights on the part of a slim majority of the U.S. Supreme Court, American federalism is now often in the news. Gillman calls debate about federalism "the biggest and deepest disagreement about the nature of our constitutional system," and in reviewing court decisions about the extent of congressional power over the states, New York Times legal reporter Linda Greenhouse notes: "These days, federalism means war" (both quoted in Kettl 2002). In policy terms, Derthick (2001) argues that states have now become the "default setting" of American government for addressing policy problems that the federal government or local governments cannot or will not solve.

To understand better the interactions between federal and state governments in regulatory policy, we must separate economic regulation of specific industries from enforcement actions related to social regulations. Despite the rhetoric of devolution, the federal government has largely preempted much of state economic regulation as part of a wider scope of preemption of state activities. Indeed, Nivola (2001) notes that more federal preemptions have occurred in recent decades than over the rest of U.S. history, as business lobbyists and federal officials seek uniformity (through preemption) on numerous regulatory policy questions. For example, the transformation from cooperative to "coercive" federalism was expedited in the 1980s when President Reagan responded to the new state attorney general activism by enacting federal preemption laws that reduced the authority initially granted to the states a few years earlier.

Within the arena of economic regulation, most transportation and financial activities of states were preempted in the 1980s and 1990s. In transportation regulation, states were specifically preempted from regulating the airlines in 1978, from most railroad regulation in 1980, from intercity bus regulation in 1982, and from economic regulation of the trucking industry in 1994. States were preempted from state chartering of S&Ls in 1989, from prohibiting branch banking in 1994, from regulating mutual funds, and, with Gramm-Leach-Bliley, the 1999 financial services reform bill, Congress gave the states until 2003 to better coordinate licensing of insurance agents, or it will be preempted. In telecommunications, the 1996 federal Telecommunications Act preempted the states from preventing entry by cable television and telephone firms into each other's markets. In nearly all of these examples, the federal preemption was designed to facilitate greater total *de*regulation, preventing the states from maintaining any active regulatory role in these industries, while also reducing, or even eliminating, the federal role.

Social regulation has presented a strikingly different pattern, in part because since World War II it has been more popular and with more voters than economic regulation.[6] Federal attempts to reduce the regulation of risk and information, and related "de-enforcement" efforts, have prompted considerable, though sporadic, state activism to fill that gap, which we might characterize as state "reenforcement." This leads to varying regulations across the states and to some reactive "second-order" federal regulations that otherwise would not have been promulgated. As a result, the relative importance of state regulation has increased, contrary to expectations from many conservative supporters of devolution, who expected the states to be coenablers of these "de-enforcement" policies.

Despite the greater popularity of social regulation, Presidents Nixon, Reagan, and George W. Bush and the 1994 Republican Congress's Contract with America mostly lumped it together with economic regulation and "big government," trying to reduce its enforcement by cutting staff and budgets and by centralizing their own authority over agency promul-

6. As demonstrated econometrically by Winston and Crandall (1994).

gation of new rule-making decisions. In response, many organized labor, environmental, and consumer groups resisted these attempts, and they often used the states as a form of venue shopping to achieve their goals. Demonstrating the popularity of some forms of social regulation, these regulatory activists have found some success in shaping policies by legislatures and state attorneys general in some states, including (but not limited to) California, New York, and Massachusetts.

Observers first noticed this balancing effect of federalism during the Reagan administration. Then, in the 1990s, Presidents Bush and Clinton moderated the federal reduction in social regulatory enforcement, but the political power and explicit antiregulatory agenda of the 1994 Republican-controlled Congress continued to make regulatory activists wary of federal activities, so they pressed on with state efforts. For example, in health care, pro-regulatory groups pressured more than half the states to adopt some version of a patient's "bill of rights" during the 1990s, when Congress would not pass such proposals. Labaton notes about such groups: "Sensing that the new regulatory battles are shifting, consumer groups like AARP, which represents millions of older Americans, are moving with it. Next month, when the organization opens an office in Louisiana, it will have established local lobbying operation in all 50 states."[7]

Since 2000, under President George W. Bush, greater skepticism from pro-regulatory activists has resurfaced. They maintain their focus at the state level, especially as several powerful Bush regulatory appointees, including John Graham, head of OMB's Office of Information and Regulatory Affairs (OIRA) and FTC chairman Muris, have written widely about the need to reduce various forms of social regulation. Labaton notes: "Sensing a growing deregulatory movement in Washington, state officials have been moving swiftly to fill what they perceive as voids in areas like antitrust, environmental law, consumer safety, telecommunications, banking, health care and energy." He adds: "Experts and state officials say the states' growing involvement is reminiscent of a movement in the Reagan administration, when the perception of lax enforcement prompted a core group of state prosecutors and lawmakers to form new alliances."[8]

Regulatory activists have used three main state-level venues to advance their policies—state legislatures, the initiative and referendum process, and

7. Stephen Labaton, "States Seek to Counter U.S. Deregulation," *New York Times,* January 12, 2002, p. A16.
    8. Ibid.

state attorneys general (SAGs). For example, in the late 1980s nearly half of state legislatures considered bills to regulate nutrition labeling, action that was preempted by the passage of the 1990 federal Food Labeling Act, as food manufacturers feared facing many different standards. Also in the late 1980s, environmental groups pressed twenty-one state legislatures to pass laws requiring plastic six-pack connectors to be biodegradable. Business groups then pushed Congress to press the U.S. Environmental Protection Agency to develop uniform national biodegradable rules, which it did in 1993. In the 1990s several states legislatures and localities passed laws banning or limiting bank ATM charges. A few states developed their own new regulatory standards for products sold in national markets—Oregon fostered new regulatory standards for baby cribs, while California developed new standards for mattress flammability. In 2001 seven states adopted the "do not call" laws against telemarketers, which proved so popular that FTC chair Muris later called for a national rule limiting telemarketing, an action he admitted would have been unlikely without the states moving first. In the most recent—and dramatic— example, in summer 2002 the California legislature passed a bill requiring steep reductions in greenhouse gases from automobiles after Congress had rejected that policy. This seems likely to force automobile manufacturers to comply with the new standards, not only in California, the biggest state market by far, but across the country, since it is not feasible to produce two separate sets of cars. Passage of this law in California, after failure at the federal level, was part of an explicit environmental group strategy to achieve national, not just state-level, goals, and California legislators were encouraged to pass the bill by U.S. senators such as John Kerry and John McCain.

While state actions vary by type of regulation, states themselves also differ, sometimes considerably. Some legislatures have not become wellsprings of social regulatory activism, nor are they likely to do so. Though more than half the states, led by California and New Hampshire, have voluntarily set carbon dioxide emissions above federal standards, another sixteen state legislatures decided to go on record opposing the Clinton administration's Kyoto treaty on climate change that called for rapid reductions in such emissions (Arrandale 2002, p. 23).[9] Still, though not all states are actively pursuing environmental enforcement above federal

9. See also Eric Pianin, "On Global Warming, States Act Locally," *Washington Post,* November 11, 2002, p. A3.

mandates, Rabe, the author of a recent study, argues: "The trend is unmistakably towards more states taking an active role in climate change" (2002, p. ix). Though it is somewhat concentrated, the overall trend is not so simple that a few well-known "progressive" states on the two coasts are dominating all state regulatory activism.

In some cases, pro-regulatory groups have pressed for state regulatory initiatives, particularly when legislatures do not act. Most prominently, in 1986 California voters passed Proposition 65, which required substantial labeling about risks and possible hazards related to food and other products. Other states were considering similar ideas at that time. Though opposed to this kind of state product-risk labeling requirements, Viscusi (1993, p. 74) admitted: "The state warning programs have served a constructive purpose by indicating a potentially fruitful area for federal involvement."

While state legislative action, initiatives, and referendums spurred this pattern of state social regulatory activism, the expanded activities of state attorneys general now play the most important role, particularly as the idea of "regulation through litigation" expands (Viscusi 2002). This relatively new form of regulatory activism has played a prominent role in tobacco litigation, advertising, and antitrust in the last twenty years. For example, aggressive SAGs active in the food nutrition labeling battles of the 1980s were called the "chowhounds." Walters (2002b) writes that "the group soon branched out into a whole range of other issues, from car sales to funeral home services . . . but in the past few years, as business has successfully made the argument for federal rather than state oversight, the Chowhounds have gradually been defanged."

Walters's argument may be premature, however. During the George W. Bush administration, SAGs again have stepped up their activities, headed by Eliot Spitzer of New York. A front-page *New York Times* article recently argued that "his assault this year on the seamier habits of leading brokerage houses has vaulted him to another plane, a national figure with a higher profile than many governors and senators. *Fortune* magazine put him on its cover in September, branding him 'The Enforcer.'"[10] More generally, Traub writes: "We are, in fact, in the midst of an era of widespread state-level judicial activism, and Eliot Spitzer is the most activist, or at least the most prominent, attorney general around. . . . Spitzer and other

10. Richard Perez-Pena and Patrick McGeehan, "Assault on Wall St. Misdeeds Raises Spitzer's U.S. Profile," *New York Times,* November 4, 2002, p. A1.

attorneys general are filling a void that was intended, by the anti-Washington right, to be filled by the marketplace—by, say, self-regulating Wall Street businesses—not by other legal actors like state AG's." Traub suggests how powerful SAGs have become: "An attorney general who interprets his consumer-protection mandate expansively can exercise a form of power that is almost more legislative than judicial. . . . I was struck by how explicitly he was seeking to forge, or at least shape, social policy."[11] Spitzer himself notes: "As the Congress and courts have succeeded in forging a new federalism, they have created an opportunity to accomplish things previously thought unsuited to state initiative" (quoted in Greenblatt 2002a).

The 2002 case of Spitzer suing Merrill Lynch using a 1921 New York State law has been cited above. Other examples include six northeastern SAGs (including Spitzer) challenging in court the Bush administration's proposal to relax environmental standards for new plants or upgrades of industrial facilities. Traub writes: "Peter Lehner, head of the attorney general's environmental protection bureau, reported that while the utilities no longer fear federal action from the deregulators in the Bush administration, they were deeply worried about the states."[12] Twenty-nine SAGs sued Bristol-Myers in a December 2001 antitrust case over the issuance of a generic drug alternative to BuSpar (an antianxiety drug), and eight SAGs sued the U.S. Department of Energy over revisions to regulations on appliance energy efficiency. SAGs do not always act in concert, of course: although nine SAGs backed a U.S. Department of Justice antitrust settlement with Microsoft in 2002, nine others insisted on continuing the case to try to achieve stricter enforcement.

SAGs have moved into the forefront of social regulatory activism, ahead of state legislatures, because they are piggybacking on the popular product liability movement in law, and they reinforce that linkage by taking on cases against big national corporations that are perceived to have deep pockets. Nearly two-thirds of SAGs are Democrats, and many SAGs of both parties are seeking to build name recognition to run for higher office, especially governor. They are collectively building new cases on the foundation of their stunning victory against tobacco firms, which appeared

11. James Traub, "The Attorney General Goes to War," *New York Times Magazine,* July 16, 2002, pp. 38–41.
12. Ibid., p. 40.

as a clear moralistic case of evil tobacco firms seducing minors to smoke, with billions of dollars generated for state budget coffers.

Business lobbying groups have not taken these state challenges lightly. They usually counter this state-level social regulatory activism in legislatures, agency hearings, business-sponsored initiatives, and in court. Business lobbyists had reacted to the trend to more regulatory action at the state level in the 1980s and 1990s. Rosenthal (1993) notes that the number of state lobbyists grew by 20 percent from 1988 to 1992. Donahue (1997, p. 49) notes that the proportion of business trade associations monitoring state policies doubled between 1982 and 1987, and lobbying expenditures grew fivefold in Connecticut from 1985 to 1995. In a recent example, a group of seventeen large corporations formed the National Business Coalition on E-Commerce and Privacy to fight proposed state-level restrictions on privacy data.

Recent campaign evidence suggests that business groups are also now working hard to shape their own agendas in SAG elections. Greenblatt (2002b, p. 45) writes: "Business groups are hoping to stop state lawsuits before they start by electing allies and defeating candidates for attorney general who are perceived as hostile toward them and too friendly toward consumers or labor. Accordingly, they are now pouring millions of dollars into attorney general races that in the past they might have ignored." Apparently, the recruitment and funding of more business-oriented SAGs is paying dividends, as ten of fifteen SAGs elected in November 2002 were Republicans, compared to a 2 to 1 (34-16) Democratic advantage before those elections. With twenty Republican SAGs, business groups hope for less aggressive action, but enough activists likely remain to continue to press a tougher regulatory agenda. Even when dealing with SAG legal actions, firms and business groups sometimes prefer more states to be involved; as Greenblatt (2003a, p. 56) writes: "The more AGs sign on to a settlement, the more protection the company has from future liability."

If business groups fail to stop aggressive state social regulatory actions, large national and international firms face the possibility of balkanized regulations, different across fifty different states, or the possibility that a large and pro-regulatory state like California will effectively dictate national standards based on the size of its market and the difficulty of adapting a single product to many different markets: the "California effect"(Vogel 1995, p. 5). They often then shift their focus to lobbying at the federal level for a single, ideally less strict, federal standard. This may be happening again in 2003, after Virginia, the home to America Online and thus half of all Internet traffic flows, leapfrogged over twenty-four other states with existing antispamming legislation with tough new legislation designed to curtail unsolicited commercial e-mail. Hansell writes: "Such anger from computer users is even causing some in the industry to support federal legislation, if only to avoid having to deal with a patchwork of state anti-spam laws."[13]

While becoming more common, this approach is not entirely new, as strict California environmental regulations prodded businesses to be more supportive of federal standards in 1969. Moe (1989, p. 312) writes: "Businesses, in fact, had actually warmed to the idea [of a federal EPA] after years of frustration with the hodge-podge of state regulations, which were gradually becoming strict enough to cause problems and confusion."

As Petersen (2002, p. 58) notes about recent events in corporate financial regulation: "Both congressional committees and corporate lobbyists (including Wall Street and accountant associations) have been trying to nip off the state-based assault on such issues as corporate governance, securities regulation and accounting practices." Business groups often seek—and achieve—these "lighter" federal standards along with preemption of the states, as with food nutrition labeling in 1990. Walters (2001, p. 20) summarizes: "It's clear that efforts to replace multiple state and local statutes with a single federal standard are on the upswing. . . . Successful or not, business lobbyists do seem to be saying that they'd rather deal with the single federal devil they know, than with the hundreds of pesky and unpredictable state and local demons they don't." Or, as Nivola (2001, p. 53) puts it, for businesses it is "better to have one 500-pound gorilla in charge of regulating the industry, its lobbyists reckoned, than to deal with 50 monkeys on steroids."

Thus federal de-enforcement of social regulation has prompted varying forms of state reenforcement. As a result, and in marked contrast to the preempted state role in economic regulation, some influential states are playing a far more important regulatory role than in the past. While political fights underlie these jurisdictional shifts in regulatory authority, it is worth considering the relative advantages and disadvantages of state regulation.

13. Seth Hansell, "Virginia Law Makes Spam, with Fraud, a Felony," *New York Times*, April 30, 2003, p. C1.

Why Regulate at the State Level?

After a decision to regulate a particular industry, a related decision is how to regulate it, including the critical jurisdictional question of whether to regulate at the national, state, or local level (or, increasingly, at some higher, supranational level of economic and political activity, such as the World Trade Organization, European Union, or North American Free Trade Agreement). In many other developed countries, in which the equivalent of American states are not nearly as important in formulating or delivering policy, this is not an issue—only the national government regulates in a meaningful way. But since the United States was originally formed as a confederation of separate states, this federal-state tension continues.

In some ways, because of the history of U.S. government, this question should be reversed—why regulate at the national level? As explained above, states were the first regulators for insurance, corporate charters, and railroads. But the appropriate locus of regulation has been an enduring issue. The issue appears simple, with the Constitution itself bearing directly on it: the federal government is given authority to regulate interstate commerce, while the states retain the right to regulate commerce within their borders. In reality, though, the separation between these two levels of commerce has been quite complex. Since the formation of the United States, the relationship has been shaped by complicated legal questions of where the boundaries between interstate and intrastate commerce should be drawn, which activities fall under these classifications, and when the federal government can preempt the states to achieve pressing national goals. Today, in the complex economic and financial environment that characterizes most major industries, it is very difficult to distinguish truly intrastate commerce that does not have some important interstate dimension, if one looks carefully at all parts of a business.

Tying jurisdictional issues to the market failure model, the economies of scale that give rise to monopolies often exceed the physical boundaries of the states, but historical path-dependence and explicit jurisdictional decisions have often limited them to within state boundaries, as with electricity monopolies or telephone monopolies in the past. Asymmetric information can occur in many kinds of transactions and commerce, and thus industries with asymmetric information could potentially be regulated at either or both levels of government. Externalities may be contained within state boundaries, as is often the case with more localized land-use planning issues, but, as with air and water pollution, externalities are likely to pass from one state into another, creating interstate dimensions to the regulatory problem.

In evaluating regulation at the state level, federal level, or some combination, several advantages and disadvantages can readily be seen. Theoretically, there are several advantages to state regulation. Allowing states to maintain the authority over intrastate commerce allows those government institutions closest to the industry to regulate it. As a result, regulators can shape policies that better match the specific needs of key participants. Moreover, state governments can enact programs that more closely reflect the desires of their political constituents. Individual states, with their smaller size, are likely to contain somewhat more homogeneous populations, so that state policies can be matched more closely to the average citizen's preferences. State regulation also has the advantage of allowing experimentation, with particular states acting as laboratories for new policies. This model has worked well in a number of cases, including railroad regulation in the 1860s, airline regulation in the 1960s, telecommunications regulation in the 1980s, and electricity deregulation in the 1990s.

Finally, in theory, maintaining state regulatory autonomy provides states with economic incentives to regulate in productive ways, since states are in competition with one another, to some degree, for mobile, productive resources. If a particular state's regulations harm these mobile resources, the resources are likely to shift their activities and jobs to more favorable jurisdictions. The fact that forty-four firms have pulled out of providing insurance in Massachusetts and New Jersey in the last fifteen years suggests that this is more than a theoretical possibility (as well as demonstrating that states do not always respond well to this issue). Still, even more than the federal government, states have a competitive motivation to be innovative in shaping effective and efficient regulatory policies, at least for firms with the threat of mobility. This may be less true for the regulation of firms with (legal or practical) geographic monopolies, such as some public utilities.

Balanced against these theoretical advantages of a dual system, with states playing a critical role, are several theoretical advantages for a unitary system that would implement regulations only through the national government. First, a single national regulatory policy promotes consistency, which can provide stability to firms in an industry, particularly if they are serving national, and increasingly international, markets. As noted above, firms often complain when states step forward with a wide range of different regulatory policies, making it difficult for firms to comply simultaneously with as many as fifty different sets of rules.

A second rationale for national regulation arises when state regulations of the industry exhibit significant effects beyond the state, called jurisdictional externalities, which are really related to the concept of interstate commerce. If a firm is engaged in truly intrastate commerce only, then regulatory choices made in one state should not adversely affect firms, shippers, or citizens in another state. If one state's regulations do affect actors in another state, that indicates interstate commerce and suggests a need for national regulation to balance conflicting jurisdictional interests. Beales and Muris (1993, p. 118) argue against state regulation of national advertising campaigns because of extrajurisdictional impacts, claiming that such regulation "in effect provides a series of central governments, responsive only to a portion of the population they govern."

A third theoretical advantage to national regulation is that one regulator may be better able to marshal the necessary analytic and oversight resources than can fifty states of varying sizes and complexity. In other words, there may be economies of scale in the development and implementation of good regulatory policy. For example, in information and risk labeling, Viscusi (1993, p. 74) argues: "The federal government is better suited than the states to develop the scientific basis for ascertaining which products merit warnings and which do not." While the federal analytic advantage may be smaller compared to large states like California and New York, smaller states like Wyoming or South Dakota might have difficulties promulgating and overseeing complex regulatory policies.

Finally, national regulation is often perceived to be less susceptible to extreme interest group manipulation than state regulation. In general, more interest groups are active in Washington, D.C. than in state capitals, including groups that support consumer, environmental, and labor perspectives. A larger number of groups seems more likely to provide balanced, pluralistic policy participation. At the state level, certain interest groups may be too powerful economically and politically for regulators to oppose, such as coal-mining interests in West Virginia, gambling firms in Nevada, or truckers in Texas. The power of some strong state groups might not be counterbalanced effectively by other groups or coalitions, allowing them to manipulate state regulators more easily than federal regulators. Potential mobility of these groups may even enhance their power when states compete for them. For example, the Kansas state banking commissioner advertised on the website that state-chartered banks will have more ability (than federal-chartered ones) to "lobby the state legislature for changes in laws and regulation."[14] And, as Dunbar and Rush write: "Lobbyists typically have greater influence in the states, where their targets are usually part-time, often under-paid legislators with little staff help."[15] Thus depending on the nature of government responsiveness, the relative "closeness" between state regulators and interest groups can be viewed either positively or negatively.

Determining whether a dual or a unitary system is the most suitable for regulating specific business activities is often difficult and controversial. In practice, though, this is not mainly a theoretical or academic exercise. Direct political influence by affected groups shapes congressional, executive, bureaucratic, and judicial decisions about the extent of federal preemption or state responsibility as much as—or more than—these theoretical factors. As noted above, most interest groups shop for the regulatory venue that will be most conducive to policy favoring them. In addition, sometimes governments charge fees for regulatory oversight, which can give states, or the federal government, an incentive to continue to hold onto regulation.[16] And new ideological perspectives on these advantages and disadvantages have shaped the degree of regulatory federalism employed in the United States over time.

The Politics of Policy

Despite the theoretical market failure framework, as in any other policy area, interest group and societal demands play a large role in determining what economic activities are regulated. Often, the basic politics of regulation appear to be fairly simple and straightforward. Businesses, labor unions, consumer and environmental groups press governments for regulatory policies that will serve their interests. Generally, we expect business groups to oppose many regulations and labor, consumer, and environmental groups to favor them. But often some businesses favor regulations that help their competitive position versus other firms or industry seg-

14. Quoted in Jess Bravin and Paul Beckett, "Dependent on Lenders' Fees, the OCC Takes Banks' Side against Local Laws," *Wall Street Journal*, January 28, 2002, p. 1.

15. John Dunbar and Meleah Rush, "The Fourth Branch: Study Finds $570 Million Spent on Lobbying in the States in 2000," Center for Public Integrity, 2002, p. 3 (www.publicintegrity.org/dtaweb/index.asp).

16. On fees for banks, see ibid.

ments, and all of these broad groups are often splintered by specific, narrow regulatory policies (see Smith 2000 for a valuable distinction between unifying, conflictual, and specific business issues).

In partisan terms, as a first cut we expect conservatives and Republicans, those associated more with business interests, to be opposed to many regulations that place governmentally authorized restrictions on private market decisions. Conversely, liberals and Democrats often favor regulations because they limit the power of businesses while protecting their core supporters in labor unions and consumer and environment groups. But in reality, the politics and economics of regulation are far more complicated when one considers the differences, noted above, between economic and social regulation. Within these categories, some regulations clearly favor (some) businesses at the expense of consumers or at the expense of other businesses. This has more often been true for economic regulation. Other regulations, often social regulations, do indeed favor consumers, organized labor, or other "enemies" of business. It is unclear what still other regulations might do, because the relationships between many regulatory policies and actual policy outcomes are quite complex, such as with the deregulation of electricity or the telecommunications markets.

Regulatory policy is made through a complicated process in the real world of American states. Public opinion establishes a wide and soft set of political parameters within which public officials must operate. When citizens seem concerned about "big government," they are likely to favor less regulation or deregulatory policies, as in the 1980s (Derthick and Quirk 1985). When concerns shift to abuse of power by large corporations, as in 2002, citizens are more likely to support tougher regulations and restrictions on businesses. Specific interest group pressure provides a more narrow and stronger set of constraints on particular regulatory issues, and sometimes interest group pressure appears to dominate the outcomes of regulatory policy. The concerns about capture and races to the bottom are due to strong interest group power in state politics generally (Renzulli and others 2002).

While regulations are usually established in statutes (at least in a general sense) by state legislators, governors, and courts, state bureaucratic officials—or "regulators"—implement specific regulations. As full-time state employees, regulators have more expertise in their areas. Many regulatory agencies were established with the explicit purpose of providing them with some degree of insulation from the political process, so that they have the ability to make complex, technical decisions that balance interests without becoming captured. Gormley (1989) argues that because of less professionalized oversight institutions—state legislatures and governors as compared to Congress and the presidency—state bureaucratic agencies probably had more scope for independent action than federal agencies, at least until after the 1970s, when many oversight reforms were introduced.

The specific case studies that form the core of evidence in this book measure the various critical elements and players that shape state regulatory politics, testing their influence over outcomes. Chapter 3, the methods and measurement chapter, gives details about how to test these influences, but it is worth making a few points here. Those who doubt whether state regulation can be effective often suspect that powerful interest groups will dominate the states' decisionmaking processes, setting off a race to the bottom. Not surprisingly, we can expect interest groups to seek the regulations that serve them best, as the Chicago School argues. Interest groups also seem to be savvy about choosing the level of government, federal or state, that is most likely to best serve their interest. The specific analyses in chapters 4–12 often show the influence of interest groups, although, interest group power is not as dominant as many expect.

The likely expectations for the influence of institutions are more complicated. We should expect legislative decisions about regulation to reflect their ideology, at least partially. That is, state legislatures controlled by Democrats should be more likely to regulate more and to regulate in favor of consumers, labor, or environmental groups, rather than business (and vice versa for legislatures controlled by Republicans). The degree of state house and senate party control and the ideological intensity of such control also probably affect how much legislatures influence regulatory decisions. We should have similar expectations for governors, but as discussed below, simple party differences may be inadequate to capture real distinctions across governors.

It also seems likely that regulation will be affected by the professionalism of state legislatures. Some states, like California and New York, have full-time, well-paid legislators and staffs. Other states meet infrequently and have low-paid, part-time legislators and scant staff resources. We can expect that more professional legislatures will be less reliant on powerful interest groups to shape their regulatory policy agendas; that is, they should be more likely to pass policy that does not necessarily correspond to the resultant outcome of a vector of interest groups pressures. Similarly, more professional state agencies, those with more autonomy and more resources, should also be more independent sources of regulatory policy. Generally, as with more professional legislatures, this means siding more often with consumer interests or notions of a broader public interest than might be captured by the concept of economic efficiency.

Horizontal Competition and Cooperation

It is important to recognize that while individual state politics shape state regulatory choices, each individual state does not operate in a vacuum. In addition to "vertical" relationships with national and international governments, states also face the challenge of "horizontal competition" with one another. States compete with one another for economic development resources—investment, jobs, and other forms of economic activity (see Brace 1993; Donohue 1997). Greater economic development stimulates state tax bases, makes program expansion easier, and is usually associated with higher reelection rates for state politicians.

Broad tax policy choices or specific incentive programs are usually the state activities we associate most with state economic development policies. But while there is not always necessarily a direct and strong relationship, regulatory policies sometimes influence, or are perceived to influence, corporate investment choices in particular states. This creates a relationship between state regulation and economic development. Sometimes scholars assume that this relationship will reduce the ability of the state to regulate businesses in a strict manner, that it will drive lax regulation and a race to the bottom. There are certainly cases in which this is true. Corporate chartering regulation, in which Delaware's regulations have attracted nearly half of all major U.S. corporations, is often assumed to be a good example of state competition driving out appropriate regulation, prompting the use of the term the "Delaware effect." Others disagree, such as Romano (1997), who argues that state chartering generally, and Delaware's chartering laws in particular, have had a positive effect on the U.S. economy by providing corporations with greater certainty about their governance rules. (For a summary of this debate, see Donahue 1997, pp. 66–68.)

While there is widespread scholarly and policy concern about a race to the bottom, some doubt that the problem is as severe as it's painted (see Ferejohn and Weingast 1997). There can also be "races to the top," such as the California effect in environmental regulation, where an innovative state pushes national regulatory policy—which, in turn, sometimes imposes the tougher regulations on all states. Recent efforts by state attorneys general may also fall into this category, as discussed in chapter 15.

To further complicate the relationship between regulation and economic development, at the same time that states are competing with one another, they sometimes cooperate over regulatory policies. Much literature has been devoted to how states innovate, in regulation and other policy arenas, and how and why those innovations diffuse to other states (Walker 1969; Berry and Berry 1990, 1992). States sometimes also work together to try to solve regulatory problems. Examples include the National Association of Insurance Commissioners (NAIC) model state laws, reciprocity agreements in interstate branch banking in the 1980s, 2003 joint state efforts to reform state licensing of insurance agents, and 2003 efforts to coordinate state Internet taxation. In some cases, greater state coordination might limit corporate pressure for federal preemption, but such coordination is difficult to achieve. Walters (2001, p. 24) writes: "no convincing evidence exists that state and local governments are ready to work together as a way to forestall business end-runs in Washington."

Assessing Reforms

Whether states are racing to the bottom, to the top, or to the middle, the focus in the specific analyses in this book is to understand better when each of these sets of critical actors has more or less influence over state regulatory choices. With that understanding, we can better assess the performance of state regulatory institutions and the likely effects of reforming them. For example, if interest groups really dominate many areas of regulation, reforming government regulatory institutions will not make much of a difference to policy outcomes. But when interest group capture does occur, there are some other reforms states might consider, including campaign finance reform that might limit that form of influence, limitations on other forms of interest groups access in the regulatory process, limiting "revolving door" contacts by regulators, or actually trying to alter the constellation of interest group power in a state (which sometimes happens as the result of policy changes, as, for example, deregulation and competition introduce new firms and interest groups into a more competitive process to achieve favorable regulations).

But much of the evidence here, consistent with the findings of other studies of state regulation, demonstrates that government regulatory institutions do shape state regulatory policy outcomes in important ways. By understanding better how different institutions shape regulatory policy, we can evaluate executive, legislative, bureaucratic, and judicial reforms. Specifically, I use evidence from several industry areas to assess some state reforms that have been implemented. First, since most of the studies herein demonstrate legislative influence over policy, I analyze reforms related to legislative professionalism and oversight, including oversight before policy implementation, as practiced in some states with state administrative procedures acts and similar procedures, and oversight during policy implementation, such as hearings and legislative reviews. Second, I examine state executive oversight of regulation, as practiced by the New York Governor's Office of Regulatory Reform and in some other large states, agencies that are modeled partly after the regulatory arm of the federal Office of Management and Budget. Third, I examine the role of bureaucratic accountability structures, in terms of elected or appointed commissioners, and the role of bureaucratic resources and professionalism. Fourth, given the growing judicialization of regulation, I analyze the role of state courts in reviewing regulation and the growing role of state attorneys general in taking a legalistic approach to regulating certain activities and industries.

CHAPTER TWO

Theoretical Perspectives

Regulation is most broadly defined as when the government bounds or restricts private economic activity. The focus here is on regulation of business activity, usually related to pricing, competition, information provision, limits on activities, and other requirements. This perspective assumes the establishment of a market-based economy, with a framework of private property rights and a judicial system developed to adjudicate controversies, enforce private contracts, and generally lay the groundwork for market transactions (Friedman 1962). Governments have generally been the entities to develop this overarching framework of property rights and a functioning judicial and police system, though there are other theoretical possibilities. The absence of such an infrastructure can lead to chaos when market activity is simply unleashed, as in the former Soviet Union in the 1990s.

With this legal framework in place, two uncoerced parties can engage in voluntary exchanges, with both parties expecting to be made better off than they were before, receiving benefits that are the gains from trade in market settings. The aggregation of many similar individual transactions forms a market, whether in a particular geographic space, a cyberspace, or in an abstract conceptual manner assessed somewhat arbitrarily by scholars. In such an aggregated market, consumers earn "consumer surplus" as their gains from trade, and producers earn "producer surplus." Using their resources of money, energy, intelligence, and whatever else can be traded in markets, all participants are made better off in this theoretical model.

The market model is quite well established in economics and rests on a foundation of individual consumer choice, subject to a budget constraint. Markets that function well require a few key elements. There must be some degree of competition among suppliers to keep prices at a competitive level. Both parties to transactions must have a reasonable degree of information transparency about the elements of transactions; that is, they know what they are trading for. Third, the transaction should directly affect only the trading parties and should not have important spillover effects on nontransacting parties. While the theoretical models of markets can be complex, most Americans understand, in commonsense terms, the basic concept of market transactions. Most of us engage in such market activities nearly every day, such that we might sometimes even take markets for granted.

With this framework in mind, which fits the U.S. political-economic environment quite well, a very useful way to conceptualize government regulation is to employ the market failure framework from microeconomics. While market failures may not be the only reasons to regulate, as there might be equity or other concerns, they provide the best rationale for government regulatory activity. Economists argue that market failures are the main normative reason to regulate. These failures are the converse of the three main requirements for well-functioning markets. They include (1) monopoly or lack of competition problems, when industries are usually regulated by public utility commissions or by antitrust regulation; (2) information asymmetries, where producers know much more about the quality of products and services than do consumers, often leading to government information provision or monitoring of the industry; and (3) externalities, in which nonparticipants or third parties to a transaction are affected, the best and classic example of which is environmental pollution.

Unregulated monopolists are able to charge prices higher than would be charged in competitive markets, and in essence steal consumer surplus away for themselves. Monopolies can develop for "natural" technological reasons, most often when an industry requires extremely high fixed costs to be spent before any consumers can be served. This is most often the case for industries that require extensive physical distribution plant, such as railroad tracks, water and sewer pipes, electric wires, or telephone or cable TV wires. Monopolies might also develop for "unnatural" reasons, which usually involve government granting of monopoly franchises while limiting entry by possible competitors. While monopolies are the extreme form of this market failure of lack of competition, a small number of firms might also work together, as a cartel, to achieve monopoly-like profits, by agreeing to raise prices collectively. Potential policy solutions to problems relating to monopolies range from leaving the market alone and hoping that monopoly profits will encourage innovative technologies to challenge the monopoly, a conservative solution; establishing some form of government price and service regulation, the typical American solution; or running the monopoly as a government agency, which is often done in other nations but rarely in the United States.

Since prices are not the only concern of consumers, the problem of asymmetric information arises when producers know considerably more about the quality of products and services than consumers do. There is almost always some degree of information asymmetry in transactions, but it would be quite inefficient to regulate every one of billions of daily transactions. The critical question is how serious the asymmetry is—whether consumers have the ability to gain enough information to make well-informed choices. Economists analyze this problem by distinguishing between search goods, for which consumers can gather information; experience goods, which they can assess only by purchasing; and postexperience goods, the quality of which might be difficult to assess even after purchase, such as pharmaceutical products or medical care. The range of solutions to asymmetric information market failures includes ignoring the problem, hoping that private "middlemen" will arise to provide information; government forcing private firms to provide information; government limits on what firms can do; government providing information itself; and government banning products.

Externalities occur because the private calculations of individuals making transactions do not include the social costs of these exchanges. Other parties are affected, and we are most concerned when those effects are large and negative. (Very large positive externalities, generally provided by governments, are called "public goods." Examples include national defense and national parks.) Externalities can be ignored, parties can be encouraged to bargain over them, or government can force the externalities to be reduced or eliminated in a variety of ways.

In historical terms, the monopoly rationale was first addressed by U.S. government regulatory policies because it was raised by the development and expansion of the railroads and later by other industry "trusts" that emerged with the development of large-scale, cross-continental capitalism in the United States (see McCraw 1984). While information asymmetries have certainly been in existence since human beings began trading goods with one another, as an issue for widespread government policy they arose as mass-market transactions became more common, first including concerns about food safety, as with meat packing in Chicago. Regulatory policies related to externalities were identified only in the midtwentieth century, when enough industrial activity had been generated to create substantial negative by-products that society recognized as a pollution problem.

As noted in chapter 1, it is often useful to combine the latter two categories, information asymmetries and externalities, under the heading of social regulation, which cuts across industries and for which enforcement is critical. Monopoly and competition regulations, which often include policies aimed at price controls and limits on competition or entry within a particular industry, are often collectively called economic regulation.

While the market failure framework is extremely valuable, like any broad framework, it provides only a conceptual map to thinking about regulation. This framework does not tell us exactly when governments should regulate, or when we should allow the market to continue to operate without regulations, or how to implement particular regulations. In the real world, in addition to market failures, ideology and political pressure determine what industries and activities actually are regulated and how those regulations operate. Thus a political economy approach to regulation must address and examine theories about the politics of regulations as well as paying heed to market failure concepts.

While we do not yet have an adequate theory of how public policy generally is made in the United States (or anywhere else, for that matter), scholars have provided some guidelines to addressing the important theoretical and empirical questions of who and what influences regulatory policy. Theory and evidence identify several major contenders for influence over policy choices, particularly when we use the variation across the American states as well as variation in policy choices made over time.

Public Interest Theories

One possibility is that public opinion shapes regulatory policy through a variety of direct and indirect mechanisms, indicating that the voters ultimately get the basic regulatory policies that they want. While there is some limited evidence for this position (Erikson, Wright, and McIver 1993; Winston and Crandall 1994), most scholars believe that public opinion provides only weak guidelines for regulators, who have considerable latitude within that range. In part, this is because the rationales for regulation and the actual procedures and processes of regulation are highly complex and technical, beyond the understanding of most citizens. Regulatory processes are also usually of low salience, so voters do not care all that much about them, except during unusual periods of crisis or media attention. Generally, while regulatory policies may occasionally engage the attentions of the mass public, such attention usually fades quickly when politicians pass a law, regulations are approved to address the problem, or the details and procedures involved in that policy prove complex and technical in nature.

Related to broad public opinion, it is also possible that the whole political process creates useful regulations ultimately based on perceptions of the need for them—in short, governments react to problems based on their severity and act accordingly. In regulation, this is the normative as positive theory, or NPT, as Joskow and Noll (1981) christened it. From this perspective, actors in society identify a significant market failure, in today's environment in explicit terms and historically either explicitly or implicitly (see Charles Francis Adams and railroad regulation in McCraw 1984), and then government is pushed to intervene to address it. Often, this occurs soon after a crisis of some kind takes place in a particular industry. These crises include industry-specific events like dramatic transportation or mining accidents (for example, Lewis-Beck and Alford 1980), or books that expose a problem publicly, such as Upton Sinclair's *The Jungle* (1907) on the meatpacking industry, Rachel Carson's *Silent Spring* (1959), which exposed the environmental damage caused by pesticides, or Ralph Nader's *Unsafe at Any Speed* (1965), which demonstrated flaws in automobile and highway safety. More generally, the crises can cut across the wider economy, such as the Great Depression in the 1930s or the stagflation of the 1970s (Eisner 1993).

The NPT can be tested over time, to see whether governments react to problems more when they are actually more severe. Or it can be tested across governments, as with the states in this book, to see if, for example, states with more toxic waste sites enact more stringent environmental regulations to control them. Largely, the NPT perspective is rooted in basic common sense: if there is a problem in society and if it gets bad enough, governments will be pressured to do something about it. But the NPT is a broad theory that may not be very useful for prediction. Whether, when, and how governments do something about the regulatory problem is the important issue for understanding the political processes behind regulation. The NPT idea does not provide much focus here. Fortunately, we have no shortage of other theoretical approaches to examine.

Closely related to the NPT idea is the public interest theory. In this "high school civics" perspective, representative democracy functions by combining the best of public opinion about what to do with more expert analytic support to solve regulatory problems, with an eye to the broad public interest. Thus a regulatory solution is crafted and implemented to improve on the market failure situation, with a benefit to society as a whole. Yet since philosophy and public choice theory have both shown that "the public interest" can be a somewhat elusive and even vacuous phrase, it must be translated into action in some manner. One useful definition is economic efficiency. If government regulatory actions serve to make markets more, rather than less, efficient, we can say that the public interest has been served, as in the NPT. Of course, this ignores equity (and potentially other) concerns that might also be important to society, but economists and philosophers do not yet have any agreed-upon formulas to clearly relate or to balance these two important concepts (but see Rawls's 1971 efforts, for example).

Another way to get at a rough conception of the public interest is through majority rule in a democratic framework. While it has been impracticable to have citizens vote on every important regulatory issue, politicians can be—and are to some extent—guided by polls of the citizens. While there are philosophical problems with such an approach, as well as identifiable social choice aggregation problems and more practical concerns, this does start to approximate what some would consider a definition of the public interest. To see if this is a useful theory, we could examine the fit between public opinion on a regulatory issue over time, or across jurisdictions, with actual regulatory policies enacted. Unfortunately, polls done over time have rarely included, and repeated, specific questions about regulation, only more general questions about the relationship of markets and government or about the size of government. While better public opinion data on the states themselves are emerging (see Erikson, Wright, and McIver 1993; Berry and others 1998), they are still not sufficient to provide confidence that we can adequately test this relationship fully across states and over time.

In any event, since regulation is rarely salient and often highly complex, we may not always expect a close correspondence between public opinion and regulatory policies. Due to regulatory complexity, in normative terms we may not want public sentiment dictating regulatory policy. Still, this relationship provides another way to think about a public interest theory of regulation.

Private Interest Theories

While public opinion sometimes influences regulation, another possibility is that concentrated interest groups, with high stakes involved and an ability to organize collectively, are highly influential in regulatory politics. One version of this theory is the well-known regulatory capture model, advanced first within political science (Huntington 1952; Bernstein 1955), but then emphasized and formalized by economists (Friedman 1962; Stigler 1971; Posner 1974; Peltzman 1976; Becker 1983). Regulatory capture is mostly assumed to happen when a single strong firm or industry group gets supportive regulation. More recent formulations of the idea involve multi–interest group capture, in which several groups compete to have their regulatory agenda approved by politicians and regulators. If enough groups compete effectively, multi-interest capture could start to look like pluralism, a more desirable normative outcome to most political philosophers.

Advocates of capture argue that it takes place either at the birth of the regulations and the regulatory agency, or it develops over a life cycle (Bernstein 1955). In either case, the firms or individuals who were supposed to be regulated end up controlling the regulators enough to get policies that favor their private interests rather than the broader public interest. Empirically, we can show this to be accurate, or at least to be probable, if we find evidence that government action is not making a market more efficient, and in making the marketplace less efficient, regulations in fact improve the profits or market position of the private interests who pressed for them.

An extreme version of capture is that regulation can only and always serve the interests of the firms that are regulated, by creating entry barriers to other possible competitors (Friedman 1962; Stigler 1971). Largely, this does not seem realistic. Usually other interests are served, too, as a political coalition may be necessary to provide support for regulation that might harm consumers, taxpayers, or some other groups. Certainly, the pursuit of such favors, which is often called "rent-seeking" (Tullock 1980), also involves payoffs, legal or illegal, to intermediaries such as consultants and lobbyists, as well as to politicians and regulators who may actually grant the regulatory favors. Another theoretical argument is that these various payoffs may dissipate much of the profits generated by the regulatory protections.

Multi–interest group capture is the more nuanced and sophisticated version of this theory. It suggests that interest groups compete for favorable policy outcomes in the regulatory arena (Posner 1974; Peltzman 1976; Becker 1983; Yandle 1983). Since collective action theories suggest that some types of interest groups will be easier to organize and hence more powerful than others (Olson 1965), usually the producer groups in regulation, the input provided by various interested groups into the regulatory process will probably not be balanced. Instead, like vectors in a physics model, the interest group pressure will act on politicians from different directions and with differential force. The groups that are able to "push" regulators harder are more likely to get resultant outcomes that they prefer, though perhaps not exactly congruent with what they want.

A sophisticated understanding of many forms of regulation reveals that often such battles are not just producer groups versus consumer groups, but some producers aligned with some consumer types versus other kinds of producers aligned with different consumer, labor, or environmental groups (see Yandle 1983). For example, in 1990s telecommunications regulatory battles over pricing, local exchange telephone companies were often aligned in regulatory battles with small consumers against the interests of cable TV firms, long-distance carriers, and large telecommunications-consuming businesses.

It is certainly true that many interest groups are active in trying to influence state regulation today. The Center for Public Integrity (Renzulli and others 2002) estimates that 37,000 businesses, trade associations, and other registered interests in the states collectively spent more than $1 billion on lobbying state officials in 2000. These figures represent an average ratio of five lobbying groups for each state legislator. The insurance industry has the most registered state lobbyists, followed by health services, education, local government, and health professionals.

In his 1980 book *The Politics of Regulation,* James Q. Wilson developed the idea that different costs and benefits for interest groups and other external actors shape the kind of regulatory politics that ensues. His 2 by 2 matrix of narrow or widely distributed costs and benefits helps us understand the new social regulation under the category of entrepreneurial politics, as well as more traditional regulatory politics such as client politics (capture), interest group politics (multi-interest group capture), and majoritarian politics. However, while this framework advanced social scientific thinking about regulation, as Shepsle (1982) criticized this descriptive, case-study oriented work by Wilson and his colleagues, it really did not have anything systematic to say about the role of government institutions in the process.

Reflecting the idea that simple, one-group capture may be relatively rare in today's regulatory environment, it follows that political institutions and actors themselves have the ability to shape regulatory policy, apart from the broader societal influences of public opinion and interest groups. These elite or institutional explanations suggest that the structure and development of governmental institutions are important. This explanation fits in well with the focus in political science on the critical role of institutions, a school of thought now two decades old but sometimes called the "New Institutionalism" or "Neo-Institutionalism" to distinguish it from early forms of institutional scholarship.

The Role of Government Institutions

So far, all of the theories outlined seem to presume that what happens within government is largely irrelevant to the regulatory outcome; that is, government is a "black box" that is acted on by outsiders, or it can be considered a "cash register" of interests. One of the most important trends in political science since the 1980s has been the reemphasis on the role of governmental institutions (Shepsle 1979; Moe 1984; March and Olsen 1989). Advocates of institutional theories argue that government actors themselves matter, regardless of what external interests are doing. Some believe that government institutions are best thought of as another set of interest groups, while others believe that they play a critical role by mediating, and sometimes redirecting, the interest group pressure they receive.

Scholars have developed considerable theoretical and empirical work in recent years focused on the role of institutions. This work has examined in greater detail the role of specific institutions—including executives, legislatures, courts, and bureaucracies—in shaping policies. In particular, a principal-agent perspective, using contractual terms and borrowed from economics, has been helpful in examining the relationships between different government actors (Moe 1984).

Principal-Agent Approaches

Economists developed the principal-agent framework to better understand relationships between shareholders and managers and between managers and workers in firms (Jensen and Meckling 1976). It can be used more broadly in any hierarchical employment relationship. Principals hire agents to perform a task, because the principals do not have the time, the expertise, or both to do the task themselves. The first part of the problem is that agents may not have the same goals as principals in performing the task. While the principal may want the task performed very well, quickly, and at a low cost, the agent may want it performed just adequately at a high cost. The second part of the problem is that the principal cannot easily monitor the activities of the agent, or it is very costly to do so, so that the principal cannot tell if the agent is performing the task well at the low cost. Thus goal conflict and lack of information (monitoring costs) together create the principal-agent problem.

In a simple way, the development of regulatory (and other) policy can be conceptualized as a chain of principal-agent relationships. Citizens are the ultimate principals in a democracy. They elect (hire) politician agents to develop laws and regulatory rules—although some would say that, because of campaign contributions and lobbying, interest groups really elect or hire the politicians, not the mass public, making politicians agents of the groups. These hired executive and legislative agents then become principals themselves as they hire bureaucrats and judges to implement and interpret the laws and regulations they pass. Higher-level bureaucrats hire lower-level bureaucrats to carry out the details of these regulations. At each step of the chain, slippage and shirking may occur, so that the agent does not perform exactly the task the principal had in mind, leading to policy results that are not exactly the same as higher-level principals might have wanted or expected. This is a classic bureaucratic problem (Miller 1992).

In particular, the main application of this approach has been to examine how government bureaucrats carry out their tasks delegated by these hierarchical superiors. Unlike business firm managers, U.S. government bureaucrats have at least two political principals, the executive and the legislature. This makes for a quite different, and far more complex, principal-agent problem (see, for example, Woolley 1993). Still, the larger federal literature on regulation has established the concept that U.S. regulatory bureaucracies respond to policy preferences held by public officials. After decades in which political scientists emphasized the relative independence of bureaucrats to implement federal regulatory policy, scholars more recently have shown that other institutional actors, including Congress (Weingast and Moran 1984; McCubbins and Schwartz 1984), the president (Moe 1982; Wood and Waterman 1991), and the courts (Melnick

1983) influence policy in significant ways. In the language of principal-agent models, scholars have clearly established that a number of competing principals influence federal bureaucratic policy implementation (see Wood and Waterman 1991; Moe 1985).

Gerber and Teske (2000) reviewed over forty studies of state regulation and categorized them into principal-agent relationships. Generally, these studies find considerable influence over regulatory policy by legislatures, bureaucratic agencies, and interest groups, the three traditional nodes of the "iron triangle." Many of the regulatory areas studied are not real iron triangles, however, because they often also demonstrate independent influence patterns as well as influence from other interest groups, including large business consumers of the regulated service, potential and actual business competitors, and "enemies of business" (Wilson 1990) such as consumer, environmental, and labor groups. The evidence is less strong for other actors, particularly for governors. There is little evidence on state courts aside from that presented in chapter 15 of this study.

Other Approaches to Institutions

Political scientists have long used government "subsystem" models that identify the key sets of actors in different policy areas. The "iron triangle" model noted above is probably the most well known metaphor in the subsystem perspective. Heclo (1979) expanded the idea into "issue networks," consistent with the idea that more parties are now involved in the regulatory arena, sometimes in shifting patterns. However, these approaches do little more than establish who is likely to be a player in a given regulatory policy arena. More recently, Sabatier and Jenkins-Smith (1993) have developed an "advocacy coalition" framework that uses the subsystem approach but addresses coalition building and long-term learning in different policy arenas. This approach is still developing and not yet highly predictive.

Other recent models of policymaking have focused on the role of rhetoric and rapid policy change in particular areas of regulation (Baumgartner and Jones 1993) or on the role of political entrepreneurs in changing policy environments (Schneider, Teske, and Mintrom 1995). Gormley (1986) advanced an issue-based framework of when different institutional actors are likely to be most influential based on the salience and complexity of the particular regulatory issue, which Gerber and Teske (2000) tested and found to have good predictive powers. Beyond the obvious difficulty of measuring appropriately complexity and salience, however, Gormley's framework does not take into account varying complexity and salience within issue areas, the fact that salience might be manipulated by interest groups and politicians, the inability to separate legislators and governors, or differences in stages of the policy process. Nor does it incorporate influence from the environment external to the state, such as state economic development competition or federal regulatory goals.

A broader theory of political influence that cuts across a number of the institutional theories is the "politics of ideas." Originated by Wilson (1980), it was developed by Derthick and Quirk (1985) in trying to explain how economic deregulation occurred in the face of opposition by the most powerful interest groups, in arenas where it seemed that iron triangles and capture were well established. Broad ideas about economics and political power can influence different institutional actors in similar ways at the same time. In some cases, including deregulation in the 1970s, the "politics of ideas" supports public interest–oriented regulation, though it need not always be so favorable, as with the idea of "destructive competition" in the 1930s.

The market failure framework helps us identify situations in which government intervention into the market might be justified, but the political process determines what regulations are passed, when, and how they are implemented in practice. We do not yet have a comprehensive theory or model of how the policy process works to develop these regulations. Instead, we have a number of theories that attempt to explain the most significant factors. Broadly, these theories fall under public interest and private interest headings. Most of these theories point to the need to assess the power of interested societal actors in regulation, especially organized interest groups. They also suggest that we need to examine the role of key government institutions in formulating and implementing these regulations.

Accordingly, this book provides a focus on these issues and actors, adding evidence from the states to the broader theoretical literature on regulation while employing these existing theories to help explain state regulation better.

CHAPTER THREE

INTRODUCTION

Measurement and Methodology

Most of the theoretical frameworks scholars have developed and tested of the political economy of regulation point toward the enduring importance of interest groups and institutional actors. This suggests that while interest group participation is critically important in shaping regulatory policy, this input might be mediated and redirected by the regulatory institutions that ultimately make the policies (see Teske 1991).

This chapter outlines the methodological and measurement tools used in the quantitative studies that follow.[1] First, it should be noted that while many issues about state regulation were raised in the introductory sections of this book, it is not possible to test all of them with quantitative data. Evidence from anecdotal and general sources helps to present as comprehensive a picture of state regulation as possible, and I return to the larger issues in the final chapters after the empirical studies. But several important questions about state regulation can be tested using quantitative data across the states and over time. Quantitative analysis is a critical approach to moving beyond anecdotes and case studies to further our understanding of regulation.

---

1. For more detailed discussions of methodological issues related to the analyses in these specific chapters, please also see the related published journal articles: for chapter 5, see Ka and Teske (2002); for chapter 6, see Ruhil and Teske (2003); for chapter 7, see Laumann and Teske (2003); for chapter 9, see Howard (1998); for chapter 10, see Broscheid and Teske (2003); for chapter 15, see Graves and Teske (2003).

The goal of this project is to develop quantitative studies that are similar in approach. The ten quantitative studies presented in chapters 4–12 and 15 are comparable to each other, but not exactly so. They are comparable in that they all employ fairly recent data, from across nearly all of the fifty states. The data mostly come from the 1990s. In a few cases, where comparable data were available, the sweep of the studies is greater, going back to the 1980s, or even the 1970s for electricity rate regulation. These studies are also comparable in that they all test the influence over regulatory policy using the same explanatory factors. These include interest groups, elected institutions—always legislatures and sometimes governors, key elements of the regulatory agencies themselves—and the election or appointment of commissioners and resources, as well as broader contextual measures of economic, social, population, or problem severity factors, where relevant.

The ten quantitative studies test a range of from five to twenty explanatory factors, all but two falling into the tighter range of five to ten. In fact, the median and modal number of explanatory factors in these studies is eight, and the mean is 9.1. These eight factors are most typically broken down as two interest group measures, two electoral institutional measures, two bureaucratic agency measures, and two broader contextual measures. The reasons for the differences in the number of explanatory factors include the availability of data and the number of cases that can be assessed in each study. It would be stretching the validity of these statistical tools to test many explanatory factors for those studies where data are lacking. Each study also takes into account the existing published literature on that particular regulated industry topic in choosing which explanatory factors, or independent variables, to test. The difference across industries also limits comparability. Two analyses employ many more variables—telecommunications rate regulation (twenty) and groundwater regulations (thirteen)—but here exact comparability is sacrificed to take advantage of the particularly rich data sets available to test in even greater detail the relative influence of interest groups and bureaucratic agencies.

In testing the concepts suggested by the theoretical perspectives, there are several issues related to appropriate methodology and measurement. While it was possible to draw some valuable conclusions by cumulating the work of previous scholars (see Gerber and Teske 2000), there are limits to how far an aggregation of these existing studies can take our knowledge. These other studies vary greatly in their purposes, approaches, time frames of analysis, and methodologies. A similar quantitative approach to all industries regulated by the states, with a similar goal, provides greater clarity about the influences over state regulation, providing a better foundation for analyzing policy reforms.

Many early studies of state policymaking were in the form of qualitative case studies. With the "behavioral revolution" in the 1960s, scholars began to use quantitative data across the fifty states, with an initial focus in state-level studies on the role of party competition in influencing welfare expenditures. While quantitative analyses across all fifty states at a point in time are valuable, methodologists have come to recognize that in some cases, especially with a noncontinuous or binary dependent variable, a sample of $N = 50$ can be too small to obtain fully reliable parameter estimates. That is, we may not be able to get enough confidence, in statistical terms, to make cause-and-effect statements by only examining the fifty states at one point in time. It is also worth noting that when we examine all fifty states, technically this is not really a "sample," as the models include the full universe of all states. While scholars have generally treated state studies with statistical discussions appropriate for data samples, Gill (2001) notes that Bayesian techniques are more appropriate. The studies presented here, however, use the long-established statistical assumptions.

To obtain better statistical results, the studies mostly go well beyond one-shot, $N = 50$ analyses, in some cases (telecommunications, electricity, hospital regulations, environmental regulations) gathering considerable data over time to develop fairly sophisticated pooled time-series, cross-sectional (TSCS) models (see, for example, Beck and Katz 1995; Beck, Katz, and Tucker 1998; Box-Steffensmeier and Jones 1997). Other cases (such as medical regulation) look at a few different points in time, or panels, across all of the states, based on the availability of new data. In still other cases (insurance and savings and loans), when it was possible to gather such data, rather than examining the actual state regulatory policy decision as the output to explain, or unit of analysis, a still larger sample size was achieved by examining the effects of state regulation on individual firms. Finally, for the regulation of lawyers, it was not possible to get data that vary over time for the central variables of interest, so the data in chapter 9 are $N = 50$, at one point in time, and I recognize some caveats that must go along with those quantitative results.

Measurement

As with any empirical studies, there are here some measurement concerns related to the explanatory factors, or independent variables, in the analyses. Political scientists have developed innovative ways to measure some of these state variables, while other measures remain more crude or limited. And new measures are being developed, tested, and analyzed every year, especially for state public opinion and the popularity of governors. Still, it is worth discussing some shortcomings and other issues about these measures, as they may influence the strength of the results and the confidence we can have in them.

Some very important recent work has been done on the growth, development, and power of interest groups in the states and the environments they have created (Hrebener and Thomas 1993; Gray and Lowery 1995; Gray and others 2003). But finding the appropriate measure for the strength of interest groups in the state regulatory process remains difficult. It would be an extremely demanding task to try to assess actual participation in legislative and bureaucratic hearings by each interest group in each area of regulation, and even that would not really measure their true strength. Arguably, the best measure would be some combination of industry- or firm-specific state-level campaign contributions, which are extremely difficult to get across all fifty states, and actual lobbying or participation efforts both in the legislative and bureaucratic arenas. Lacking data to capture such measures, we generally must rely on proxy measures that capture the general economic power of the interest group (such as its share of state gross economic product or employment) or some notion of political or organizational power (such as number of members compared to state population), or similar measures (such as its reputation for power). These are probably fairly good measures of interest group political power in some cases, but may be less appropriate in others.

In a few large states, legislatures are like "mini Congresses" with full-time legislators, good pay, large staffs, and frequent meetings. In other— usually smaller—states, legislatures meet infrequently, serve part-time, and have very little staff support. Given this continuing variation in state legislatures around the United States, political scientists have developed good measures of legislative professionalism (Squire 1992; Mooney 1994). And, of course, good measures of state party control are easily constructed. We now have some measures of state elite ideology beyond simple party identification that recognizes, for example, that Democrats around the country do not all necessarily share the same ideology (Berry and others 1998). We can be fairly confident about these overall measures of state legislative ideology and professionalism and use them in a variety of ways. These studies employ a mix of party control and ideology variables, depending on which seems most appropriate in the particular regulatory context. The finding that most of these studies show a strong substantive and statistically significant influence for state legislative party control or ideology suggests that these are good measures. No study of which I am aware has yet examined the makeup of specific state committees overseeing the efforts of particular state regulatory agencies, an approach that has been used successfully at the federal level and holds promise for future state scholarship.

For governors, scholars often use party identification as a proxy for ideology, though this is clearly not ideal, given the variation in party ideology around the country. We also have available some scales of gubernatorial power, but these often capture in part the number of appointments governors make—in a particular area of regulation, this may not be directly relevant, or it may already be measured by an appointed or elected regulator variable. Scholars are beginning to develop some measures of gubernatorial popularity, but these are just being refined. Since we have considerable anecdotal evidence about their importance in the state regulatory process, finding better measures of gubernatorial ideology and power should be an issue high on research agendas for state politics (see Ferguson 2003). I return to the policy role of governors with a broader discussion in chapter 14.

Finding good measures of the influence of bureaucracies themselves is difficult. Scholars have used regulatory budgets and number of personnel involved, per capita state population, to measure the size of regulatory bureaucracies, or state budgetary commitments to that specific regulatory activity. Measures of whether regulators are appointed or elected are easy to find. Measures of bureaucratic budgetary dependence on the legislature are often available. But few scholars have measured differences in detailed bureaucratic structures across the states and the effect they may have on policy outcomes. Some of the studies here go much further, especially that of telecommunications regulation in chapter 4.

Political scientists have done some innovative research on the connection between public opinion and state policy outcomes, though not often directly in regulatory policy (Erikson, Wright, and McIver 1993; Berry and others 1998). But there is room for scholars to improve the measures and especially to test the connection to outcomes in a wider array of policy domains. Since it is less likely that public opinion influences some of the detailed regulatory policy decisions analyzed in these studies, public opinion is assessed only in a few instances, where policies are more salient to the public at large.

Methodology

Several studies in this book employ pooled time-series, cross-sectional models that take advantage of variation in policies both across the states and over time within states. The cross-sections are generally all of the fifty states, though occasionally a few are not included due to data problems or to issues related to the differences of Alaska and Hawaii, in particular. The time series are usually some number of years in the 1990s, or sometimes in the 1980s when the particular regulatory policy was fairly high on the political agenda.

In almost all cases, the regulatory policy, or dependent variable, is some form of state regulatory policy output. What did the state decide to do? Did it allow electricity deregulation or not? What telecommunications price ratio does it apply across residential versus business customers? Did it maintain a hospital certificate-of-need program after the federal government dropped that requirement? How much continuing education for lawyers does it require? How quickly did the state develop an EPA-approved state implementation plan for clean air? In other cases, the dependent variable explained is a regulatory outcome, measuring what actually happened as a result of state regulation; this is the dependent variable for S&L regulation and insurance regulation, where I examine failures and insolvencies of firms as regulatory outcomes. In these cases, the dependent variables are also individual firm failures, as partly explained by state regulation, rather than specific state-level decisions. All cases use these techniques to explain the regulatory output or outcome, with a series of independent, or explanatory, variables that capture various aspects of state interest group strength, differences in state institutions and institutional actors, and variations in economic conditions or in problem severity.

Many of these models employ standard OLS regression analysis, retrofitted for pooled models to include robust or panel-corrected standard errors (PCSE). Since Stimson (1985), this technique also sometimes incorporates the use of dummy variables for years, to isolate the cross-state effects of particular points in time. Some models, where appropriate, use event history analysis, or EHA. EHA has some similarities to regression analysis but is really a hazard model, or duration design, which is appropriate when there are dependent variables that take on either 0,1 outcomes. These EHA models explain how "susceptible" a state is to adopting a particular policy at a particular point in time. In a few cases, other related techniques are employed.

Broadly, these studies come under the category of time-series cross-sectional data. Since analysis of TSCS data is relatively new but is catching on among many scholars, it is worth a little discussion about some of the relevant statistical issues. Scholars have been making great strides in the theory and political science application of these models in recent years (see, for example, Box-Steffensmeier and Jones 2002). TSCS data can raise statistical problems in at least three ways: autocorrelation over time, cross-correlations within each panel-year, and nonconstant error variance (or heteroscedasticity). Currently, there are no generally accepted diagnostic procedures for TSCS data that solve all of these problems simultaneously. Thus researchers must use a mixture of theory-based assumptions and empirical tests to guide the selection of an appropriate model and estimator.

Autocorrelation, the first potential problem, is a challenge to diagnose in TSCS analysis. Given that difficulty, some researchers suggest a compromise approach, assuming an AR-1 autoregressive structure and modeling it by including lagged values of the dependent variable from prior years as a predictor or explanatory variable (for example, Beck and Katz 1996).

The problem of cross-correlation among errors arises in many analyses because researchers often find that observations are densely connected with one another in the U.S. states (Peterson and Rom 1990; Ringquist and Garand 1999). Unlike randomly collected data, observations collected across U.S. states have complex statistical dependence structures. Thus researchers must be aware of possible cross-dependency among model error terms.

Heteroscedasticity is the third potential problem with these TSCS data. Differences in states and similar groupings within regions of the country may contribute to nonconstant error variance—panel heteroscedasticity—within a given panel-year of the analysis. If they are not accounted for, these differences in variance within panel-years can greatly reduce the efficiency of the estimators employed. Thus researchers often have to address problems with TSCS data related to correlated and nonconstant errors within each panel. Accordingly, I generally follow Beck and Katz (1995, 1996) and apply the ordinary least squares estimator with PCSE in these models. This method is flexible, efficient, and arguably superior to other methods used in finite samples.

For greater readability, rather than addressing the specific methodological concerns that arise with each empirical chapter, the focus there is simply on the nature of the regulatory measures, or dependent variables, and the explanatory, or independent, predictor variables that are used to explain the measured form of regulation. I discuss the overall fit of the models to the data, the significance and substantive influence of key predictor variables, and the effects the explanatory variables have on the regulatory measures. For any particularly complicated methods, there are additional citations and some methodological endnotes for the reader who is attuned to such issues and wants more explanation of the specific research decisions that were made in a particular chapter. For example, the insurance solvency chapter (chapter 6) employs both a two-stage methodology, to address the fact that inspections of insurance firms are an endogenous choice made by political and bureaucratic actors, and a more complicated analysis designed for event counts of rare events (such as the insolvency of firms in a particular state in a given year).

PART TWO

Monopoly Regulation

Monopoly industries have been regulated in their intrastate operations by state public utility commissions (PUCs) for nearly a hundred years. Regulation of these industries is usually also performed in parallel, to some degree, at the interstate level by federal regulators. The analyses in this section focus on two of the most important infrastructural industries in a modern economy—telecommunications and electricity. These are critical industries upon which nearly all Americans depend, at home and at work, for communication and energy, to engage in their normal daily tasks. Americans literally could not live normal twenty-first-century lives without the services of these industries, which we often take for granted, except when they are disrupted, as with the rolling blackouts of power in California in 2000, or with the huge 2003 blackout in the northeastern United States. Each study examines the factors that help explain the decisions regulators make in apportioning rates to different classes of customers—specifically, the ratio of residential to business intrastate prices for services. For telecommunications over the period 1990–98, Junseok Kim, Jack Buckley, and I find that an array of factors related to the state regulators' attitudes, structures, and resources best explain pricing decisions.

For electricity, Sangjoon Ka and I find that state legislative ideology influences the rate ratio, as does the manner in which regulators are selected: appointed by the governor or elected directly by voters. In addition, because electricity deregulation has been the most prominent element of state regulation in recent years—and controversial given the price hikes and blackouts in California's deregulated markets and problems with an aging electrical grid across the nation—a second analysis in chapter 5 examines the factors that explain state decisions on this complex matter. The findings show that state legislative professionalism is quite important in prompting deregulation, as well as the actual prices that customers pay for electricity.

Historical Development

Federal regulation of the telephone industry began in 1913, with the so-called Kingsbury Commitment, an agreement by AT&T and the federal government that the industry would be a regulated monopoly, initially regulated by the Interstate Commerce Commission (ICC) and after 1934 by the Federal Communications Commission (FCC). The Federal Power Commission (FPC) began regulating the interstate aspects of electric power in 1920; the Federal Energy Regulatory Commission (FERC) replaced the FPC in 1977. With the development and activities of these federal institutions, politicians and courts have defined the legal and political reasoning behind the traditional interstate and intrastate commerce split, which started with railroads in the 1860s, proceeded through trucking in the 1930s, and focused on telecommunications in the 1980s and 1990s and electricity in the twenty-first century.

Natural monopoly industries are characterized by extremely high initial fixed costs, usually associated with the construction of a widespread physical distribution plant to serve many, or all, consumers in a given geographic region. After sinking these high fixed costs, variable costs of serving new customers are quite low for the firm and they tend to decline over a wide range of industry output, making it very difficult for would-be competitive firms to price at a level near that of the incumbent firm.

The basic economics of natural monopoly are now well developed and can be understood from Economics 101 textbooks. They stand in marked contrast to the way that fully competitive markets operate. But in the 1860s, when railroads were expanding across America, the idea of natural monopoly—and whether and how to regulate it—was just developing. Some states began to establish "weak" regulatory commissions to provide information about services, prices, and safety, led by Charles Francis Adams in Massachusetts. Different institutional models of regulation emerged; while northeastern states emphasized an independent commission model of regulation, the midwestern states, influenced heavily by the

Grange agricultural interests, opted for direct legislative forms of regulation. Eventually, these states pushed for some form of federal regulation,
and the inability of states to control growing interstate commerce by railroads led to the establishment of the first federal regulatory agency, the
ICC, in 1887.

The ICC was weak at first, and when railroads challenged ICC attempts to push the envelope of their regulatory powers, the U.S. Supreme
Court generally backed the railroads. But as the Progressive political movement grew, Congress gave the ICC more "teeth" in the early twentieth
century. In 1907 New York and Wisconsin established "strong"' public
utility commissions, with power over rates. Fully forty-five states established PUCs between 1907 and 1922. Even though the economics of natural
monopoly firms did not necessarily dictate that firm boundaries match
those of the states, those political jurisdictions evolved into regulatory
boundaries.

The basic intrastate-interstate regulatory split has evolved over time
but is still largely in place today in these industries. The states generally
regulate the physical connections from the distributed networks to the
houses and businesses themselves, as well as the other intrastate elements
of these industries. The local connections are just beginning to get some
competition, after being perceived as the clearest parts of the monopolies
in the past. In parallel, the FCC and the FERC regulate pricing, competition, and service activities that flow across the states.

The political environment that seeks to influence regulation of these
industries, at both the federal and state levels, is filled with industry interest groups, often with opposing agendas. These include, most prominently,
the regulated firms themselves, which are involved in all aspects of their
regulation. In recent years, as most of these industries have experienced
technological changes and some degree of deregulation, the environment
also includes firms that are the emerging competitors of entrenched monopolists, as well as large organized groups of businesses that use electricity, telecommunications, or transportation services. In addition, at least
since the 1970s, both grass-roots and government-sponsored consumer
advocates provide significant input into the policy decisions made by PUCs
on behalf of dispersed, small residential consumers.

Most state PUCs are made up of regulators appointed by the state governors, with some overlapping of terms, though regulators are elected in
about one-quarter of the states, mostly directly by voters but indirectly by
the state legislature in a couple of states. The state PUCs jointly form a

national group, the National Association of Regulatory Utility Commissioners (NARUC), which also has a research operation, the National Regulatory Research Institute.

Within each state, the PUC regulatory process generally is quite structured around administrative hearings, and a large body of legal precedent has emerged over time. Rate change and other regulatory proceedings take a long time, are highly technical, and typically involve massive amounts of testimony and economic evidence from the variety of interested parties noted above. At the same time that these slow-moving, traditional, and sometimes cumbersome regulatory proceedings are in force, most of these industries themselves have changed very rapidly in recent years. Both technological changes and policy movements toward deregulation have made these formerly lumbering and stagnant industries far more competitive and nimble in recent years, as well as chaotic (including firms like Enron, WorldCom, Global Crossing, and others).

Other PUC-Regulated Industries

We can learn more about the regulation of telecommunications and electricity by examining a few other natural monopoly industries that are no longer regulated by the states. As noted, railroads were the first monopolistic industry regulated by the states. Over time, however, most railroad transportation became interstate in nature, and court decisions tended to establish the primacy of the ICC over state regulators when there were disputes about jurisdiction. With the federal deregulation of railroads in 1980, the Staggers Act, designed to revitalize a dying U.S. railroad industry, Congress preempted the economic regulatory role of the states. Similarly, in 1982 Congress preempted further economic regulation of the intercity bus industry. There has been no movement to bring state regulation back in these transportation industries since.

In earlier work I examined in great detail a less prominent industry formerly also regulated on the intrastate level by the states, economic regulation of the trucking industry (Teske, Best, and Mintrom 1995). For trucking the natural monopoly case probably never applied well, but truckers were able to use regulation to limit new entry of competitors. Also for trucking, unlike railroads and intercity buses, Congress did not preempt the states when it deregulated trucking in 1980. Following that large-scale federal deregulation of interstate prices and entry, however, only a few states gradually made corresponding deregulatory changes over the next fourteen years. Powerful entrenched intrastate trucking interests managed to maintain archaic regulations that harmed their states' economies and kept competition at bay, despite near unanimous agreement (or as near as it gets in public policy circles) that economic deregulation of trucking had proven to be beneficial to everyone but the entrenched monopolists and good for the public interest, however it was defined.

Large business shippers and potential trucking competitors attempted to reverse this regulatory capture politically in the states but largely were not successful. They also attempted to get the ICC and the courts to preempt state regulation by making the interstate commerce argument more pervasively to include areas of transportation that formerly fell under intrastate commerce definitions. While these state-level efforts succeeded to some degree in reducing some economic inefficiencies, it was only in 1994, when UPS and Federal Express found their own trucking delivery of packages limited by state regulations, that enough heavy political pressure was brought to bear on Congress to preempt state economic regulation of the trucking industry. This expensive lobbying effort proved successful, and it provides another recent example of "nondevolution," or preemption, and an example of federal politicians not trusting state regulatory decisions. While state economic regulation of trucking was preempted in 1994, the states continue to have the power to regulate noneconomic aspects of the industry, such as weight and height limitations, carriage of hazardous materials, and other related safety and environmental issues.

In political terms, state deregulation was explained largely by interest group pressure from truckers, shippers, and agricultural interests. This parallels the simple explanation that the powerful interests at the federal level, Fed Ex and UPS, also appeared to be the dominant forces behind the federal preemption decision in 1994, as they contributed more money toward federal political campaigns than any other industry.

In trucking as in telecommunications and electricity, analysis finds an important role for state interest groups, generally the regulated firms, but also for new competitors and concentrated business consumer groups. Certainly interest groups are very active in formal PUC proceedings, as well as in legislative lobbying about broader structural issues. And when the regulated firms are most dominant, as with state trucking regulation, the structure and resources of the regulatory institutions do not seem to play a critical role. But when many interest groups compete and perhaps counterbalance each other's input and pressure to some degree, the strongest influence over policy decisions comes from the combination of the state legislature and the state bureaucratic actors themselves. Differing legislative ideologies, regulatory resources, and accountability structures clearly lead to different policy outputs across the U.S. states as they regulate these monopolistic industries.

CHAPTER FOUR

Telecommunications

with

JUNSEOK KIM
JACK BUCKLEY

Telecommunications is the infrastructure industry behind the information economy that has developed in the United States and in other advanced nations. In the past the most important element of telecommunications was that it allowed humans to communicate at a distance. While this is still critically important to the exchange of information, the digital convergence of computer technology and telecommunications, as epitomized by the development of the Internet, has made the telecommunications backbone even more critical to the way that Americans will live and work in the future. Every nation needs healthy and technologically advanced telecommunications systems to support economic growth and data exchange.

For virtually all of its history, the telecommunications industry has been regulated. In most other countries, rather than regulate this presumed natural monopoly, the government itself took over and ran the telecommunications industry. This trend has been reversed somewhat in the last twenty years, as most advanced countries, stimulated by 1992 European Union and 1996 World Trade Organization policy reforms, have privatized their national telecommunications carrier and encouraged competition by other firms. But regulation is still in place in all nations in some form. No country features a completely free telecommunications marketplace.

In the United States, the breakup of AT&T in 1984 was one of the most important events in the history of U.S. regulation. Based on an antitrust court case that AT&T agreed to settle in 1982, the 1984 breakup ended a long period in which AT&T provided all U.S. long-distance telephone service and about 80 percent of local services through its subsidiaries. The breakup led to a new era of competition, first in long-distance services and later in local services, as well as to competition in newly emerging telecommunications technologies and services, including wireless and Internet services.

History of State Role

Throughout the entire history of the telephone industry, the states have played a critical role. Starting with New York and Wisconsin in 1907, state PUCs regulated telephone services well before Congress created the FCC at the federal level in 1934 and even before earlier federal regulation by the ICC in 1914. After 1934 the FCC played the leading role in creating a fairly uniform and harmonious regulatory environment, with the state PUCs generally making corresponding changes in their own policies. The FCC and the states established a stable relationship in which long-distance and business rates were priced higher than costs to cross-subsidize lower-than-cost rates for residential access and local calling. This fit well with the dominant political consensus on telephone rates, which favored widespread access for all Americans, a goal that was largely achieved (though Mueller (1997) argues that competition achieved universal access more efficiently than regulation). However, when technology later allowed competition, these cross-subsidies fed the pressure for competition to emerge and grow, especially in those segments of the industry that were priced well above costs.

The events leading up to the AT&T breakup, and policy developments afterward, have been chronicled well in many sources (Temin and Galambos 1987; Cole 1991; Brock 1994). In addition, Teske (1990) and Cohen (1992) wrote books explicitly focused on the early decisions of the states after the 1984 AT&T breakup, when state policy choices became much more open to change and much more important to the development of this industry than they had been since 1934.

The federal-state regulatory relationship since 1984 has been complex in its economic, political, and legal dimensions (see Teske 1995). Judge Harold Greene, who heard the AT&T antitrust court case, oversaw the federal regulatory process after the breakup. Greene had to make decisions about when, and if, the "Baby Bells" that were spun off from AT&T, and which most analysts perceived to retain considerable monopoly market power after 1984, could enter manufacturing, information services, and long-distance markets. The process of allowing the Baby Bells into these markets moved very slowly and was highly contentious. Considerable criticism was launched that the U.S. telecommunications industry was essentially being regulated by a single, unelected D.C. Circuit judge, and that he was dragging his feet.

However, with so many contentious interest group battles, including long-distance firms versus local firms, new competitors versus entrenched incumbent firms, telecommunications versus cable television firms, and firms generally versus consumer groups, both large business users of telecom services and residential consumers, Congress had great difficulty passing legislation to restructure this industry and its overall relationship with the cable television and computer industries. Finally, after many false starts, Congress did pass a massive compromise bill, the 1996 federal Telecommunications Act (FTA). The compromise Congress made was basically to establish a variety of "quid pro quo" standards for entry in new markets, requiring firms to prove first that they had adequately opened their own markets to competition before they would be allowed to enter other markets, to seek economies of scope in their service provisions. Overall, the FTA encouraged competition and to some extent based its ideas on models of local competition and regulated interconnection that had been developed in leading states, like New York and Illinois. It explicitly preempted some forms of state and local regulation that prohibited or limited competition. Still, as the FCC has implemented various aspects of the FTA, firms have gone to court to try to achieve their interpretations of the broad rules established by Congress, and this continued political and legal wrangling has slowed the movement to greater local market competition.

While these events have received considerable scrutiny by scholars, especially at the federal level, we do not have a comprehensive analysis of state regulatory choices over the nearly twenty-year period since divestiture, a period that allowed for numerous political and regulatory interventions. The industry evolved substantially over that period—interstate and intrastate long-distance competition became realities, and the long-distance industry, like many other U.S. industries, has become a concentrated oligopoly with a few dominant firms and a fringe of smaller niche players. Local competition has moved considerably more slowly and is only a viable option for business users and for residents in a few large cities, though it is expected to expand in the near future. Wireless communications has emerged to become so inexpensive and convenient that

some customers use it for much of their telecommunications services, and
it has become directly competitive with wireline services in many cases.
Finally, Internet access has become a critical component of telecommunications services in recent years, and an important service offering for many
telephone companies.

Factors Likely to Influence Regulation

With this history in mind, we present a quantitative analysis of telecommunications regulation by the states over the period 1990–98. Historical
and empirical studies have emphasized the importance of interest groups
in telecommunications regulation. Telecommunications firms have been
among the largest contributors to state legislative campaigns in recent
years. At times regulatory battles in this industry have resembled fights
between industry segments or interest group politics more than classic
producer versus consumer battles in traditional monopoly regulatory politics (Wilson 1980). Any quantitative analysis of state decisionmaking must
measure these different industry interests. A few studies have also pointed
to the importance of state institutions in these policy decisions, including
state elected officials, the legislature, and the governor as well as the regulatory agencies themselves (Teske 1990; Cohen 1992). This study goes
further than prior analyses to consider the influence of a wider range of
institutional factors. In addition, economic and competitive factors are
likely to shape regulatory decisions. State markets are different, rural and
more urban states face different pricing structures, and the presence of
concentrated large users can influence policy choices. These measures are
included as explanatory factors in the analyses below.

Measuring Regulation

The critical issues in telecommunications regulation are competition and
pricing of several services, including local access services, access prices for
long-distance firms, and intrastate long-distance rates. State PUCs still
regulate prices in many markets or have influence over many other factors that affect prices, such as interconnection policies. In addition, state
regulation influences competition, as does market size and other factors,
but how regulators price, how they set up interconnections agreements,
and other factors will affect how fast competition develops and how far it
goes into different segments of the telecommunications industry. Unfortu-

nately, it is not possible to analyze all of these possible elements of state regulation over a longer period because the data are not available.[1] Instead, this analysis focuses on one important regulatory measure that has clear political implications—the price ratio that state regulators establish between local residential services and local business services. This ratio reflects, at least in part, the degree to which regulators are trying to protect residential consumers in their state, which could be one definition of the public interest. This variable allows analysis of an issue of classical redistribution—who gets what at whose expense—in local telephone markets.

After divestiture, the states could no longer rely as much on interstate long-distance revenues to subsidize their local operations, putting pressure on local prices. States have also been pressured to maintain substantial cross-subsidies to rural and high-cost areas, but now without as much of a cross-subsidy from interstate funds, leading frequently to increases in local rates for other, nonrural consumers in a state. Often this increase has taken the form of another cross-subsidy: from business to residential consumers. The issue of local business to residential cross-subsidy is the central variable of interest here since it raises the classical political issue of redistribution and evokes tensions among state political actors. Less well-off users and users in high-cost areas might be excluded from the telephone network if local residential rates become too high. However, raising local business rates might force local businesses to shop around for communications alternatives (private networks, cable services, and so on). This could eventually lead, in turn, to higher residential rates, as the sources of the subsidy disappear.

To capture this trade-off, the measure of regulation is the ratio of consumer intrastate phone rates to business rates.[2] A small ratio indicates

1. We would have preferred to analyze from 1982 until the present. But the FCC collected telecommunications data before 1989 and after 1989 in an inconsistent manner, not easily reconciled. Thus we employ the more recent data.

2. Because of the complications of telecommunications pricing, it is worth understanding the specifics of this measure. The residential rate is gathered from city-level data and averaged for all cities across a state. It includes the monthly connection charge and the monthly flat rate, if that city has flat rate service. If the city does not have flat rate service, a measured rate for a hundred local calls is employed instead. In addition, the local charge includes touch-tone service, 911 charges, any surcharges, and taxes. The equivalent information is used to create the business rate for that state. In essence, this captures what most consumers think of as their local payment for telecommunications services.

that consumers are benefiting relative to business groups, while a high ratio suggests the opposite, ceteris paribus. The ratio varies from 0.25 to 1.32 across the states and years.

Although this ratio is an important measure, it is not the only important policy outcome. The ratio could be set at a certain level, but the absolute level of prices for both sets of users could be high, if regulators allow the incumbent firm to earn high profits at the expense of all consumers. Similarly, the ratio could be set at the same overall level, but absolute prices could be lower for both groups in another state that tries to squeeze more efficiency out of the local carrier, or affords them a lower rate of return. Still, this is a very useful measure to examine.

Explaining Regulation

To explain the price ratio, four sets of independent variables are examined in the analysis: (1) those related to interest groups and the larger public; (2) those related to elected state political actors; (3) PUC institutional factors; and (4) other control variables.

Several interest groups merit attention. The local incumbents are probably the most powerful, and they have learned to use the regulatory process in a strategic manner (see Campbell 1996). So the first thing to examine is the relative power of the Baby Bells over this regulatory decision. Local dominant carriers (mainly Baby Bells) want to keep residential rates down for two reasons: to justify the existence of the access fee as a revenue source from long-distance carriers and further defend their universal service claim, and to use low residential rates as an implicit entry barrier against potential competitors in the local market. If residential prices are low, competitors will not see market entry as viable. Thus the Baby Bell variable is a proxy for the pressure from local dominant carriers on the PUC—the regional Bell operating company (RBOC) percentage of market share in prescribed telephone lines by state.

Second, I examine the influence of AT&T's market share, a proxy for the dominant long-distance carriers' influence on state regulators, using the percentage of AT&T market share of prescribed telephone lines by state. Since accelerated competition in local telephony is directly linked to the reduction of their burden of cross-subsidy from interstate to intrastate telephony, AT&T and other long-distance carriers want to become local competitors, which requires more market-based local rates for residential consumers of incumbent firms. Since the AT&T breakup, AT&T has still remained a market leader, holding about 63 percent of the nation's lines in 1998 but gaining only a minimal share of the local telephony market.

As a control variable, we also include the ratio of residential to business presubscribed intraLATA (local access and transport area) lines. This partially captures the local market share of the two groups for which state policymakers are determining prices.

There is a body of evidence that differences in public opinion are strongly correlated with state policy differences (Stimson 1991; Hanson 1999). This can be examined using Berry and others' (1998) state ideology scores, which are constructed on a zero to one hundred scale, with higher values indicating a more liberal citizenry. States with a more liberal ideology should tend to push PUCs to favor residential consumers over the business sector in the price ratio.

The second set of variables tests the political influence exercised by elected officials over the PUCs across the states. For state legislatures, we test the ratio of Democrat to Republican legislators in both the lower and upper houses.[3] Assuming that Republicans are more likely to favor business groups whereas Democrats support consumer interests, an increase in the party ratio in either house should lead to relatively lower residential rates, meaning a decrease in the ratio.

Governors seem likely to play a similar role in their state to the president in the federal government. Governors have their own agendas that may depart substantially from what even their more prominent supporters might want. More so than individual legislators, this is likely to lead them to promote moderation, compromise, responsive regulation, and concern for the public interest. Governors' partisanship may therefore have only a negligible effect on state regulatory decisionmaking. The variable that captures the percentage of votes cast for the elected governor stands as a proxy for relative strength of the governor's power in a state. The larger the vote share of the governor, theoretically the more authority he or she can exercise in a state. However, the prediction for this variable is ambiguous as well, and it is included more for completeness than for an explicit theoretical assumption.

Also included as a variable is a state office in Washington, D.C., which equals one if a state has its lobbying office in the capital and zero otherwise. This is a proxy for how seriously each state lobbies the federal gov-

3. Unicameral and nonpartisan Nebraska is treated as having a ratio of 0.50.

ernment; it is included more as a control measure and may not prove significant.

Turning to the PUCs themselves, several variables measure differences in accountability structures and institutions across three dimensions: statutory PUC authority over regulatory matters, PUC institutional structure, and the presence of restrictions on PUC commissioners. PUC authority refers to the size and purview of the commission's authority. Four variables measure this concept: statutory PUC authority over telephone rates and facilities, statutory PUC authority over accounting and audits, statutory PUC authority over financial and corporate regulation, and the total number of commissioners in a state PUC.

Data on PUC authority came from all available written information on regulatory statutes from the National Association of Regulatory Utility Commissioners (NARUC), government publications, state reports, and state PUC web pages on the Internet. For each state, we obtained forty-five dichotomous indicators varying over time and across states; they are grouped into three categories and scaled in order to measure the scope of PUC decisionmaking authority over intrastate telecommunications firms. Larger values are coded to indicate greater PUC authority over the regulated firms. The range is from seven to forty-three. The following elements make up the PUC authority indexes. First, for PUC authority over telephony rates and facilities, the agency has the authority to:

—authorize temporary/interim rates pending investigation;
—require prior authorization of rate change;
—suspend proposed rate changes;
—initiate rate investigation upon its own motion;
—regulate or control rates on sales to ultimate consumers;
—regulate or control rates on retail sales to ultimate consumers (basic local exchange service—Bell LEC and Non-Bell LEC);
—regulate standards by setting safety standard;
—authorize interconnections;
—require interconnections;
—regulate standards by requiring utilities to act as common carriers;
—regulate standards by requiring joint use facilities;
—regulate standards by requiring line extension within the area served;
—require certificates of convenience and necessity for initiating service;
—require certificates of convenience and necessity for constructing major additions (generating plants);

—require certificates of convenience and necessity for constructing major additions (transmissions lines);

—require certificates of convenience and necessity for constructing major additions (distribution lines);

—require certificates of convenience and necessity for constructing major additions (other plants);

—require certificates of convenience and necessity for abandonment of facilities or service;

—issue indeterminate permits;

—allocate unincorporated territory among utilities.

In the second category, PUC authority over accounting and audits, the agency has the authority to:

—prescribe a uniform system of accounts;

—require specific entries or adjustments in accounts;

—prescribe rules for preserving records;

—interpret uniform systems of accounts;

—prescribe units of property;

—require annual audits by independent accountants (or another interval);

—require annual audits by independent accountants under either a general statute or a specific status;

—require copies of independent audit report.

The third category is PUC authority over financial and corporate issues, measuring if approval of the agency is required prior to:

—sale of facilities (entire operating units);

—purchase of facilities (entire operating units);

—merger or consolidation;

—issuance of securities (mortgage bonds);

—issuance of securities (debentures);

—issuance of securities (notes over one year);

—issuance of securities (notes under one year);

—issuance of securities (preferred stocks);

—issuance of securities (underwriting of new common stock);

—purchase or issuance of securities by utilities operating in the state but incorporated in another;

—issuance of restricted stock options;

—entrance into lease transactions.

The third category inquires also whether the agency has the authority to:

—disqualify directors and officers where interlocking directorates and conflicts of interests are involved;

—require advance submission of budgets on capital expenditures;

—regulate the declaration of dividends;

—regulate the entry of utility into nonutility activities either directly or through an affiliate;

—regulate approved diversification.

Consistent with public interest theory and prior studies (Berry 1984; Gormley 1983), the more authority for a state PUC over the regulated industry, the less likely it should be to be captured by the regulated firms and thus the more likely that it will support residential interests over the private business groups. An increase in the number of commissioners, which ranges from three to seven in the states, consequently should increase the cost of regulatory decisionmaking within a PUC, leading to a greater likelihood of capture by private industry groups.

Three indicators measure the accountability relationship of the PUC—elected PUC commissioners, the PUC as an official arm of the legislature, and bureaucratic independence. The variable elected PUC commissioners is a dummy variable, equaling one if the PUC commissioners are elected and zero otherwise. Teske (1991) found that commissioners elected by popular votes are more responsive to the public in telecommunications regulation and enjoy wider discretion than political appointees. Those elected by popular vote should be more likely to represent and implement voters' interests, leading to a majoritarian outcome favoring residential consumers over business.

The next two variables, taken together, categorize the institutional form of the PUC. The variable PUC as legislative arm is also dichotomous, equaling one if the PUC is officially an arm of the state legislature and zero otherwise. Bureaucratic independence is coded one if the PUC is neither an arm of state legislature nor under the executive branch, and zero otherwise. Taking the concept of a neutral and competent bureaucracy as the benchmark, state PUCs that are independent should be more likely to enjoy freedom from external pressures and thus support voters' interests (Wilson 1989). There is no clear theoretical prediction for the variable PUC as a legislative arm.

Two variables—a statutory requirement for PUC commissioners' qualifications and the revolving door hypothesis—capture institutional restrictions on state PUC commissioners. Here, the goal is to measure the substantive constraints on the qualifications and opportunistic behaviors of state PUC commissioners. The statutory requirement for PUC commissioners is a dichotomous variable, equaling one if the commissioners need to have a professional background in order to be eligible to serve on the commission under state legislation. This professional background usually stipulates some economic, legal, engineering, or accounting experience in related areas. While the academic literature provides little direction on how this statutory requirement for PUC commissioners might affect state PUC policy decisions, it is included for completeness, with the expectation that regulators with professional backgrounds are more likely to have the analytic ability to support the broader consumer interest rather than narrow business groups.

The second commissioner variable relates to the revolving doors hypothesis, and it assesses the imposition of restrictions on how long after service on a PUC a commissioner must wait before taking a job with the regulated industry. Following previous discussions of the revolving door issue (Gormley 1979), if PUC commissioners are restricted from working for the regulated firms for a certain period after departure from PUC, they should be less likely to be captured by regulated firms and business interests while actually making decisions.

The last set of independent variables includes general economic controls. The first two indicators are yearly differences in telephone penetration rates in a state, which range from 89 percent to over 100 percent (more telephone lines than people), and the unemployment rate in the previous fiscal year. The state unemployment rate (lagged by one year's time) is a proxy for the overall state economy. Some scholars argue that innovation toward a new regulatory regime is more likely when there are substantial economic disruptions (Rose 1989). An increase in the unemployment rate in a state may lower the probability of increasing residential rates.

The variable penetration rate is defined as the yearly difference in telephone penetration rate within a state, given by the number of main telephone lines per capita, which ranges from 89 percent to 105 percent, as a proxy for the stock of telecommunications infrastructure in a state. Greenstein, Lizardo, and Spiller (2002) survey several studies that investigate the impact of telecommunication and information technology infrastructure on economic performance. Policymakers probably perceive the possible trade-off between economic efficiency and equality. If state policymakers interpret the penetration rate as a determinant of the need for further expansion of service (toward universal service), then for a given level of cost and telecom infrastructure within a state, the higher the penetration rate, the more weight toward economic efficiency in policy (thus increasing the consumer to business ratio).

Results

We analyze state regulation using the least squares estimator with panel-corrected standard errors (for methodological discussion of these techniques, see chapter 3). The results are presented in table 4-1, with a focus on the level of statistical significance for variables with substantive importance.

The PUC statutory measures (PUC authority 1, 2, and 3) all have statistically significant coefficient estimates with the expected negative signs (thus supporting lower consumer rates). These findings support the contention that the level of substantive rules, resources, and political design significantly influences decisions by state regulatory agencies. How state PUCs are constituted and organized matters—they are institutions with independent sources of power and influence over regulatory policy. They act here in a manner consistent with the public interest, defined as lower consumer prices, while exercising considerable discretionary authority and operating on the basis of specialized knowledge.

The elected PUCs and statutory requirements for PUC commissioner variables are also statistically significant with the expected signs. These results indicate that accountability structures established by legislators influence policy decisions. The coefficient on the revolving door hypothesis variable is statistically significant, but in the opposite direction from the expectation. In other words, mandatory waiting periods preventing commissioners from immediately working for regulated industries after leaving the PUC are correlated with more residential consumer-friendly rate structures. This unexpected outcome may occur because we only measure the "exit" phase of the revolving door. As Gormley (1979) points out, the revolving door hypothesis can also involve prior service or employment within the regulated industry. This may effectively limit the pool of potential applicants for the post of commissioner and thus bias the effect of this variable.

None of the variables capturing the elected political players are statistically significant—the ratio of Democrats to Republicans in the upper and lower houses and the measures of governor's party affiliation and percentage of votes received. Because of measurement issues, this result is

Table 4-1. *Telecommunications Rate Ratios, 1990–98*[a]

Explanatory factors	Coefficient
AT&T market share	−0.00025
	(0.00038)
RBOC intrastate market share	−0.00066***
	(0.00018)
Ratio of residential/business	−0.0231
presubscribed intraLATA lines	(0.1440)
Elected PUC commissioners	−.034257**
	(0.016342)
Number of PUC commissioners in a state	0.008832**
	(0.00263)
Revolving door hypothesis	0.0522***
	(0.00752)
Statutory requirements for PUC commissioners	−0.01040*
	(0.00579)
State PUC as a legislative arm	0.5283***
	(0.01079)
Bureaucratic independence	−0.00936
	(0.00967)
PUC authority 1 (rates and facilities)	−0.00681***
	(0.00177)
PUC authority 2 (accounting and audits)	−0.02299***
	(0.00609)
PUC authority 3 (financial and corporate	−0.00404**
regulation)	(0.00181)
Yearly differences in telephone penetration rates	−0.015226***
	(0.002319)
Unemployment rates $(t-1)$	−0.01161**
	(0.00366)
Ratio of Democrats to Republicans (lower house)	0.00130
	(0.00279)
Ratio of Democrats to Republicans (upper house)	0.00038
	(0.00252)
Votes cast for governor (%)	−0.00123
	(0.00096)
Party affiliation of governor	0.00067
	(0.00386)
State office in D.C.	0.04905**
	(0.1595)
Citizen ideology	−0.00095**
	(0.00042)
Constant	2.5180***
	(0.2577)
Summary statistics	
$AR^2 = 0.2485***$	
$N = 364$	

*Significant at .1 level; **significant at .05 level; ***significant at .01 level.
a. Standard errors are in parentheses.

not unexpected in the case of the governor (see chapter 3), but it is more difficult to explain for the legislature. Partisan legislative politics probably matters for regulatory policymaking, but perhaps an equally important question is how long it takes until the effects of changes in politics are established. If partisan legislative politics shapes bureaucratic structure at one point in time and the design of a bureaucracy reflects the interests, strategies, and compromises of those who exercise political power, then changes in bureaucratic behavior as a result of politics might only be noticed when there are major shifts in the ruling coalition—and even then the changes may take a long time to be measurable. The data here were measured over a relatively short period (1990–98), and the partisan balance in legislatures may shift slowly in the states. Several of the differences in regulatory authority examined here may be partially endogenous, in the long run, to the legislative ideology of the state and thus are reflected in the variables in PUC measures rather than in current legislative party control variables.

Consistent with expectations, the Baby Bell share variable is statistically significant with the expected sign, whereas the AT&T market share is not significant. The variable for a state lobbying office in Washington, D.C., is statistically significant and predicts that having such an office is favorable to residential consumers, although exactly why this should be the case is unclear. Citizen ideology is significant and in the expected direction: more liberal states are found to have lower relative residential telephone rates. Finally, telephone penetration rates and unemployment rates (t-1) are also significant and in the expected directions.

Discussion

These findings demonstrate that a range of interest group and institutional factors influence state telecommunications regulation. In this analysis, we have been particularly careful to include an unusually wide range of bureaucratic variables, capturing many different elements of PUC incentives, accountability structures, resources, and other factors. Most of these factors have a significant and substantive influence over the regulated price ratio, suggesting that the manner in which state PUCs are established and operated has an important effect on regulatory policy outcomes.

Overall, state telecommunications regulation is neither a simple form of protection of the public interest nor is it the product of capture by regulated industries. Regulation instead seems to be the result of a delicate balance of different and competing interests—political, bureaucratic, and economic. How the ultimate decisionmakers, the PUC regulators, get to their positions, and the powers they hold, have a large influence over the price that consumers pay relative to business users.

This result supports the idea that the political process designed PUCs to be somewhat insulated politically to make difficult technical decisions when required to do so. PUCs are not completely free of the influence of interest groups and other political actors, but they are certainly far from captured by them.

CHAPTER FIVE

MONOPOLY REGULATION

Electricity

with

SANGJOON KA

Since Thomas Edison invented electricity and opened the first U.S. power plant on Pearl Street in lower Manhattan, interested parties have debated how to deliver the service, including whether and how to regulate it. For most of this period, given the very high fixed costs necessary to construct and maintain generation and distribution facilities, most analysts have assumed that electricity has inherent elements of a natural monopoly, pointing toward a need for regulating prices and service delivery. And since electricity is difficult to store and transmit over a long distance, it has inherently local qualities that have made it most ripe for regulation at the state level.

American political attention to electricity regulation has varied substantially over its history. The initial establishment of "strong" state public utility commissions to regulate electricity, as well as railroads and telephones, was a contentious political battle of the first rank. However, after all fifty states established such bodies, the actual regulation itself became a highly technical process involving the frequent participation of lawyers, engineers, and accountants. It generally became much less salient politically. This was particularly true because controversy was avoidable; advancing technologies allowed prices to fall for long periods of time, providing state and federal regulators with the happy chore of allocating benefits to consumers and producers rather than hiking costs.

In more recent years, however, electricity regulation captured national attention after the energy crisis of 1973 as prices spiked upward, effectively punctuating the existing low salience, subgovernment equilibrium.

While this provided years of intense scrutiny and more of a focus on consumer representation in the state electricity pricing process (see Gormley 1983; Berry 1984), mass attention faded again as prices stabilized and even fell in the 1980s and 1990s.

Yet years after prices stabilized, technological and federal policy changes created the opportunity for state electricity regulators to join in a newer regulatory policy regime—by deregulating and allowing competition in the industry. As of 2003 about half of the states had deregulated state markets. Problems with the deregulated electricity market in California, and with pricing schemes by firms like Enron, again made regulatory issues more salient politically, and caused several states to stop or slow down their deregulatory movement. The giant blackout in the northeastern United States in summer 2003 makes further deregulation even less likely.

History of State Role

In the early part of the twentieth century, electricity industry leaders realized that Progressive reformers had gained the political advantage in seeking to regulate or otherwise control politically this industry. They faced the possibility of municipalities regulating the firms or even taking them over as a public service—not a favorable outcome for electricity firm owners and managers since urban political machines hostile to large business owners controlled the politics of many cities at that time. Nationalization of these firms was another possibility they faced, and indeed most other nations made this choice at that time. In 1907 Edison protégé Samuel Insull, with backing from banker J. P. Morgan, coalesced business support for a system of state regulation, which fit in nicely with the political agenda of reformers like Charles Evans Hughes in New York and Robert LaFollete in Wisconsin, both of whose states established PUCs in that year. While Insull hoped for toothless state regulation that he and his colleagues could easily capture and control, the reformers hoped for real powers to limit prices to consumers and force responsive service. Soon most other states had established similar PUCs to regulate the electricity industry, as well as telephones, railroads, and sometimes other industries, such as insurance. In return for this regulation, firms generally were given an exclusive franchise to provide electricity in a given geographic region of the state.

As the scope of the industry grew, the federal government also began to regulate, starting with the Federal Power Commission in 1920. Actual federal involvement in electricity production as an economic development activity, exemplified most clearly with the Tennessee Valley Authority in the 1930s, expanded the degree of federal regulatory involvement in electricity. By 1950, 25 percent of Americans received power directly from federally controlled sources. In the 1920s and 1930s the mechanisms of state regulation were often frustrated by the ownership of electricity firms by large interstate holding companies, which operated outside of state authority. Thus Congress passed the Public Utility Holding Company Act of 1935 to eliminate the holding companies, the first of several important federal interventions that affected state regulation.

In terms of the actual regulatory process that developed at this time, state PUCs regulated the monopoly firms by determining the appropriate rate of return, or profit level, for electric utilities, and then determined the price for each class of captive customers. This basic system worked fairly well before the 1970s, and there was little conflict over electricity prices; consumers were satisfied with falling rates, as utilities exploited growing demand to achieve greater economies of scale.

Electricity prices became a salient issue, however, when they spiked upward because of the 1973 energy crisis and increasing environmental constraints on coal-fired and nuclear plants after the 1970 Clean Air Act. After rates increased, in 1978 Congress passed the National Energy Act, made up of five related statutes, to reduce dependence on foreign oil, promote energy conservation, and develop alternative energy sources. The Public Utility Regulatory Policies Act (PURPA) was the most significant component, as it allowed nonutility companies to enter the wholesale electric market by requiring electric utilities to interconnect with and buy energy offered from any nonutility "qualifying facility" (QF) registered with the Federal Energy Regulatory Commision (FERC).

Fourteen years later in 1992, after energy prices had stabilized, Congress passed the Energy Policy Act (EPACT), designed to promote energy conservation and efficiency by opening access to transmission networks and making it easier for nonutility power generators to enter the wholesale market. EPACT created a new category of independent power producers called exempt wholesale generators (EWGs) that could generate and sell wholesale electricity.[1] EPACT allowed utilities the right to shop

---

1. EWGs are different from QFs because they do not have to meet PURPA's cogeneration or renewable fuels limitation, and utilities are not required to purchase power from EWGs.

for wholesale power supplies, creating a national open-access electricity transmission grid for wholesale transactions. Building on these competitive actions by Congress, in 1996 the FERC issued Order 888 to open transmission access to nonutilities and Order 889 to build electronic systems for sharing information about transmission capacity. Thus in the 1990s, federal policies promoted competitive access to make the electricity market more efficient, which made it possible for states to deregulate the retail electric utility market. But the decision to actually deregulate or not remained in the hands of state political actors.

Factors Likely to Influence Regulation

There are several important players in state electricity regulation in addition to the PUCs and the state politicians that appoint them, pass relevant legislation, and partly control their budgets. Akridge (1979) argues that five sets of actors play the most critical roles in influencing rate design decisions: public interest groups, electric utilities, manufacturing firms, governments, and state utilities commissioners and staff. Berry (1979, 1984) and Gormley (1983) suggest that industry groups and PUCs themselves are the actors most directly involved in the process of setting rate structures. The utility firms themselves are critical repeat players in the regulatory game, with substantial resources and the most incentives of any one party to try to influence the regulatory process. They are involved intimately in all aspects of the state regulatory process.

On the consumption side, there are three classes of electricity consumers. Historically, based on usage patterns, the industry and regulators classified consumers into residential, commercial, and industrial categories. In general, residential customers pay more than the other two customer classes and industrial customers pay less, as regulators have believed that it costs more to serve residential customers. But how much more it costs is the issue here, and the answer regulators have found has varied by state and over time.

Large industrial and commercial users of electricity also have considerable incentives to be concerned about prices and supply of electricity. They often form user associations to participate in state regulatory proceedings. Sometimes they will argue that they will leave a state, taking many jobs with them, if electricity prices are too high or service too unpredictable.

Regular "consumers" are also important players in the regulatory game. Since the 1970s, explicit government or "proxy" advocates have represented the interests of residential electric consumers (Gormley 1983; Berry 1984). As in many other areas of regulations, however, residential consumers are dispersed and, individually, they have far lower incentives to participate, or pay others to participate on their behalf, than do commercial and industrial users, or electric utilities firms.

Since the 1978 PURPA, some additional actors have emerged to try to influence state regulators, including the QF generators. Since the 1992 EPACT, when Congress created the EWGs, these firms have tried to influence state regulation in their favor.

Measuring Regulation

Examining rate design and the ensuing price ratio of the utility industry provides a directly parallel analysis to the telecommunications study in chapter 4. While utility rate design can be a vastly complicated process in actual practice, the ultimate results are fairly straightforward.[2] Who pays for more of the huge shared infrastructure that is necessary to provide electricity services to all customers? This decision comes after an equally complicated decision about how much the utilities themselves are allowed to earn as a rate of return on their assets, a decision upon which most regulatory analysts have focused most of their attention.

A simple way to understand these rate differences is to examine the industrial sector price as a percentage of the residential sector price, a ratio that becomes the dependent variable in the first electricity analysis in this chapter.[3] A high ratio value indicates that the industrial sector pays relatively more and the residential sector pays relatively less. In 1995, for example, the last year of this analysis, the ratio ranged from about 0.41 in New York State to 0.77 in Rhode Island. These ratios are established, though usually not explicitly, by decisions made by the PUCs.

Explaining Regulation

We analyze variance in the price ratio by examining a range of explanatory variables, capturing the influence of industry and consumer groups,

2. Economists and regulators have employed four different methods to design rate structures: declining block rate structure, inverted rate structure, flat rate structure, and peak-loading pricing rate structure.
3. The commercial sector is generally not as important in the state politics of rate design.

the party identification of governors, the ideology of the state legislature, the selection method for public utility commissions, and the professionalism of PUCs. While the institutional actors actually make rate design decisions, they receive pressure from a range of interest groups. Utilities themselves might be the most powerful because of their constant participation and the high stakes in regulatory issues, but they are generally more concerned about the absolute level of rates (and profits) than they are about the ratio between industrial and residential users. Industrial electricity user groups are one of the most powerful interests in rate design, as they are well organized and have incentives to participate actively in the regulatory process by offering information to elected officials and to regulators and by offering resources to elected officials. As a proxy for the power of industrial user groups, the study divides the work force employed in manufacturing by the total state work force.[4]

Consumer groups also attempt to influence electricity regulation, though scholars find mixed evidence of their success in influencing rates (Joskow 1972; Gormley 1983; Berry 1984; Teske 1991; Campbell 1996). As data on actual state consumer activity are limited, a proxy measure is necessary here. We use variables initially measured by Gormley (1981) for consumer participation in each state in the late 1970s and then update these measures in our own survey of commissioners in 1999 using the exact same set of questions.[5] A check of these 1999 survey results compared to Gormley's reveals some decline in overall consumer involvement over time, probably because rate levels stabilized in the 1980s and 1990s, but also considerable comparability within specific states. With this limited mea-

---

4. State-by-state reputational rankings of interest group power, such as those put together by Hrebener and Thomas (1993), might be useful, but they are not available over time and thus would show no temporal variation.

5. From late 1999 to mid-2000, we mailed up to three rounds of a two-page survey questionnaire to all 194 state public utility commissioners, following up with telephone calls when responses were not forthcoming. The main purpose of the survey was to update and extend the measures gathered by Gormley (1983), to gauge the perceived influence of several participants and related actors in state public utility commission proceedings in the 1990s. Survey responses eventually came back from 100 of these 194 commissioners, for an overall response rate of 53 percent, compared to Gormley's 84 percent. Gormley received at least one respondent from all fifty states and the District of Columbia; we received at least one respondent from forty-eight states, but no responses from Arkansas and Wisconsin.

sure, Gormley's single score for each state is used over the period 1973 to 1984, and the newer survey score for the period 1985 to 1995.[6]

In most states, governors appoint the PUC members. Democratic governors are likely to prefer a rate design that benefits residential users. This variable is coded as one if the governor is from the Democratic Party and zero otherwise. Democratic state legislatures are also more likely to prefer rate design that favors residential consumers. State legislatures can influence PUC decisions by approving appointees in most states, by some influence over PUC funding levels, and by the scope of industry review that commissioners and staff can undertake. Here we multiply the ideology score of elected Democrats given by Erikson, Wright, and McIver (1993) by the proportion of the Democratic Party in both houses and the ideology score of elected Republicans by a proportion of the Republican Party in both houses.[7] The two scores are summed and divided by two, yielding a composite legislative ideology score.

The structure of a regulatory agency may also be an important factor in explaining state policy choices. The literature has been quite mixed on whether elected commissioners make significantly different decisions than appointed commissioners (Costello 1984; Hagerman and Ratchford 1978; Harris and Navarro 1983; Gormley 1983; Primeaux and Mann 1985; Boyes and McDowell 1989), though Besley and Coates (2000) make the strongest theoretical and empirical case for more pro-consumer regulatory decisions (lower prices) being made by elected commissioners. While the appointed commissioners are aligned more with the governor, elected commissions need to be more attuned to the demand of voters, mainly consumers, leading to a likelihood of their favoring lower residential price ratios. In most states, the governor appoints commissioners with the consent of the state legislature. In twelve states in 1996 (and thirteen by 1998), voters elected the regulatory commissioners directly.[8] Besley and Coates

6. Lacking responses from Arkansas and Wisconsin, rather than simply extrapolating Gormley's figures, we transformed Gormley's results for these two states to our survey results by using a Z-score transformation, which extrapolates data based on relative changes in other states according to the Z-distribution.

7. The legislative ideology scores measured by Erikson, Wright, and McIver (1993) are used instead of the Berry and others (1998) government ideology scores, since the Berry measures combine the ideology of the governor and the legislature into a single measure rather than separating their influences.

8. The twelve states are Alabama, Arizona, Georgia, Louisiana, Mississippi, Montana, Nebraska, North Dakota, Oklahoma, South Carolina, South Dakota, and Tennessee. New Mexico changed its selection method from appointment to election in 1998.

(2000) note that states with elected commissioners tend to be smaller, poorer, and more likely to have Democratic governors. States sometimes change their PUCs—Texas switched from elections to appointments in 1977, as did Florida in 1981; South Carolina switched to elections in 1996, while Minnesota employed elections from 1960 to 1971, appointments from 1972 to 1975, elections again in 1976 and 1977, and appointments after 1977.

Turning to the PUCs themselves, some scholars have emphasized the independent role of professional bureaucrats, especially on technical issues (Wilson 1989; Eisner and Meier 1990). Studies have demonstrated that professionalism (Gormley 1983; Berry 1984; Meier 1987; Brudney and Hebert 1987), regulatory resources (Brudney and Hebert 1987; Teske 1991), and task factors (Lester and others 1983; Thompson and Scicchitano 1985; Scholz and Wei 1986) are sources of differential bureaucratic influence in the states. The current study examines the influence of regulatory resources held by a commission, measured as full-time PUC employees per one thousand employees in the state.[9]

Thus we test a pooled cross-sectional analysis of rate structures for forty-six states over the period 1973–95.[10] The technique is ordinary least squares with panel-corrected standard errors (see Chapter 3 for more detailed methodological discussions). This technique is appropriate when the number of time periods is small relative to the number of panels (Beck and Katz 1995); there are twenty-three time periods in these data and forty-six states (panels).[11] The price ratio in a given state and a given year is explained as functions of the governor's party, legislature ideology, the PUC selection mechanism, PUC resources, business user power, and citizen ideology.

Results

The results in table 5-1 show two explanatory variables with high statistical significance—legislative ideology and the selection method of regula-

9. State regulatory budgets demonstrate a very high correlation with the employment measure.

10. Alaska, Hawaii, Nebraska, and Nevada are excluded due to lack of a full set of appropriate data.

11. For a comparison of statistical techniques, other models were tested using feasible generalized least squares. While there were some differences, the results were largely similar. Since OLS with PCSE is the preferred technique, these results are reported.

Table 5-1. *Electricity Rate Ratios, 1973–95*[a]

Explanatory factors	Coefficient
Industrial power	−.0222
	(.0689)
Governor's party	.0006
	(.0040)
Legislative ideology	.0398***
	(.0091)
PUC selection	.0285**
	(.0119)
PUC resources	−.0073
	(.0266)
Citizens' ideology	.0012
	(.0018)
Constant	.607
	(.02)
Summary statistics	
$AR^2 = 0.09$	
Wald Chi^2 = 23.1***	
Log likelihood = 2033***	
N = 1,052	

*Significant at .1 level; **significant at .05 level; ***significant at .01 level.
a. Standard errors are in parentheses.

tory commissioners. As expected, rate structures are designed in favor of residential consumers where the state legislature is more liberal. Similarly, the price ratio favors residential consumers in states where the public elects PUC commissioners directly. Other variables are not significant at high levels of confidence, though the signs of coefficients are in the expected directions.

These significant variables have substantive effects on rate design. A change in the ideology of the state legislature from one standard deviation below the mean to one standard deviation above, while holding other variables at their means, leads to a increase of nearly 8 percentage points in the price ratio. A change in the selection method of commissioners from elected to appointed leads to an increase of over 5 percentage points in the price ratio.

To test whether the analysis of this long time period might have obscured the influence of some variables for part of this time, especially as the most intense and salient focus on price levels occurred in the 1970s and early 1980s, the twenty-two-year analysis is broken into two eleven-year periods. For the first period, 1973–84, as in the full model, only the legislative ideology and selection of the commissioner are significant. But for the 1984–95 period, when prices became less salient, in addition to these two variables the party of the governor, the resources of the PUC, and the power of industrial interests are also significant. In that period, as hypothesized, Democratic governors and PUCs with more resources favor residential interests, but the direction of industrial power is not as expected; in states with relatively more industrial interests, the ratio tends to favor residential consumers. Overall, these results suggest that when rate levels were most salient, legislative ideology and PUC responsiveness to voters drove the ratio of prices, but when the issue became less salient, a wider range of influences became significant.

Discussion

While the process behind electricity rate design is complex, the final results are fairly clear to involved parties, making this a redistributive issue. Variation by state and over time is explained best by the ideology of the legislature and by the mechanism with which PUC commissioners are selected and, thus, to whom regulators are most directly accountable. The finding for elected commissioners is similar to Besley and Coates (2000), who studied state electricity pricing from 1960 to 1997 and found that elected commissioners are associated with lower prices for all categories of consumers. In short, institutional politics mattered a great deal in rate design in the post–energy crisis environment. The role of interest groups was not significant over the entire period, though this may be partly a function of our relatively weak measures of group influence.

Comparison of these quantitative results with the findings from the 1999 survey of PUC commissioners can determine if they are replicated by the opinions of the regulators themselves. Following Gormley's survey (1983), commissioners were asked to evaluate the influence of several sets of actors in state public utility commission proceedings, with 1 representing the lowest level of influence and 10 representing the highest. They provided scores for the influence of the state attorney general, business groups, citizens' groups, individual citizens, labor groups, municipalities, public utility commission staff, and utility companies. Overall, commissioners rated PUC staff members as the most influential, with an average score of 8.0, followed by utility companies at 6.8. They rated the importance of the state legislature next, at 5.7, while the governor's role was

rated much lower, at 4.1. These influence rankings replicate fairly well
the results of this quantitative study.

Deregulation of State Markets

As noted above, technological changes and federal policy choices in the
1990s allowed for the possibility of partial deregulation of and competition within the electric power industry at the wholesale and retail levels.
The dependent variable in this model is whether a state deregulated in a
given year from 1996 to 2000. The policy failures associated with deregulation in California in 2001 brought considerable attention to state choices;
before those problems, however, deregulation was seen as innovative. After California's problems, at least seven of the twenty-four deregulated
states delayed or suspended implementation. The massive blackout in
the northeastern United States in summer 2003 will likely further delay
deregulation.

Measuring Deregulation

Deregulation can occur by legislative statute or from a comprehensive
regulatory order by the state PUC. As of January 2000, twenty-four states
had deregulated their electricity markets: twenty-two by legislative actions and two as a result of only PUC action (see Andrews 2000 for a
more detailed analysis of the timing and interaction of legislative and PUC
deregulatory actions). As Vermont's regulatory decision was subsequently
overturned in the courts and not actually implemented, here twenty-three
states are coded as having deregulated.[12] These states are coded 1 in the
year of the choice to deregulate and in subsequent years; other states are
coded 0 each year.[13]

12. Including Vermont in the model as a deregulated state does not change the
results appreciably.
13. While the actual implementation of deregulation has varied somewhat by
state, with California's process viewed most negatively in 2001, the actual
deregulatory bills or PUC orders are quite similar to each other. Thus a zero-one
binary variable captures the important variance, certainly as well as other studies
of state innovations that employ event history models. Further, states could potentially reverse their decisions, returning them to the "risk set," a result that will
be more likely if some of the problems from California appear in other states and
they are blamed on deregulation rather than on supply shortages.

Explaining Deregulation

While this analysis employs the same explanatory variables as the price ratio analysis, a few adjustments are necessary due to the more technical nature of this issue. In particular, since legislative ideology is not predictive in this model, as it was for the price ratio, the professionalism of the state legislature is more likely to predict a more technical decision than a purely redistributive one.[14]

Interest groups are likely to influence deregulatory decisions. Here we measure the influence of industrial users in terms of competitive demand, by subtracting the proportion of total electricity consumed from utilities by industrial users in 1986 from the proportion of total electricity consumed by industrial users in 1996. In addition, the federal policies behind the 1992 EPACT created a new category of competitive firms, exempt wholesale generators, which compete with utilities and try to sell their electricity in the wholesale market. This makes it possible for transmission-dependent utilities, previously dependent on surrounding investor-owned utilities, to shop for cheaper electricity, threatening the wholesale customers of the former utility monopoly. Thus states in which the percentage of electricity generated by nonutilities is high are likely to have a stronger incentive to introduce competition.

Legislative professionalism has been defined by Mooney (1994, p. 71) as "the enhancement of the capacity of the legislature to perform its role in the policymaking process with an expertise, seriousness, and effort comparable to that of other actors" (see also Ringquist and Garand 1999). Initially, most state legislatures created a study commission or a task force on electricity deregulation. After these findings were reported, some legislatures decided to enact deregulatory legislation, while others deferred. Since various interest groups attempt to influence legislators, a more professional state legislature seems better able to analyze complicated reports, pacify interest group demands, and propel the legislation forward. Several scholars have found that legislative professionalism is a strong predictor of state energy policy variation (Lester and others 1983; Ringquist 1993b; Altman 1997). The Squire (1992) Index is used to measure professionalism, which incorporates member pay, staff members per legislator,

14. Specifically, we also ran the model described below with the ideology variable instead of the professionalism of the state legislature, but the coefficient of legislative ideology was not significant (it was .204, and the standard error was .202).

and total days in session; scholars have found this measure to work well in replications and comparisons across time (Mooney 1994).

For consistency, as in the price ratio analysis above, the same measure of PUC professionalism is employed here: the number of PUC employees per one thousand total employees in a state. Also incorporated into this analysis, as in the price ratio analysis, is the influence of commissioner selection. In addition to these factors from the price ratio model, scholars who study the development and passage of new state policy innovations often examine the proximity of an election (Berry and Berry 1990, 1992; Mooney and Lee 1995). Though electricity regulation may not usually be highly salient in electoral terms, the analysis also tests this explanation of deregulation.

States may also be pressured to deregulate by all sets of consumers because their overall rates are high in absolute terms. Electric rates vary greatly across states; for example, in 1995 residential rates ranged from $14.55 per million Btu (in Washington) to $40.73 per million Btu (in New York).

Scholars of policy innovation also examine diffusion patterns of new policies across geographic space. Mooney and Lee (1995, p. 604) argue that policy diffusion refers "to the patterns by which organizations adopt a particular innovation across both space and time." After one state adopts a new policy, the expectation is that other surrounding states are more likely to follow suit (Berry and Berry 1990, 1992; Walker 1969); thus the analysis examines the ratio of surrounding states that adopt electricity deregulation to the total number of surrounding states in each year.

An S-shaped curve in the cumulative distribution of the diffusion of innovation implies that time alone may play a role in leading state governments to adopt innovation. As the number of states having adopted an innovation increases, state governments that have not done so consider innovation as a more common, and perhaps safer, event, and various groups are more likely to pressure states for adoption. To control for these time maturation effects, the analysis incorporates a series of dummy variables, treating 1996 as the baseline year (Beck, Katz, and Tucker 1998).

Results

An event history analysis, a pooled time-series cross-sectional technique, is the proper technique to explore what factors led state governments to adopt energy deregulation in what year (Allison 1984; Box-Steffensmeier and Jones 1997). The starting point is 1996 because states started to adopt deregulatory policy innovations in that year. Therefore, all of the forty-eight states are in the 1996 "risk set."[15] Only forty-three states reappear in the 1997 risk set, because the five states that adopted deregulatory policy innovation in 1996 are no longer observed in the risk set; and so on for the next three years, until twenty-three total states deregulated.[16]

The model tested in table 5-2 is highly significant and it predicts 87 percent of the cases correctly, compared to a baseline of 71 percent if one guessed, a priori, that all states would not deregulate in these years, for a reduction of more than 50 percent of unexplained cases. Four variables are highly significant in this model. Both the professionalism of the state legislators and the professionalism of PUCs, based upon resources, increase the likelihood that a state adopts deregulation.[17] High electricity prices make a state significantly more likely to deregulate. And the presence of more competitors matters; the greater development of nonutilities increases the probability that a state deregulates.

Three of these significant effects are in the expected direction and their influences are substantial. A change in the professionalism of the PUC from one standard deviation below the mean to one standard deviation above, while holding other variables at their mean value, leads to a 41 percent increase in the likelihood of deregulation. Likewise, a change in the professionalism of the state legislature from one standard deviation below the mean to one standard deviation above leads to a 35 percent increase. These effects of institutional professionalism are nearly as large as actual price effects; a change in electricity price from one standard deviation below the mean to one standard deviation above leads to a 46 percent increase in the likelihood of deregulation.[18] The other variables in

15. Alaska and Hawaii are left out of this analysis.

16. In 1996 forty-eight states were in the risk set and five (California, New Hampshire, New York, Pennsylvania, and Rhode Island) adopted deregulation, for a hazard rate of 0.104 (5/48). With these five states deregulating, in 1997 the risk set included forty-three states, of which seven deregulated, for a hazard rate of 0.163. With thirty-six states in the risk set in 1998 and three states adopting, the hazard rate was 0.083. In 1999 the risk set included thirty-three states, of which eight adopted deregulation, for a hazard rate of 0.242.

17. These findings for professionalism are similar to those of Andrews (2000), who examined the state-by-state diffusion of several levels of deregulatory policy decisions.

18. A change in the development of nonutilities from one standard deviation below the mean to one standard deviation above leads to a 32 percent increase in the likelihood that a state government adopts deregulation.

Table 5-2. *Electricity Deregulation, 1995–2000*
(Event History Analysis)[a]

Explanatory factors	Maximum likelihood estimate
Demand of industrial users	−.020
	(.034)
Development of nonutilities	.021*
	(.013)
Legislative professionalism	3.37**
	(1.37)
PUC professionalism	2.76***
	(.96)
PUC selection	.273
	(.411)
Election cycle	−.502
	(.470
Electricity price	.317**
	(.152)
Innovation in neighboring states	−.939
	(.928)
1997 time maturation dummy	.890
	(.660)
1998 time maturation dummy	1.14
	(.711)
1999 time maturation dummy	1.91**
	(.790)
Constant	−5.72
	(1.41)

Summary statistics
Pseudo R^2 = 0.328
Wald Chi^2 = 42.9***
Log likelihood = 87.6***
Cases correctly predicted (percentage) = 87
N = 156

*Significant at .1 level; **significant at .05 level; ***significant at .01 level.
a. Standard errors are in parentheses.

the model, including elections, commissioner selection methods, decisions of neighboring states, and demands of industrial users, do not have statistically significant effects on state government decisions.

Discussion

As with the analysis of energy pricing, it is useful to compare these quantitative results with data from the 1999 survey of commissioners. Asked to rate the role that each set of actors played in deregulation efforts, with 1 representing "not important at all" and 10 representing "extremely important," commissioners viewed the state legislature as the most important player in restructuring the electric utility industry, with a mean score of 8.5. Commissioners rated their own staff as important, at 7.0. These results are consistent with findings from the event history analysis model. In contrast, commissioners rated the effect of nearby states as the least important factor in deregulating the electric utility market, with an average score of 5.0, validating the quantitative model's lack of finding for neighboring state decisions.

For much of the twentieth century, state PUCs regulated the rates and service of monopoly electricity firms in times of stable or even falling prices, and this activity was not highly salient in political terms. Incremental policymaking ruled the day, until the energy crisis of 1973 punctuated that equilibrium, an exogenous shock to a stable subgovernment system that caused consumers to focus more closely on the rates they paid. Thus the findings of the price ratio analysis make sense; in the new regime that followed that change for the next quarter century, and especially in the first decade after the price shock, the degree to which the ratio favored residential consumers is best explained by the more liberal ideology of some state legislatures and by PUC commissioners who are elected directly by the voters, rather than appointed, a structural change that some consumer groups fought for during this period.

This finding demonstrates that nonincremental change and increased salience generate political and institutional responsiveness at the state level, particularly for a policy decision that is essentially redistributive in nature. The importance of political institutions is also demonstrated by the results of the second analysis, which focuses on policy change—deregulation is driven faster by more professional state legislatures and regulatory agencies. Paralleling a relationship identified by Derthick and Quirk (1985) for federal deregulation, state legislatures are critical players in making policy changes that are likely to last, but they are also more likely to do so when supported by strong bureaucracies with the resources to develop and implement the policy change.

In the rate-focused regulatory regime and in the transition period toward deregulation, both the quantitative models and the data from the survey demonstrate the critical role of the state legislatures. In the period in which redistributive questions dominated, state legislative ideology was central, while professionalism was the significant legislative dimension in the period of the more technical policy change of deregulation. That different dimensions of state legislatures influence salient redistributive and more technical policy decisions over long time periods is an important finding about political influence over bureaucratic decisionmaking, particularly for this relatively "strong case" of state PUC bureaucracies that are more insulated than many other types of bureaucratic agencies.

PART THREE

Information Asymmetries

Information asymmetries occur when producers know considerably more about the nature and quality of a product or service they sell than do consumers. As a consequence of this market failure of asymmetric information, governments have often stepped in to regulate by providing information or forcing businesses to provide information, or by overseeing certain elements of an industry to ensure that the information asymmetry does not ruin fair market competition. Generally, such regulation does not primarily address prices and competitive entry, but it may sometimes influence prices and competition, as in insurance.

Many citizens identify with this type of "protective" regulation, as it seems motivated by both a sense of justice and common sense. Consumers often believe that government agencies should be protecting them from abuses or deceptions by businesses. If businesses are gaining an advantage by misleading the public at large or some consumers, there is often a political impetus, or even sometimes a groundswell after highly salient scandals or crises like the current corporate accounting problems, to regulate, or even to punish, those businesses in some manner. In the extreme case, this would be fraud or misleading information, but more common is an asymmetric balance of information.

This section examines state regulation of three industries—in chapter 6, insurance, which is regulated only by the American states and not by the federal government; in chapter 7, savings and loan firms, which before 1989 had the choice of being chartered and regulated at either the federal or the state level; and in chapter 8, regulation of hospital expansion choices, via the state certificate-of-need (CON) program, which formerly was a required regulation by the federal government but is now a policy of choice for the states. In each of these cases, the public interest idea behind the regulation is that consumers will be protected through government actions, while competition among firms is maintained and encouraged. In reality, the politics of such information-oriented regulation may protect the public interest, but it may also provide advantages to certain firms or segments of the industry, often entrenched firms, at the expense of new firms or potential competitors.

In a complex and risky economy, insurance is a necessity for most consumers, including automobile insurance (which is mandated in most states) and health, property, casualty, and life insurance. Insurance policies themselves are complicated, filled with clauses to address many potential contractual contingencies and to treat possible problems with moral hazard, where consumers behave in a more risky manner simply because they have insurance coverage. Often consumers find insurance policies confusing, and they usually cannot easily determine whether the premiums they pay to insurance firms are being invested wisely. The financial solvency of insurance firms is critical, so that firms can pay out claims. With Ani Ruhil, I examine liquidations of insolvent insurance firms across the states from 1987 to 1997. This was a period when many analysts were concerned that insurance firms might experience financial problems similar to those suffered in the banking and savings and loan field in the late 1980s, leaving policyholders unable to collect payments after accidents. While there are many other important issues in insurance regulation (see Meier 1988 for a detailed examination of pricing and other policies), consumers at least can compare prices, while the financial solvency of insurance firms is particularly difficult for consumers to gauge. The results show that the stronger the power of the insurance industry, the less often states will liquidate firms, preferring to find other options. Elected commissioners are associated with fewer liquidations of firms, and when state commissions perform more financial audits of firms, there are fewer liquidations, as regulators presumably are able to address problems before they become more severe.

Similar to insurance, depositors and investors want to be sure that financial institutions are safe places in which to place their savings. Before 1989 savings and loan firms (S&Ls) had the option of a federal or a state charter, with nearly half choosing state charters (now only federal charters are available). The financial failure of about one-quarter of S&Ls in the late 1980s created one of the worst domestic policy problems in recent history, leading to nearly $200 billion in resolution costs—ultimately paid for by taxpayers. With Julie Laumann, I test a database that includes all S&Ls as of the late 1980s. State charters were associated with a greater likelihood of failure than federal charters, suggesting greater capture of state regulators. Interestingly, this higher state failure rate is completely a result of the large number of failures in Texas, and it disappears by separating Texas out of the analysis. In principal-agent terms, stricter state regulatory accountability structures led to fewer failures, and more stock-owned S&Ls failed (compared to mutually owned firms). As with insurance, this analysis suggests that how and to whom regulated firms are accountable is important, and that more focused bureaucratic resources devoted to oversight earlier in the process might have reduced the number of subsequent financial problems.

Rising health care costs have been at the forefront of public policy debates for thirty years. Concern about overinvestment in hospital facilities led to a mix of federal and state policies, including a federal requirement for state hospital certificates-of-need regulation in the 1970s. CON regulations are an explicit entry barrier to limit the number of hospitals investing in certain areas of medicine. Following a more deregulatory philosophy, in the 1980s the federal government withdrew its financial and regulatory support for CON regulation and left it up to the states to continue, which some have done, while about one-third have dropped CONs. With Richard Chard, I examine state choices from 1982 to 1996. The findings show that, following the Chicago-school and capture arguments, CON regulations are more likely to be retained in states with more powerful hospital interest groups. But states with more Democratic legislative chambers are also more likely to retain CONs, as are states whose citizens have higher incomes and educational levels, and states that have higher per diem hospital charges.

Thus for these areas of information regulation, a mix of interest group and governmental actors are influential. Stricter state regulation and enforcement are associated with better outcomes for consumers in insurance and savings and loan regulation, though the case is less clear for state hospital regulations. While these current issues are most important to public policy, a complete understanding requires some historical background.

Historical Development

It was only in the twentieth century that the federal government began to play a major role in regulation based on asymmetric information, when the U.S. Department of Agriculture inspected processed meat after Upton Sinclair's 1907 book *The Jungle* prompted a 50 percent drop in meat sales. In the 1930s such regulations accelerated at the federal level, as the Food and Drug Administration addressed unsubstantiated claims of miracle cures. In addition, responding to the financial panics associated with the Great Depression, the federal government established stricter financial information requirements, along with the development of the Securities and Exchange Commission (SEC), to assure investors that corporations were reporting their assets and liabilities in a fair and understandable manner. Related to that, during the New Deal Congress also passed the 1935 Public Utilities Holding Company Act and bank reforms to provide a stronger foundation for investor confidence.

Much of this New Deal expansion of regulation was focused at the federal level. Although federal officials did not always preempt state regulations, they did create new agencies and new regulations that were national in scope. Still, state banking regulations continued and states were free to establish their own regulations on an intrastate basis, although courts also made decisions that often expanded the jurisdiction of interstate commerce. And the 1945 Congressional McCarran-Ferguson Act maintained state regulation over the insurance industry, even after the Supreme Court reversed older rulings and deemed that insurance was "commerce."

As noted in chapter 1, in recent years there has been considerable interaction between federal and state regulation related to information regulation and enforcement. Starting with President Reagan, conservative administrations tried to eliminate some social regulatory agencies, but Democratic resistance forced them to reduce enforcement instead. In response, groups favoring greater information regulation have pressed their claims at the state level—with successes in some large states, like California and New York, through legislative action, popular initiatives, or, increasingly, litigation by state attorneys general (see chapter 15).

Other State-Regulated Industries

The cases examined here—insurance, savings and loan, and CON regulations—are just three examples of state regulation that has its basis in information and monitoring issues. There are many others. As discussed in much more detail in part IV, occupational regulation is based on a mix of asymmetric information justifications and economic entry issues.

Corporate chartering is the oldest form of information regulation. States charter all corporations; none are chartered at the federal level. The first federal foray into any form of regulating corporate governance did not come until the 1933 Securities Act. Corporate chartering began in 1752 in Pennsylvania, but New Jersey became the dominant state of incorporation after it liberalized its laws in 1896. After Woodrow Wilson pushed New Jersey to toughen its requirements in 1913, Delaware famously became the main chartering state, with 300,000 firms now officially chartered there, including 40 percent of all New York Stock Exchange listed firms. Many have argued that Delaware's chartering laws are very pro-management and anti-shareholder, but there is a large and controversial literature on whether or not corporate chartering in Delaware truly represents a race to the bottom (see Donahue 1997, pp. 66–69). Still, many scholars refer to the "Delaware effect" as a prime example of when a single state can influence national regulatory policy, as it seeks to gain economic development, taxes, and jobs for lawyers, accountants, and other workers within that state. Delaware has also earned that role for the usury laws it relaxed in 1981, so that eight of the biggest ten firms that issue credit cards now do so from within Delaware. Despite the prominent role for states in corporate chartering and governance throughout most of American history, some observers are concerned that recent legislation, particularly the Sarbanes-Oxley Act passed to respond to Enron and other corporate scandals, provides a much greater role for federal regulation of corporations (Bainbridge 2003).

Moreover, states play an important regulatory enforcement role in workers' safety and enforcement of federal Occupational Safety and Health Administration (OSHA) rules. Workers do not know as much about an employer's safety record and practices as their employers know, so government safety regulation is justified on that basis. When Congress established OSHA in 1970 after a major fight between business and labor groups (see Moe 1989), states were given the opportunity to establish their own state safety enforcement agencies to enforce the OSHA standards, if approved by OSHA. Although there has been some minor change over time, about half the states established their own safety agencies, and there has only been one effort by OSHA to actually de-certify a state-run program, after a 1991 fire in a chicken processing plant in

North Carolina killed several workers and exposed a weak state enforcement effort.

Studies attempting to explain why some states enforce worker safety rules themselves have uncovered few political explanations; instead, states further geographically from Washington, D.C., are more likely to operate independently. Scholars have found some mixed evidence for the idea that states with their own safety agencies are likely to pursue less stringent enforcement designed to favor in-state business interests (Marvel 1982; Thompson and Scicchitano 1985). Scholz and Wei (1986) find that state agencies are more responsive to state political influences; in some states that means fewer inspections, in others with a pro-employee attitude, like California, it means more inspections. States also have the option of having safety laws apply to their own public sector workers, which is not a requirement of the federal legislation. About half the states have passed laws covering public sector workers in a similar manner to their private sector counterparts. In recent years, a few states have been frustrated by slow or static OSHA requirements and have passed their own regulations in the areas of ergonomics and other worker safety issues. Under President Clinton, this state action accelerated OSHA's argument for a single national ergonomic standard, one that was promulgated with some controversy at the very end of the Clinton presidency, but then reversed under President George W. Bush.

Related to OSHA and worker safety issues, states administer workers' compensation programs and regulations to compensate workers actually injured on the job. Most of these programs are similar to no-fault insurance, as employers often are required to participate in some form of the program. Several states have government-run monopoly programs, while others allow some choices for employers. While OSHA tries to prevent accidents, workers' compensation programs provide a legalistic compensatory process after an actual workplace accident. There is some evidence that state flexibility is leading to better performance (Conerly 2003).

In a more minor, but not trivial, industry, states regulate funeral practices and competition. Harrington (2003) argues that the states have provided substantial barriers to entry that serve to protect funeral home providers against new competition and have raised costs for consumers. After failing to achieve his goal of national funeral home regulations when serving as FTC chair, Pertshuck (1982) suggested that funeral home owners are among the most powerful political groups because they are spread across all legislative districts and they have considerable free time during the day to lobby.

Aside from the case of state regulation of savings and loans (analyzed specifically in chapter 7), states also have regulated other aspects of banking, though this role has been reduced over time as the federal government has preempted many state restrictions on branch banking, interstate mergers, and other elements. Research has focused on how banking and insurance interest groups influenced the timing of state banking deregulation before federal preemption (Kroszner and Strahan 1999), and on why some states formed reciprocal compacts with each other, to encourage interstate banking, before the 1994 federal preemption (Skalaban 1992). Today, though S&Ls no longer have a state-chartered option, banks can still choose to be chartered at the federal or the state level. While state chartering is generally cheaper for banks, larger banks tend to prefer a national charter, and they hope to gain some degree of legal and regulatory protection from the Office of the Comptroller of the Currency (OCC) in the U.S. Treasury Department. Fees from banks are important to regulators at both levels; for example, the country's largest bank, Bank of America, pays $40 million in fees each year, or fully 10 percent of the OCC budget.[1]

Since 1934 the federal SEC regulates most financial market activity, but even here states retain some regulatory authority. Says Joseph Borg, director of the Alabama Securities Commission and president of the North American Securities Administrators Association: "State securities cops have a duty to protect investors in their states, something they have been doing longer than the SEC's been around."[2] For example, as noted in chapter 1, in 2002 when the SEC and the NYSE did not take action, New York state attorney general Eliot Spitzer sued Merrill Lynch for the lack of objectivity of its stock analysts, with a winning settlement spawning related investigations by the SEC, NYSE, NASD, and others. As he presses his case to other firms, "regulators from several other states, including California and New Jersey, have agreed to help Mr. Spitzer."[3]

The federalism aspects of financial regulation are likely to shake out further since the 1999 federal Gramm-Leach-Bliley Act, which broke down Depression-era walls that had been established between investment, commercial banking, and insurance, encouraging a more competitive and in-

1. Jess Bravin and Paul Beckett, "Dependent on Lenders' Fees, the OCC Takes Banks' Side against Local Laws," *Wall Street Journal,* January 28, 2002, p. 1.

2. Gretchen Morgenson, "A Wall St. Push to Water Down Securities Law," *New York Times,* June 18, 2002, p. A1.

3. Ibid.

novative financial sector. In the short run, this means that states must work together to develop comparable regulations to certify insurance agents; if twenty-nine states do not agree by 2004, some forms of state insurance regulation will be preempted by the federal government. More than any time since 1945, there is now serious discussion of a federal role in insurance regulation. If national financial firms continue to see state regulation as a problem for them, they are likely to lobby hard for this cause. Furthermore, evidence that state regulation has not been effective (see Cummins 2002) is likely to strengthen the case for state deregulation, federal preemption or both which, as noted in chapter 1, has been the dominant pattern in other areas of economic regulation over the past twenty-five years.

CHAPTER SIX

Insurance Solvency

with

ANI RUHIL

Insurance is the largest and most important industry that is regulated only by the states. States regulate prices, services, and the solvency of firms in the industry. Some recent research and a natural experiment in Illinois, which does not require preapproval of price changes by insurance firms, suggest that competition might serve consumers better than the approved price, entry, and exit regulation as practiced in most states (Cummins 2002).

Most of the authors of quantitative case studies of five states that vary in their degree of regulation—South Carolina, Illinois, California, Massachusetts, and New Jersey—do not find price regulation effective (Cummins 2002). But even if price regulation is relaxed, the free-market advocates opposing price regulation argue that solvency information regulation is still important, as Cummins (2002, p. 20) writes: "Solvency regulation also appears to provide a net benefit to insurance buyers and is another instance of an appropriate informational and bonding role for regulators. By providing information on insurer financial quality, regulators allow buyers to choose an insurer with low solvency risk. Furthermore, by effectively monitoring insurers that experience deteriorating financial conditions, the regulator can help minimize the number of policyholders having claims settled by guaranty funds rather than by solvent insurers."

Thus this chapter examines the factors associated with state solvency regulation of the insurance industry from 1987 to 1997, which has influenced the need for liquidations of some insurance firms. Only a few scholars have studied the political economy of state insurance regulation (Cheit

97

1993; Meier 1988), and their efforts do not include long time-series studies that link state policymaking institutions to actual policy outcomes. While one might assume that random processes generate most insurance firm failures, or deteriorating state or regional economic conditions, or perhaps risk-taking behavior by insurance company executives, the findings demonstrate that state political and bureaucratic institutions exert an important influence over firm solvency.

History of State Role

Regulation of insurance is the oldest form of government regulation in the United States, dating from Ben Franklin's firm in 1752 and later efforts to charter and regulate insurance firms in Pennsylvania in the 1790s. As these early efforts proved ineffective, in the 1850s Elizur Wright, a Boston mathematician, pressed the Massachusetts legislature to set tougher regulatory standards for insurance firm operations, and New York and other states followed suit. By the 1860s, however, insurance firms felt crippled by varying state regulations and challenged them on the grounds that insurance was interstate commerce, properly under federal jurisdiction. In 1868, however, the U.S. Supreme Court ruled that insurance was not "commerce." This approach held until 1944, when the Court reversed the earlier decisions to hold that insurance was, in fact, commerce. But by then insurance firms were comfortably familiar with state regulation and did not want a regulatory upheaval that might include a mix of federal and state regulations. They generally supported the 1945 Congressional McCarran-Ferguson Act, which upheld the exclusive state regulatory role, though now in effect under Congress's choice, not the Court's interpretation of the Constitution's commerce clause.

Generally, state insurance regulation has remained in place because it has not produced major disasters, although it has not been as efficient as it could be (Cummins 2002). As many insurance firms faced financial problems in the 1980s, parallel to financial problems in the S&L and banking industries (see chapter 7), however, more observers, including federal politicians, questioned the effectiveness of state insurance regulation. Critics argued that the states were unable to effectively regulate a rapidly diversifying global insurance market because states lack adequate resources and cannot coordinate their regulations (Dingle 1990; Hollman, Hayes, and Burton 1993; but see Pommeroy 1992; Haase 1992). In response, Representative John Dingle drafted plans for a federal insurance regulator in

1993. The National Association of Insurance Commissioners (NAIC) and the states responded with new data-sharing efforts and an accreditation plan to press state legislatures for adequate funding to create more effective state insurance regulatory commissions.

More recently, the 1999 Financial Services Act (FSA), called Gramm-Leach-Bliley, opened the door for firms in these financial industries to disagree on whether state regulation serves their interests. Some insurers are concerned that the breakdown of barriers between banks and insurance firms, combined with significant state regulation of insurance firms only, will slow their competitive responses to bank incursions on their businesses. The American Bankers Association Insurance Association has proposed a federal insurance regulator, rather than continuing with state regulation. State insurance regulation seems to be at a critical juncture, its future uncertain, as many federal officials have not been pleased with its recent performance. A 2001 GAO report noted (Gurwitt 2001, p. 18): "We observed repeated instances of inadequate tools, policies, procedures and practices, as well as a lack of information sharing among different regulators, within and outside the insurance industry. . . . Washington is intrigued with the idea of junking the entire structure of state insurance oversight and switching to a federal regulatory system."

Specifically, national insurance firms have become concerned about their agents being required to meet varying standards to become licensed in different states. The FSA did mandate more state coordination—at least twenty-nine states were required to adopt a uniform method of regulating insurance agents by 2004; otherwise, the states will be preempted by a federal system. Firms are also concerned about slow state-by-state approval of contracts for new services; ten states have responded with a Coordinated Advertising, Rate, and Form Review Authority (CARFRA) within NAIC to address this concern.

Not all firms are opposed to continued state regulation, particularly firms without a national scope. Jack Ramirez of the National Association of Independent Insurers says: "Insurance markets, especially in property/casualty insurance, are local in nature—they vary from place to place depending on the weather, traffic congestion, population density, and so on. We think that state regulation is more responsive to those local needs and variances" (quoted in Gurwitt 2001, p. 24). In defense of an important continuing state role, NAIC president Kathleen Sebelius argues: "The heart of the system, which involves consumer protection and solvency regulation, stands up well compared to any federal system" (Gurwitt 2001,

p. 20). States also want to retain regulatory authority, in part because it generates considerable funds; insurance firms pay over $10 billion in fees and premium taxes to states, while the states collectively spend less than $1 billion on the process of insurance regulation.

The questions of who regulates, and how, are important because insurance performs a crucial function in a complex economy: the reduction of risk. Insurance firms invest customer premiums into asset portfolios to generate income over time and purchase reinsurance to dilute the underwriting risks of primary insurers.[1] Given this chain of financial transactions, if one link collapses, other parties will feel ripple effects. Indeed, the need for "safety and soundness" regulation of solvency comes from the liabilities of insurance firms and the fact that primary liability holders are likely to be considerably underinformed about the investment portfolios of their insurance providers (see Meier 1988; Joskow 1973); this asymmetric information calls for some form of governmental regulatory protection (White 1995, p. 3; see also Munch and Smallwood 1980).

The consequences of insurance insolvencies can be severe: policyholders can lose the entire value of the assets they thought they had protected. While most states have established guaranty fund systems that assess premiums on healthy insurance companies to compensate policyholders of the failed company, these funds are often inadequate. And postcollapse assessments are usually followed by increases in premiums that subsequently force low-income consumers out of the insurance market. Moreover, because insurers operate in multiple states, bailout plans require extraordinary coordination efforts that delay final payouts to policyholders of failed companies.

Factors Likely to Influence Regulation

In insurance solvency regulation, state regulatory bodies try to prevent problems by monitoring the market conduct of domiciled firms. Model laws and acts that govern transactions are generally based on regulations of the multistate NAIC, a voluntary organization that recommends that state insurance departments conduct periodic financial examinations. Relying on historical data submitted annually by insurance firms and on

1. Adiel (1995, p. 23) points out that on average insurers spend more than 25 percent of the premiums collected on reinsurance purchases, which creates complications for the current regulatory framework since reinsurance is largely exempt from any state regulation and not covered by guaranty funds.

performance benchmarks, state insurance departments assess firm finances. Should regulators detect problems, they are authorized to place firms under conservation and to try to rehabilitate the company to maintain availability of coverage and avoid an outright insolvency. However, sometimes this intervention fails, and the situation may require regulators to liquidate a company.

While this regulatory blueprint looks good on paper, an example demonstrates some of the conflicts involved in state regulation of firms that operate in several states. In 1991 New Jersey regulators seized the failing Mutual Benefit–Executive Life Insurance Company and developed a bailout plan together with an industry consortium and NAIC. The plan needed the approval of the forty-two states where Mutual Benefit's shareholders resided and a bitter struggle ensued. New Jersey's regulators might have prevented the collapse but they conducted financial examinations only every five years and the state lacked a guaranty fund. The first omission allowed the firm to undertake risky investments in the real estate market, while the second led New Jersey legislators to pass a law establishing a guaranty fund on the day Mutual Benefit was seized.

Thus the critical regulatory institutions for insurance regulation are NAIC, state legislatures, and the state insurance departments. NAIC, essentially made up of the fifty state insurance commissioners, is responsible for drafting and coordinating insurance regulations. NAIC drafts bills that become model acts for all state legislative consideration if approved by twenty-five state commissioners. However, states are not bound by NAIC proposals, and state legislatures sometimes demonstrate their independence by rejecting or adapting them. Laws passed by states are implemented and enforced by insurance departments, typically headed by an insurance commissioner appointed by the governor, although commissioners are elected directly by voters in twelve states.

In an attempt to develop more uniform state policies, in 1989 NAIC adopted a set of minimum effective Financial Regulation Standards, followed by an accreditation program to promote and reward state compliance. Accredited states are required to hire and retain qualified staff to conduct timely analysis of domestic insurers. Every three to five years, the state insurance department reports on the financial health of domiciled private insurers. However, lacking coercive authority, this accreditation program has proved ineffective so far.

NAIC accreditation or not, states do not always regulate closely. For example, in 1999 the Center for Insurance Research argued that loose regulation by the Massachusetts Insurance Division allowed the near failure of Harvard Pilgrim Health Care, prompting a state takeover.[2] A more recent furor over lost NAIC accreditation involved the Tennessee Department of Commerce and Insurance; in 2000 the state lost the accreditation earned in 1994 because of inadequate oversight of firms linked to Martin Frankel, who stole more than $200 million from insurers in five states.

Measuring Regulation

The intensity and success of state regulation varies greatly across states and over time. Consequently, the data for the analysis are a pool of cross-sectionally dominated annual time series for the fifty states for the 1987–97 period. Constraints related to data availability from NAIC force a restriction of attention to this ten-year period.[3]

Initially, this study was to examine two measures of solvency regulation: (1) conservations, or rehabilitations—the explicit preemptive regulatory action undertaken to prevent outright failure of the firm; and (2) liquidations—the number of domiciled companies actually liquidated in each state in a given year.[4] However, while some firms proceed from conservation to liquidation, available data do not allow a clear distinction between individual firms that lapse into conservation but survive and firms that do not survive and are then liquidated; only aggregate numbers are available in each category of insolvency. Thus we analyze only liquidations, the final policy outcome.

States with fewer firms lapsing into insolvency are monitoring their domestic industry better than others.[5] The peak year for insolvencies was 1989, when 123 firms across the nation were liquidated, while the aver-

2. Scot Paltrow, "How Insurance Firms Beat Back an Effort for Stricter Controls," *Wall Street Journal*, February 5, 1998, p. B1.

3. Specifically, complete NAIC data are available only for the 1987–97 period.

4. We are also combining insolvencies from all different lines of insurance, health, life, and property/casualty, for two reasons: because firms often write insurance in multiple lines simultaneously, and because data limitations do not allow us to disaggregate insolvencies by line.

5. In the insurance sector, "domestic" firms are those domiciled in a state, "foreign" firms are out-of-state firms, and "alien" firms are internationally based insurers. Insurance departments are responsible for monitoring only domiciled firms, although foreign firms do operate in nondomiciliary states via licensing and subsidiary arrangements.

age has been about 53 firms each year, with most years in the late 1990s under 30 a year.[6] Note that not all states experienced insolvencies in every year under consideration. Rather, for any given year about 60 percent of the states report no insolvencies, while in another 20 percent there is only a single insolvency. At the other extreme, some states experienced a rash of insolvencies, with the maximum of 39 in a state in a single year. The preponderance of zero liquidations in the data means that an event count model is appropriate for this analysis.[7] The combination of many zeros and wide variance in the data argues for the use of the ZIP model (see Michener and Tighe 1992; Dionne and others 1997).[8]

Explaining Regulation

Scholars of regulatory politics typically portray insurance regulation as a highly complex and weakly salient issue (see Gormley 1984; Eisner, Worsham, and Ringquist 2000). As a result, industry groups and bureaucratic regulators are most likely to exert the greatest influence on regulatory outcomes because, compared to elected political actors and consumers, they possess detailed industry knowledge.

Renzulli and others (2002) provide evidence that there are more insurance lobbyists in the fifty states than for any other industry. Further, their political clout is enhanced by the fact that about 15 percent of state lawmakers who serve on committees overseeing insurance legislation are either insurance agents, company executives, or otherwise connected to the industry. The insurance industry also outpaces securities firms and the

6. Liquidations data for 1998 and 1999 come from Standard and Poor's annual industry reports.

7. If we modeled these "count data" with ordinary least squares regression, that would yield inefficient parameters estimates and inconsistent standard errors (King 1989, p. 763).

8. See Ruhil and Teske (2003) for further technical and modeling details. The Poisson distribution is premised on the assumption that the events are independent across time—that is, there is no contagion (or alternatively, no occurrence dependence). Ideally, one would like to test for both positive (past insolvencies increase the likelihood of future insolvencies) and negative (past insolvencies decrease the likelihood of future insolvencies) contagion. In practice, unfortunately, it is well nigh impossible to distinguish between true and spurious contagion, especially when, as is apparent in the present case, the count data contain an excess of zeros.

banks in campaign contributions to electoral activities.[9] In addition, many insurance commissioners are involved in the "revolving door" phenomenon; Paltrow indicates that in 1995, for example, seven of the twenty-one appointed state insurance commissioners came from the industry, while in 1997 alone four commissioners left their posts for high-paying jobs in the industry.[10] Moreover, insurance firms may threaten to leave a state to provide pressure to relax regulations, as has occurred in Texas and Wisconsin and in large numbers recently in New Jersey and Massachusetts. Given this lobbying power of insurance firms within states, the expectation is that states with relatively more powerful insurance industries will press for less aggressive regulatory monitoring and fewer liquidations. The study analyzes industry influence in solvency regulation by including a measure of the financial influence of the state insurance industry—per capita insurance carriers' contribution (in millions of dollars) to the gross state product (GSP).

When insurance issues become salient, politicians sometimes become involved. In 1993, for example, the New York legislature refused to pass two NAIC model laws and lost accreditation. State legislatures have also intervened directly in rate regulatory decisions, and in at least two recent cases, governors have overturned or suspended rate increases approved by their own state's insurance commissioner. Compared to insurance commissioners and bureaucrats, politicians are more likely to hold general goals related to industry solvency, while commissioners are more concerned about availability, pricing, quality of service, and solvency (Chidambaram, Pugel, and Saunders 1995, p. 9).

Since insurance regulators actually cite state legislators as an important influence on them, even more than pressure from regulated firms (Miles and Bhambri 1983), the means by which insurance commissioners hold office matters greatly. Elected commissioners are more likely to be able to act on their preferences than appointed commissioners. Some participants certainly believe that this distinction matters—in 1988 a consumer organization affiliated with Ralph Nader urged Californians to switch to an elected commissioner, who would be more responsive to voters. Thus states with elected commissioners should exhibit fewer insolvencies; elected commissioners are measured with a dummy variable = 1, and 0 otherwise.

9. Walter L. Updegrave, "How the Insurance Industry Collects an Extra $65 Billion a Year from You by Stacking the Deck," *Money*, August 1996, p. 52.

10. Paltrow, "How Insurance Firms Beat Back an Effort for Stricter Controls."

Even elected commissioners are constrained (see Klein, Nordman, and Fritz 1993, pp. 136–39). While insurance commissioners are more likely than politicians to intervene and liquidate firms if necessary, their freedom to do so is limited by the state's political environment. Specifically, elected commissioners should better regulate the solvency of the domiciled industry when the state government is under divided party control; threats of legislative sanctions for regulatory actions at odds with the average preferences of the legislators are less tenable under divided government. Empirical research on divided government at the state level is mixed (see Fiorina 1992, p. 86; Mayhew 1991; Alt and Stewart 1990; Clingermayer and Wood 1995; Alt and Lowry 1994). We measure divided government via a dummy variable that assumes the value of one when no party simultaneously controls the governor's office, the state house, and the state senate. The analysis also tests an interaction variable, examining the joint influence of elected commissioners and divided government simultaneously.

With the high complexity of insurance regulation, enhanced bureaucratic expertise requires appropriate resources. We examine a measure of state budgetary dollars available for each insurance carrier domiciled in the state (budgetary resources per domiciled firm), expecting that better-funded departments can better monitor their firms. While budget is often used as a proxy for resources or effort and is also generally viewed as a way for elected politicians to influence bureaucratic activities, it is also true that merely allocating dollars does not automatically translate into aggressive monitoring and regulation (for example, see Meier 1988). For example, while the Massachusetts Division of Insurance had a budget exceeding $8 million in 1997, it conducted only one examination of Harvard Pilgrim Health Care from 1991 to 1997, a firm that eventually went into receivership. To better specify bureaucratic monitoring, the analysis also includes a variable capturing the number of financial examinations actually conducted by the insurance department in a given state in each year.[11] The number of financial examinations is not an exogenous variable; that is, it is the outcome of related legislative and bureaucratic choices. Thus we first model examinations as a function of other factors that are likely to explain it, including budgetary resources, elected commissioners, divided government, their interaction, the influence of state insurance carriers, and state population.[12] The results demonstrate that, not surprisingly,

11. While budgetary resources significantly influence financial examinations of firms in the first-stage analysis, the simple correlation is only 0.51.

12. This is a first-stage negative binomial regression analysis.

more budgetary resources lead to more financial examinations, as well as elected commissioners, divided government, and smaller populations resulting in more financial examinations on average in a state.

Some control variables may also influence insurance firm liquidations apart from political and regulatory activity. For example, cyclical pricing and severe loss shocks, significant cost changes, and increased competition between insurance carriers can trigger insurance financial crises (see Klein 1995). Lacking state-specific or national indicators of the financial health of the insurance industry, the analysis employs temporal dummy variables that assume the value one in a given year and zero otherwise.[13] These dummy variables capture year-specific nationwide insolvency trends that are common to all insurance firms in all states.[14]

The size of state insurance markets, and related consumer demand, may influence insolvencies. A proxy variable—state population—tests whether states that are more populous experience greater insolvencies because regulators are hesitant to worsen the excess demand problem. In terms of normal probabilities, more insolvencies should occur in states with relatively larger markets regardless of specific political and economic circumstances (see, for example, Michener and Tighe 1992; Dionne and others 1997). As states regulate their domestic firms and not those registered in other states, the number of domiciled insurance firms is the scale variable in the analysis.[15]

Results

The results are reported in table 6-1.[16] The main focus on bureaucratic monitoring is productive; the more financial exams conducted by state

13. The dummy variable identifying the 1987 period is the excluded category in all models estimated here.

14. Ruhil and I also experimented with an alternative specification—the insurance industry component of the gross domestic product—under the assumption that severe declines in this proportion should be indicative of deteriorating financial health of the U.S. insurance industry. However, the temporal proxies are preferred because of insufficient variance in the insurance component of the GDP over 1987–97.

15. Note that by construction the scale parameter is constrained to unity. Hence we do not include the coefficient on the scale variable when reporting the results.

16. The Vuong test statistic (V) indicates that the ZIP specification is a better fit to the data than the basic Poisson regression model. Likewise, the Wald tests for the joint significance of the variables entering the binary (logit) model lend additional credence to the ZIP formulation.

Table 6-1. *Insurance Firm Liquidations, 1987–97*[a]

Explanatory factors	Poisson coefficient
State insurance industry strength	−2.645***
	(0.67)
Elected commissioner	−0.089**
	(0.035)
Divided government	−0.603**
	(0.144)
Elected commissioner/divided government	0.309
	(0.409)
Financial exams conducted[b]	−0.0058***
	(0.0006)
State population	0.005**
	(0.0008)
Constant	−1.985**
	(0.232)

Summary statistics
Wald Chi^2 = 39.41***
Log likelihood = 1624***
ZIPχ^2 = 377.90***
$V_{(ZIP\,V,\,PRM)}$ = 2.69
N = 541, with 216 nonzero and 325 zero observations

*Significant at .1 level; **significant at .05 level; ***significant at .01 level.
a. Coefficients for temporal (1988–97) dummy variables are not reported. Standard errors are in parentheses.
b. Predicted financial exams conducted generated from the first-stage model.

insurance departments, the fewer insolvencies occur in that state. For example, an additional examination reduces liquidations by about 30 percent. The insurance department's budgetary resources have the opposite effect, though to a much smaller extent, suggesting that the budgetary variable is a probably a weak proxy for the actual usage of regulatory resources and may be picking up some of the market-size effects.

In addition, there are important institutional effects. States with elected commissioners are significantly less likely than those with appointed commissioners to liquidate insurance companies, experiencing 25 percent fewer insolvencies, holding all else constant. As expected, states with more powerful insurance industries have fewer domiciled firms that become liquidated, demonstrating their power over regulatory outcomes.

Discussion

State insurance regulation is complex and probably influenced by many factors, not all of which are identified or measured perfectly here. The procedures for declaring insurance firms insolvent are arduous, requiring coordination across bureaucracies, legislatures, governors, and even state courts. Explicit state institutional and policy choices affect the number of firms that become insolvent and unable to pay off on the claims of policyholders. Specifically, the power of the state insurance industry affects solvency regulation. As with the regulation of telecommunications and electricity, whether insurance commissioners are accountable directly to voters (when they are elected) or to governors (through appointments) also shapes different outcomes. Finally, the manner in which insurance commissions use the resources they are given by legislatures affects how many firms fail in a state. This evidence for solvency regulation supports recent studies that demonstrate great variation in the effectiveness of state insurance price regulation (see Cummins 2002). Though the insurer insolvency crisis of the early 1990s is past, faced with possible federal preemption related to broader financial deregulation, states and NAIC need to improve their regulatory and monitoring policies if they want to retain their authority.

CHAPTER SEVEN

INFORMATION ASYMMETRIES

Savings and Loan
Solvency

with

JULIE LAUMANN

Historically, the states and the federal government have shared the regulation and oversight of financial institutions. Recently, the federal government has expanded its role and preempted the states in a number of areas. Before 1990 savings and loan firms had an option to be chartered at the state level. Banks, however, still have a choice of federal or state chartering; state charters tend to be cheaper, but federal rules may be more stable and uniform for the banks. Still, many specific aspects of state banking regulation have been preempted in recent years.

Many analysts have been concerned that state chartering and regulation of financial institutions creates to a race to the bottom or a "Delaware effect" similar to corporate chartering (but see Ferejohn and Weingast 1997). In this view, states create lax regulations, which they hope will allow them to obtain mobile jobs, economic development, and fees that state-chartered institutions might bring to them. On the other hand, other scholars believe that state competition leads to more innovative and efficient regulation than a single, national regulatory option (Romano 1997).

At the height of the S&L crisis in 1989, the federal government preempted further state regulation. Before that action, states had played a critical role in regulating this segment of the financial industry for decades. Congress preempted the states because it perceived that lax state regulation contributed to the S&L crisis of the late 1980s, which was resolved a few years later with the expenditure of about $200 billion in taxpayer funds, and because it wanted to shift blame away from its own responsibilities.[1] The crisis was viewed as a monumental failure of de-regulation and the worst domestic policy failure in recent history. Ana-lysts articulated many reasons for the S&L failures, including extreme fluctuations in interest rates, new competition from emerging financial institutions, surprisingly sharp economic downturns in some regional economies and, perhaps most important, a moral hazard problem in which federal and state deregulatory laws and regulations encouraged S&L man-agers to take risks while the deposits of S&L investors were insured by the federal government. Yet while these general explanations partly clarify the problem in retrospect, they do not explain why some S&Ls failed and others did not. The goal of this chapter is to assess how and to what degree state regulation contributed to this problem. As about half of the S&Ls were chartered and regulated by the states and the other half by the federal government, we can assess the relative role of state policymaking.

Many books have been written about the crisis, some suggesting in their title that they provide the "inside" story (Adams 1989; Lowy 1991; Pilzer and Dietz 1989). Others emphasize the severity of the problem in their titles, calling it a "debacle" (Barth 1991; Eichler 1989; Romer and Weingast 1991; White 1991), a "mess" (Kane 1989; Pilzer and Dietz 1989), a robbery (Waldman 1990), a "fix" (Adams 1989), or simply "hell" (Day 1993).[2] These books suggest extreme corruption, fraud, or at least sheer incompetence as the primary causes, damning such S&L executives as Charles Keating and Neil Bush. In addition to the corrupt S&L managers, a number of analysts focus most of the blame on politicians, such as the "Keating Five" in Congress, and regulators, for incompetence in address-ing industry problems. Mayer (1996, p. 21), for example, cites the laxity of states like California in allowing S&Ls to invest in real estate, the in-competence of regulators, and "the systematic, sometimes ignorant, and sometimes deliberate misdiagnosis of the disease that was wasting the business, and the administration of quack remedies in response."

While specific examples are easy to find, corruption and incompetence are hardly complete explanations: Strunk and Case (1988, p. 136) cite studies that show 20–23 percent of S&L losses were related to criminal or

1. Although Day (1993) and others cited potential S&L loss figures as high as $1 trillion, most estimates range from $150 to $300 million, depending on what costs are included. A 1993 Congressional Budget Office report pegged the figure at $180 billion from 1981 to 1996.

2. One book (Brewton 1992) even links the Mafia, the CIA, and the presi-dency to the S&Ls.

fraudulent activities. Other estimates are lower: Rom (1996, p. 3) cites Ely and Lowy as arguing that only 3 percent of S&L losses were related to fraud, while Barth (1991) estimates about 10 percent, and Litan (1991, p. 210) estimates about 20 percent. Rom believes that as much as 25 percent can be attributed to the total combination of fraud, junk bond investments, delay, and incompetent regulation. White (1991, p. 117), a former Federal Home Loan Bank Board (FHLBB) member, argues that while there was considerable corruption by bankers and politicians, this was not the primary cause: "Thrifts had little incentive to behave otherwise [that is, in a less risky manner], and the excessively lenient and ill-equipped regulatory environment tolerated these business practices for far too long."

Though many others focused on changing economic trends that made the S&Ls highly vulnerable (Brumbaugh 1988; Strunk and Case 1988), some scholars have offered explanations based more in politics and institutions. Romer and Weingast (1991, p. 178) argue that normal congressional politics drove this issue more than any extraordinary events, as Congress delayed taking regulatory steps because it had few incentives to do so, which ultimately made the problem far worse. Litan (1991, p. 209) summarizes: "Romer and Weingast are correct when they argue that the fundamental causes of the thrift mess are political rather than economic or criminal." Rom (1996) argues that most politicians and regulators sincerely tried to solve problems, but made honest mistakes and suffered the electoral consequences. He also maintains that compared to other public policy problems, the S&L mess was not necessarily a true "crisis."[3] Hill (1991) argues that the system of dual federal-state regulation may partly be to blame.

History of State Role

S&Ls were created mainly to fund home mortgages for American families. Politicians and scholars have debated about who should regulate them and in what manner. All S&Ls were initially organized in a mutual form,

3. Using the Congressional Budget Office figure of $180 billion for resolving S&Ls over the period 1981–96, this is about $11 billion a year, which Rom calls a "tragedy" but not a "crisis." Rom argues that other public policies "waste" far more resources—for example, $15 billion on annual agricultural price supports, a program with little public policy justification, or $100 billion a year in estimated uncollected tax revenues.

in which depositors were also the direct owners. Starting with New York in 1875, states became the exclusive regulators of S&Ls. By 1932 all but two states regulated S&Ls and most had deposit insurance funds to deal with potential financial crises. During the Great Depression, however, nearly all these state deposit insurance funds went insolvent and were unable to bail out depositors, which led to a jurisdictional debate. To restore public confidence in the industry, the U.S. League of Savings Associations successfully lobbied the federal government to back up S&L deposits with its own funds, which it did by establishing the Federal Savings and Loan Insurance Corporation (FSLIC) in 1934. In addition, Congress passed a new federal chartering option for S&Ls, empowering the FHLBB to charter and regulate thrifts at the federal level.[4]

With this congressionally established dual regulatory system, federally chartered S&Ls were automatically covered by the FSLIC, but state-chartered thrifts could also be covered by federal insurance if they complied with FSLIC net worth and capital standards, while states remained the primary regulators of their other activities. The FHLBB retained authority even over state-chartered institutions, including the power to declare an S&L insolvent, but in reality, the FHLBB shared power with state agencies and did not use it aggressively (Rom 1996, p. 82).

S&L charters split over time fairly evenly between federal and state regulators. States competed with the national government, as well as with other states, to attract firms. Politicians and regulators, in pursuit of campaign contributions and fee revenues from S&Ls, respectively, tried to attract firms through innovative or lenient regulation.

Congress repeatedly failed to pass bills that would have abrogated state jurisdiction over S&Ls, in part because state innovations led to many positive new developments, including the use of automated teller machines, adjustable rate mortgages, and negotiated orders of withdrawal for checking accounts. Using their states as laboratories, Texas, California, and a few other states expanded considerably the options for S&L activity in the 1960s and 1970s.

In 1963 the Texas legislature revised its 1929 S&L statute, providing thrifts with extraordinary freedom and providing regulators with considerable discretion, with the S&L commissioner and three members of the

4. Note that the federal government first chartered banks in 1863 after considerable debate. See Khademian (1996, pp. 94–99) for more details on this federal-state interaction in banking.

finance commission able to enact regulations without legislative approval. Texas-chartered S&Ls were the first in the nation to be allowed to conduct commercial lending and to invest in corporate debt and nonresidential real estate, leading many Texas S&Ls to engage in speculative activities. These relaxed rules led to 75 percent of Texas S&Ls opting to hold state charters in 1980, compared to 50 percent in 1950. Ironically in retrospect, as Texas thrifts prospered through 1982, their regulation was considered a model for the nation (Fabritius and Borges 1989, p. 74; Rom 1996, p. 78). But the sharp decline in the Texas economy in 1983, as oil prices dropped, led to massive problems for Texas S&Ls.

California's S&L regulation demonstrates how state officials adapted their actions to benefit state-chartered institutions. In a 1960s innovation, California S&Ls introduced adjustable rate mortgages for adaptation to interest rates fluctuations. Relaxed regulations also permitted S&Ls to invest more heavily in construction projects, rather than residential mortgages. Many California S&Ls converted to stock rather than mutual ownership and exploited liberal regulations to expand substantially, leading to some financial problems in the late 1960s and 1970s. Governor Brown and the legislature tightened regulations in 1975, which led large numbers of state S&Ls to convert to federal charters, resulting in declining contributions to state legislators and a 50 percent drop in state regulatory fees. The shift away from state charters, from 172 in 1978 to 55 by 1983, convinced Governor Brown to support, and the legislature to pass, a more relaxed bill that abolished limits on investments in government securities, commercial paper, corporate debt securities, and real estate. Seeking to promote the industry, Governor Deukmejian's administration approved many applications for new charters, and federal regulators slowed this expansion only a little.

Although Texas and California were the most prominent, other states also promoted innovation for their state-chartered S&Ls. Florida had virtually no state-chartered thrifts before 1980, when a new state law allowed them to make consumer and commercial loans without restrictions and to engage in real estate development. Relative to federally chartered institutions in Florida, state S&Ls rapidly became more heavily invested in commercial lending and liquid investments. Florida's S&Ls were regulated by the state comptroller, not by a separate banking regulatory agency.

Before the 1980s both federally and state-chartered S&Ls mostly fulfilled their role as secure savings institutions. Protected by regulation and facing little competition, S&Ls were generally profitable. Rapid advances in information technology, however, transformed the financial sector, enabling consumers to pursue far more sophisticated investment alternatives. Thus as interest rates escalated wildly in the late 1970s, consumers explored other financial options. Proscribed by law from offering competitive interest rates and faced with a serious threat from new mutual funds, the S&Ls faced their "first crisis"—of profitability—in the early 1980s. As a result, Romer and Weingast (1991, p. 177) note that 85 percent of FSLIC-insured thrifts had negative earnings in 1981.

Politicians intended that federal (and state) deregulation would allow S&Ls to adjust to this shifting competitive environment. Specifically, in 1980 Congress passed the Depositary Institutions Deregulatory and Monetary Control Act, which eliminated restrictions on the interest rates S&Ls could pay and allowed them to make investments previously prohibited. Soon thereafter, the federal 1982 Garn–St. Germain Act greatly expanded the allowed range of services and investments. The 1982 act also allowed federally chartered institutions to become stock-owned, as all had been required to be mutual firms in the past.

These acts came in the midst of state actions. Fabritius and Borges (1989, p. 143) argue: "To a very great extent, the Garn–St. Germain Act was patterned after rules that had governed Texas state-chartered S&Ls for nearly two decades." Although not all states followed suit after these federal acts, many states, like Florida, did relax regulations on state-chartered thrifts. Interestingly, the authors of a book published by the U.S. League of Savings Institutions write: "The new liberal laws for these state-chartered systems went far beyond what the Garn–St. Germain provided for the federal system and what most people in the business thought was needed. In retrospect, the leadership of the state leagues and savings and loan executives in those states generally should have exercised *greater oversight of their state legislatures*" (Strunk and Case 1988, pp. 59–60; emphasis added).

A more apparent "second crisis" followed from these permissive changes in the mid- to late 1980s, caused not by interest rate fluctuations but by risky investments, especially in regions facing severe economic downturns, such as Texas and Arizona. Thus a "snowball" (Hammond and Knott 1988) had developed: federal and state politicians and regulators addressed S&L failures with more relaxed, rather than tighter, regulation. Partly these were poor decisions, partly they were captured by the S&L industry. Adding to this problem, officials cut federal regulatory staff, consistent with prevalent deregulatory philosophy, as White (1991, p. 89) notes that examinations per S&L asset dollar fell by one-half from 1980 to 1984 as the problem grew. In 1984 Ed Gray, the head of the FHLBB, requested a thousand new examiners but was rejected by the deregulatory goals of President Reagan's Office of Management and Budget.

FSLIC insurance underlay this set of poor policy choices, and in 1980 Congress actually raised the FSLIC deposit guarantee from $40,000 to $100,000. FSLIC insurance also reduced the incentives for states to place meaningful restrictions on state-chartered S&Ls, since losses would be borne by the federal insurance fund, while benefits from liberal state regulations were enjoyed solely by the state actors.

As more S&Ls failed in the mid-1980s, the FHLBB finally began to tighten S&L standards and established programs to reduce the impact of losses on the FSLIC. But by 1986 failed S&Ls made the FSLIC insolvent, leading to legislation to recapitalize the fund. The issue now became politically salient as the media made it clear to U.S. taxpayers that they would foot much of the bill to bail out the S&Ls. Extensive congressional hearings attempted to shift blame from federal politicians onto the states. As Hill (1991, p. 28) wrote: "The perception of many members of Congress . . . is that state-chartered thrifts incurred an inordinate share of the losses." Congress thus passed new legislation, the Financial Institutions Reform, Recovery, and Enforcement Act of 1989.

Reversing the trend of relaxing regulations, the act restricted risky investment and lending. Congress preempted states from allowing state-chartered thrifts to engage in any activities that were not approved for federal S&Ls. The law gave federal agencies expansive supervisory and enforcement powers over both federally and state-chartered S&Ls, encouraging a return to less risky residential lending. The act was designed to curtail, and ultimately eliminate altogether, state-chartered S&Ls. Congress also established the Resolution Trust Corporation (RTC) to sell the remaining assets of failed S&Ls to reduce federal bailout expenditures. The RTC was aided by economic recovery and its sales reduced some of the expected losses.

Thus the deregulation of S&Ls was insured and backed by the credit of the U.S. government. Federal deposit insurance served to discourage depositors, shareholders, politicians, or regulators from monitoring adequately the performance of thrift managers, whom regulations had encouraged to become risk-seeking. But even under these circumstances, not all S&Ls failed. White (1991, p. 148) notes that in 1987, although one-third of S&Ls were running losses, the other two-thirds were still making profits. What role did state chartering and oversight play in the failures of S&Ls?

Factors Likely to Influence Regulation

Delegation relationships were clearly important in the failure of S&Ls. Political scientists increasingly employ principal-agent approaches to understand delegation relationships (see Mitnick 1980; Moe 1984; Pratt and Zeckhauser 1985; Bendor 1988; Wood 1989; but for critiques see Cook 1989; Meier, Wrinkle, and Polinard 1995; Waterman and Meier 1998; Worsham, Eisner, and Ringquist 1997). This study focuses on three important relationships in which the failures of principals to control or monitor agents contributed heavily to the S&L problem. First and most important are delegation relationships in terms of federalism and the role of the states in chartering S&Ls. Abstracting to treat the federal principals as a unitary actor, their goals were to maintain healthy S&Ls that served customers well, as supported by FSLIC insurance, and to avoid losses that taxpayers would have to cover. These goals conflicted with state goals, which often emphasized their own financial, political, and economic development rewards from state-chartered S&Ls that were attracted by lenient regulations. This federalism relationship also implies high levels of information asymmetry, due to geography and traditions of jurisdictional fiefdoms. Combining goal conflict and information asymmetry, it would not be surprising to see considerable "slippage" between the actions of federal principals and state agents in S&L regulation.

The second important relationship to examine is more commonly explored: the delegation and oversight relationship between political actors, most prominently the legislature, and bureaucratic actors at the same level of government (state or federal, depending on the S&L's charter). Following Waterman and Meier's (1998) approach of treating the parameters as variables, the degree of conflict between these institutions appears less strong than for the federalism relationship, as an "iron triangle" or "capture" relationship held at least partially through much of the crisis. While Romer and Weingast (1991) argued that Congress largely knew what was happening, others have suggested a greater information asymmetry problem between politicians and regulators as the problem evolved (Rom 1996). We analyze the degree of independence held by regulatory agencies from legislative, executive, and public influence, which clearly gave some regulatory agencies a relatively greater ability to use their information advantages than others (Khademian 1996).

Third, at the level of corporate governance, from which original principal-agent models derived, some S&Ls were owned directly by their depositors, in mutual form, while others were stockholder-owned, a difference in monitoring incentives that has been associated with differential financial success (Jensen and Warner 1988). We examine whether S&Ls organized as stock entities, with an intervening board of directors and with shareholders holding somewhat smaller incentives to monitor, were more likely to fail than those with mutual ownership.

The expectation is that state-chartered S&Ls, stock-owned S&Ls, and S&Ls regulated by a less politically accountable agency were more likely to fail. The largest degrees of conflict and information asymmetry between principals and agents should be in the federalism relationship, with somewhat smaller, but still important, differences in the bureaucratic and corporate governance arenas.

Measuring Regulatory Failures

The data set for this analysis includes 3,816 S&Ls from 1987, as provided by the U.S. Office of Thrift Supervision, virtually all S&Ls then in existence.[5] Of these 3,816 thrifts, 1,003 (or 26 percent) actually failed, which is defined as meaning that they incurred some resolution costs by the U.S. government. This means that 74 percent did not fail at all. This defines the measure of regulation, or dependent variable, which is one if an S&L failed and zero otherwise. Some 24 percent of the failing S&Ls were located in Texas, a figure far above its national population share.

Explaining Regulatory Failures

Laumann and I explain the failure of individual S&Ls using a logit model that incorporates measures of three important delegation relationships, as well as several other control variables. For each of the independent vari-

5. While this is a great data set, particularly in size, the ideal model for this type of study would be a pooled time series, which would enable a researcher to track changes in the independent variables over time at both the state and federal levels. Control over any possible confounds, such as intervening historical events, would be greatly enhanced as a result. Unfortunately, the requisite data over time are not available. Thus the analysis employs a cross-sectional design. Most of the variables are sufficiently stable across the mid-1980s to allow a reasonable degree of confidence in the model.

ables in the models, when the S&L was state-chartered, the relevant state measure is used; when an S&L was federally chartered, the appropriate federal government measure is employed.

The state charter dummy variable equals one for state-chartered S&Ls and zero for federally chartered ones. Regulatory accountability measures the accountability of regulators to their horizontal-level political principals. The range is from zero to seven, with seven representing the lowest accountability. This comes from the American Council of State Savings Supervisors (1989) and Murphy (1989). The scale is created such that one point is scored if: (1) the regulatory agency is not a subordinate unit of a department; (2) the regulatory agency is not solely responsible for S&L regulations; (3) the regulatory agency's decisions are not subject to approval by administrative or legislative authority; (4) the agency is responsible for approving S&L charters; (5) public hearings are not held on charter applications; (6) there is no right of appeal to charter applications; or (7) the agency is not required to submit budget requests to the legislature.

In the ownership category, the dummy variable equals one for mutual ownership of S&L and zero for stock ownership. Assets refers to the total assets of the S&L when it failed, unemployment to the unemployment rate in the state or federal jurisdiction.

Next party identifications are measured, for the governor (or president)—Republican = 1, Democrat = 0—and on a scale of 1 to 5 for the legislature or Congress (upper and lower houses jointly), with 1 equaling strongly Democratic; 2, moderately Democratic; 3, split control; 4, moderately Republican; and 5, strongly Republican.

The dummy variable equals 1 if states allowed S&Ls to branch out of the state and 0 otherwise. The dummy variable is 1 if states allowed external S&Ls to branch into their state and 0 otherwise. Finally, the dummy variable is 1 for Texas S&Ls and 0 otherwise.

The first issue is whether state-chartered S&Ls were more likely to fail. Despite the growth of state-chartered thrifts in relaxed states like Texas and California, the nationwide percentage of state-chartered S&Ls actually dropped a little over time, from 54 percent in 1960 to a level of 42 percent in the present data set. In terms of monitoring, Rom (1996, p. 81) argues that the FHLBB examined about as many state-chartered S&Ls as federally chartered ones from 1979 to 1985, although he also notes that the FHLBB probably did not use as much leverage from these examinations of state S&Ls as they did with federal ones. State-chartered firms may have operated under more lenient regulatory environments and were therefore more likely to fail. A previous study found that a disproportionate number of the insolvent thrifts addressed in 1988 were state-chartered (Barth and Bradley 1988). In addition, the special role of Texas, which incurred such a large proportion of failed S&Ls, must be looked at. White (1991, p. 151) notes that unprofitable Texas S&Ls accounted for fully 50 percent of the total losses by unprofitable S&Ls nationwide. Thus to sort out the influence of Texas, added to the full model (model 1) are models that use a dummy variable to account for Texas's special role (model 2) and a model that leaves Texas out (model 3).

One would expect that the differing accountability relationship between regulators, politicians, and other interested parties across states and the federal government affected S&L failures. Greater public and democratic accountability generally should yield more regulatory warnings and fewer failures in that jurisdiction.[6] The specific measure of accountability reflects multiple principals, as many elements are tied to legislative interactions (oversight, budgets, approvals), but others include aspects of executive (agency structure) and public accountability (public hearings).

In terms of ownership form, S&Ls changed over time: 87 percent of S&Ls were mutuals in 1960, but by 1985 only 67 percent were, as managers found that the stock ownership form was more autonomous and made it easier to raise capital. Given monitoring incentives, mutually owned firms should be less likely to fail, as stock ownership creates an additional layer between principals and agents, and as Strunk and Case (1988, p. 107) argue: "At some institutions, management did not tell their board members about activities in which the institution was engaged, even large compensation plans for management. Board complacency made it possible for management to keep many key facts from directors."

To achieve a comprehensive model, other explanatory variables are incorporated. First is the amount of assets held by thrifts, a measure of size and possibly their political clout. Second, the economic health of each state, as measured by unemployment, should also play a role in the likelihood of failure. Third is the partisanship of elected officials in determining their regulatory orientation. Although neither party is solely associated with the S&L crisis, Republicans traditionally favor policies to reduce regulations, while Democrats have been more favorable toward government regulation. Failures might be greater in states where the legislature,

---

6. Khademian (1996) argues that overlapping agencies and agency autonomy are preferred to a single consolidated bank regulatory agency.

the governorship, or both was controlled by Republicans; for time consistency, we measure the party identification in 1987. Also measured are state regulations that allowed "out-of-state" financial institutions to develop branches within their state ("branch-in") and those that allowed "domestic" institutions to develop branches in other states ("branch-out"), expecting that more competition led to more failures.

Results

The results of the three models are presented in table 7-1. Model 1 uses all 3,816 S&Ls in the United States. Model 2 is exactly the same but adds a dummy variable for location of an S&L in Texas (either federally or state-chartered). The third model excludes all Texas S&Ls, to examine more closely the overwhelming impact of Texas S&Ls in the failure statistics.

The results support several expectations. First note that state-chartered institutions were significantly more likely to fail than federally chartered S&Ls in the full model. However, the next two models illustrate that this is largely because Texas had so many failed S&Ls, so many of which were state-chartered. In the third model, excluding Texas, state-chartered S&Ls were actually a little less likely to fail than federal ones (though not significantly so). Thus state-chartered S&Ls did fail more often, but that result is driven entirely by Texas, where the case study evidence illustrates that S&Ls had clearly captured legislators and regulators.

In terms of public accountability, the findings of all three models show that when regulatory agencies were less accountable to legislators and other political actors in their jurisdiction (whether federal or state, depending on the charter), more S&Ls failed. Texas again was the most prominent example of a regulatory body that was not accountable, as it was given the right to make rules without any legislative oversight. But this result is still significant, though a little smaller, even when Texas S&Ls are excluded, as the Florida case study exemplifies. Although these results are not presented in table 7-1, we also examined only the state-chartered S&Ls across the country. Here, less accountable regulatory agencies led to more failures, so this result is not only a function of the accountability relationships of federal government regulators.

In all models, mutually owned S&Ls were less likely to fail, as their owners had greater incentives than stock shareholders to monitor firm performance. Some S&Ls made a choice to convert from mutual to stock to raise capital more easily, but perhaps also with the idea of taking more

Table 7-1. *S&L Failures, 1989*[a]

Explanatory factors	All S&Ls	All S&Ls (with Texas dummy variable)	Excluding Texas S&Ls
State charter	2.28***	0.61*	−0.52
	(0.33)	(0.37)	(0.42)
Regulatory accountability	0.52***	0.30***	0.16**
	(0.07)	(0.07)	(0.08)
Mutual ownership	−0.57***	−0.77***	−0.60***
	(0.09)	(0.09)	(0.09)
S&L assets (thousands)	0.12	0.08	0.24
	(0.26)	(0.28)	(0.27)
Unemployment	0.001	0.001	0.001
	(0.001)	(0.001)	(0.001)
Governor's party	0.31**	−0.16	−0.08
	(0.13)	(0.12)	(0.18)
Legislative party control	−0.34***	−0.07	−0.03
	(0.07)	(0.07)	(0.07)
Branch-out	0.14	0.18	0.18
	(0.16)	(0.16)	(0.16)
Branch-in	−0.03	−0.03	−0.007
	(0.14)	(0.14)	(0.15)
Texas dummy	. . .	1.94***	. . .
		(0.16)	
Constant	−3.95***	−2.50***	−1.59**
	(0.50)	(0.54)	(0.58)
N	3,816	3,816	3,289

*Significant at .1 level; **significant at .05 level; ***significant at .01 level.
a. Standard errors are in parentheses.

risk, to seek more rewards for managers. Other analysts have found a higher failure rate for stock firms (White 1991), but not while controlling for other explanatory factors.

In addition to these results for the core hypotheses, there were generally unstable results for the party control of key political actors, seemingly related to the large influence of Texas. In the full model, jurisdictions with Republican executives and Democratic-controlled legislatures were more likely to have failing S&Ls. This appears to be largely a function of Texas, which had a Republican governor and Democratic-controlled legislature when most of the failures took place. When the Texas dummy variable is added in model 2 and when Texas is excluded completely in model 3, the partisan control variables become insignificant, confirming anecdotal federal-level evidence that party differences were not the key issues behind the S&L problems.

The other independent variables that measure economic factors related to the jurisdiction and competitive factors related to the S&Ls were not significant in any of the models.

It is useful to consider the magnitude of these statistically significant explanatory factors. With all model variables set at their mean level, the mean likelihood of an S&L failing is 29 percent in model 1. When all variables are converted to their maximum that is associated with more failures, the average predicted failure rate shoots up to 88 percent; in the opposite direction for all variables, the likelihood of failure becomes only 1 percent, demonstrating substantial joint explanatory power from the variables in the model. Again the Texas effect is apparent; in model 3, the range of likelihood bounded by the joint influence of these variables narrows substantially, from a low of 21 percent up to 44 percent.

With Texas included, states are associated with considerably higher failure rates—the probability of failure is 49 percent higher for state-chartered thrifts, ceteris paribus. With Texas excluded, state S&Ls are less likely to fail, by 9 percent, although this is not statistically significant.

There are also large differences for the accountability relationships. In the full model, the least accountable regulatory agencies are associated with a 56 percent higher likelihood of failures compared to the most accountable. However, when only the non-Texas S&Ls are examined, this drops to a 16 percent difference, suggesting that, absent Texas, there was some mutual adaptation between legislators and regulators.[7]

The full model yields a 13 percent greater likelihood that stock-owned S&Ls failed; with Texas S&Ls excluded, stock-owned firms are still 10 percent more likely to fail, ceteris paribus.

7. There are some potential issues with endogeneity. State legislatures that passed relaxed laws may have wanted relatively unaccountable agencies that they knew could be captured by the S&Ls. This parallels Romer and Weingast's (1991) argument at the federal level. However, it is also possible that laws were written with policy-oriented goals and agencies were given varying autonomy to regulate, closer to Rom's (1996) perspective. It is also true that S&Ls choose to be state- or federally chartered and to be mutual or stock firms. Here again endogeneity is a potential concern. S&L managers may have wanted to take more risks and therefore found the appropriate charter and form that most allowed that to take place. However, in a temporal sense, many of these decisions were made years before the actual failure. Even if some unmeasured elements of the S&L managers really "caused" the failures, how they were regulated remains highly relevant in a situation where fully 25 percent of S&Ls actually failed. In any case, it was not possible to find appropriate exclusion variables in the data set to test for the potential endogeneity issues.

Discussion

Many factors contributed to the S&L crisis, all of which were underscored by the moral hazard situation of FSLIC insurance guarantees. State-chartered S&Ls failed more often than did federally chartered ones (but only when Texas is included in the analysis), suggesting less effective oversight by state legislators and regulators, at least in Texas. This quantitative evidence supports the case studies that some states wanted to attract jobs and fees from S&Ls and were willing to accept more risk to get these benefits, risks that were underwritten by federal insurance. Including Texas, we see a race to the bottom here, with Texas winning that race, in terms of attracting state-chartered S&Ls and then "losing" when so many failed during the economic downturn. Excluding the large influence of Texas, however, it seems that state bureaucratic capabilities, relative to federal capabilities, were not the major problem in the S&L case.

Ultimately, the massive insolvencies of the one-quarter of all U.S. S&Ls in the 1980s cost taxpayers nearly $200 billion dollars and shook their confidence in further deregulatory policies. There is no question that the familiar reasons given for these failures were important—extreme fluctuations in interest rates, competition from emerging financial institutions, and the encouragement of risk-taking behaviors by new federal deregulatory laws while, at the same time, the deposits of investors were insured by the federal government. But these factors were fairly similar across all S&Ls. This analysis goes further to explain why some S&Ls failed and others did not. The relative ease of policy monitoring, in both the economic and political spheres, by owners of the S&Ls themselves and by federal and state regulators, respectively, helps explain failures.

In terms of future policy guidance, these findings suggest establishing tighter monitoring relationships when easing other kinds of market regulations on firms insured by or funded by the public sector (see Wood and Waterman 1993). For example, this may provide a lesson for states as they establish and monitor larger numbers of new charter schools. There is a trade-off, of course, as monitoring is always costly, and policymakers do not want to blunt the incentives for policy innovation by the states as experimental laboratories. But consider the request made by FHLBB head Gray in 1984 for one thousand new S&L examiners that was turned down by President Reagan's Office of Management and Budget. Rom (1996) estimates that 25 percent of the $200 billion in taxpayer losses were caused by fraud and the like and another 25 percent by bad loans made from 1983 to 1985 (the other 50 percent was from interest rate losses in the "first" crisis in 1981 and thus were not salvageable). If the thousand proposed new examiners could have salvaged only 1 percent of these 50 percent of losses that were potentially preventable, that would have represented $1 billion saved. Using these savings, each new examiner could have been paid $1 million; as examiners can be hired probably for less than $100,000 total cost a year, in a cost-benefit sense, this would have been a good investment to make in 1984.

CHAPTER EIGHT

Hospital
Certificates-of-Need

with

RICHARD CHARD

Rising health care costs have been one of the most critical problems faced by national and state policymakers in the past two decades. While much of health care policy is shaped by national politics, states are responsible for a considerable amount of health care costs, directly and indirectly. States also administer a number of regulations across the health care industry, including professional licensing related to medical practitioners, as analyzed in chapter 10.

With mixed success, politicians and bureaucrats have crafted regulations attempting to control health care costs while still maintaining quality of care and access. One of the most important state-level policies aimed at cost control has been hospital certificate-of-need (CON) regulation. This chapter analyzes the politics of state decisions from 1982 to 1996 to determine why about one-third of states dropped CON regulation after the federal government no longer supported it, while others have maintained it.

History of State Role

Certificate-of-need regulation is a supply-oriented intervention requiring government approval of all hospital and service enhancements before construction. The basic origins of CON regulation can be traced to the 1946 Hill-Burton Act, which provided government financing for hospitals for needy populations; first operated in rural areas, the politically popular distributive program was expanded by Congress to urban areas as well.[1] The concept behind the CON regulatory mechanism developed after Blue Cross, blaming growing hospital expenditures, instituted drastic rate increases in the 1950s. This caused the insurance commissioners of several states to threaten to impose mandatory price controls on hospitals. In response, the insurance industry offered its own cost containment system, the certificate-of-need, arguing that hospital expenses were increasing due to Medicare retrospective reimbursements and growing capital expenses made necessary by intense competition over quality. As Feldstein (1998, p. 261) notes, "the most frequent reasons given for supply regulation are the duplication of expensive services which are subject to economies of scale, the excess of beds in communities, and . . . the lack of provider incentives to be efficient."

In 1968 the American Hospital Association endorsed CONs, and in 1970 New York became the first state to enact a comprehensive CON law, followed by Florida in 1972. In 1974 the federal government mandated CONs for all states. The specific federal impetus behind state health planning agencies' use of CON was the Health Planning and Development Act of 1974, which employed financial disincentives rather than command-and-control regulations. The federal Department of Health and Human Services would not pay for noncertified hospital construction, either directly through the Hill-Burton mechanism, or indirectly through Medicaid and Medicare payments to the hospital.

CONs created a slow and expensive process for hospitals to expand their services, with requirements including letters of intent, formal applications, witnesses, financial projections, public hearings, and often a lengthy appeals process for the losing side. In one celebrated case, the University of Florida's hospital successfully opposed the Mayo Clinic from performing liver transplants for six years, at a cost of millions in legal and consulting fees (Doherty 2001, p. 16).

With some evidence that CONs were not working to control costs and a broader switch to more prospective reimbursement policies that could limit costs, the federal government repealed the CON mandate in 1986. Policy debates over CON regulation were transferred to the states. As Weissert and Weissert (1996, p. 274) write: "The program and the era of federal support for health planning were allowed to die a quiet death,

---

1. Weisert and Weisert (1996, chapter 7) provide a discussion of the larger historical attempts to regulate health care costs.

starved of both dollars and supporters. Some states dropped their own programs immediately . . . while others kept them in place."[2]

In 1982, the first year in this data set, forty-eight states had CON regulations in place (only California and Idaho had none); this dropped quickly after withdrawal of federal support to forty states with CONs in 1987 and gradually declined to thirty-three states by 1996, the last year of our data set. Only one state, Texas, has reversed its initial decision to drop the CON laws, as Texas insurers and providers had grown comfortable with the system.

In economic terms, CON regulation is an attempt to lower aggregate hospital costs by restricting entry. Specifically, as Ford and Kasserman (1993, p. 783) explain: "The applicant must demonstrate: (1) a market demand (or 'need') for the incremental output, investment, or new service being proposed, and (2) the inability or unwillingness of existing firms to meet that demand with facilities already in place." Economists have long been skeptical of this method of regulation, as they perceive these kinds of barriers to entry as likely to raise costs and limit valuable competition. (See, for example, discussions by Derthick and Quirk 1985 and Teske, Best, and Mintrom 1995 on economists' consensus about the harm from similar restrictions in the airline and trucking industries.)

Despite such skepticism, hospital groups argued that competition was a unique problem in the health care industry for two specific reasons. First, the identity of the paying health care consumer is not clear because of third-party insurance. Second, the demand for hospital care is often relatively inelastic. These elements combine to partly reduce the consumers' cost sensitivity, creating a moral hazard situation. Thus the hospital industry argued that, rather than price regulation, supply regulation was necessary to reduce total costs and to provide a marketlike equilibrium.

Factors Likely to Influence Regulation

The hospitals' approach appears to be a classic example of the Chicago School "economic theory" of regulation as proposed by Stigler (1971; see also Friedman 1962). Stigler argues that all producers with enough political power will seek entry protection from government to reduce competition and raise their profits. Chicago School economists argue that these

2. At the state level the regulation is more direct, with all capital improvements of $100,000 or more requiring approval from the state CON board.

models hold up well, even in explaining much of the deregulation of the 1970s and 1980s (Peltzman 1989). Thus the analysis will need to include measures of the power of hospital and medical interests in the states to assess their role in retaining CON regulations.

Public interest theories imply a more complete political model of regulation, recognizing that a single, stylized politician or regulator does not determine state policies (for example, Meier 1988; Teske, Best, and Mintrom 1995). A number of elected and unelected political actors and institutions have some degree of influence over CON regulations. Thus in this broader model, politicians may support state CON regulation, or its removal, for reasons other than producer group "capture," including broad ideology or a more specific and genuine sense that CON regulation might serve the public interest by reducing costs and inefficient hospital duplication of facilities.

While no scholars have yet tested fully these competing political explanations for the emergence and persistence of state CON regulations, there is a related economic literature on the effect of CON regulations once they are in place. On one hand, Sloan (1981) found that CON regulation did not decrease or increase health costs in the 1960s and 1970s. On the other hand, Nyman (1994) found that CON regulations created barriers to entry for nursing homes and drove up nursing home costs. Conover and Sloan (1998) found that CON regulations do not affect health costs overall, but that they do reduce acute care costs by about 5 percent. Thus the existing literature on the economic effects of CON regulation shows mixed results about its effectiveness.

Measuring Regulation

Chard and I examine the degree to which the political power of various actors is associated with the continuation or removal of CON regulations using a pooled cross-sectional time-series analysis for the fifty states over the period from 1982 to 1996, yielding a sample with 750 observations. U.S. Census Bureau records are the source for much of the data, supplemented by questionnaires sent directly to the state commissioners of health. The measure of regulation, or dependent variable, CON, is coded as a dummy variable—one for years in which a state had a CON regulation on record and zero otherwise. It is reasonable to treat state CON regulations as similar to each other because they were established under a federal framework, rather than representing fifty separate state decisions, and they cover the same essential set of hospital regulations. Given the dichotomous (zero or one) nature of the dependent variable, this equation is estimated using logistic regression (logit). The model includes fourteen dummy variables in order to control for autocorrelation in the regression analyses of the pooled time-series data (see also Box-Steffensmeier and Jones 1997).[3]

Explaining Regulation

The explanatory factors, or independent variables, measure interest group strength, political party strength in the state legislatures, actual hospital costs in the states, and other conditions that might influence health regulation and hospital costs. The variable measuring hospital interests is the number of hospital industry–related interest groups active in a particular state multiplied by their average political action committee spending. If the economic theory of regulation applies here, more hospital groups in a state should successfully help to retain CONs.

The variable of uninsured citizens is the percentage of the population not covered by insurance within a state, which is a partial measure of consumer price sensitivity in the absence of third-party payer arrangements. On average, about 9 percent are uninsured. The variable of physicians is the number of physicians (in thousands) in a state, used as a control variable that may be related to the number of hospital facilities required to serve patients.

The house party variable captures the percentage of Democrats in the lower house of the state legislature, while the senate party variable measures the percentage of Democrats in the upper house of the state legislature.[4] Generally, Democrats should be more favorable toward marketplace regulations than are Republicans, as a matter of party platforms and ideology. The variables education and income represent, respectively, the percentage of state residents with a high school diploma and the inflation-adjusted average per capita income of state residents, both used as

3. Stimson's (1985) method to correct for autocorrelation in pooled cross-sectional time-series data employs the creation of $N - 1$ dummy variables, where N is the number of years in the series.

4. For unicameral Nebraska we used county-level federal congressional voting data as a proxy. Legislative party percentages are examined rather than Berry and others' (1998) elite ideology scores in order to focus on the legislative party role specifically, not combined with other state measures of ideology.

control variables. Finally, a per diem hospital costs variable is included with the expectation that, ceteris paribus, states with high costs are more likely to retain CON regulations in the belief that CON lowers costs, even if the economic research evidence is still unclear on this point.

Results

Table 8-1 presents the results of the logistic regression, which is highly significant in statistical terms, with seven of the eight explanatory variables showing high levels of significance. Hospital interests are indeed significantly and positively associated with state retention of CONs, as predicted by the Chicago School theories. States with a higher percentage of Democrats, in both the lower and the upper houses, are more likely to retain CON regulations, supporting the partisan politics model of ideological preference. States with higher hospital costs are more likely to retain CON regulations. In addition, states with more affluent and better-educated citizens and states with fewer physicians are more likely to retain the CON regulations.

With several variables that are significant in statistical terms, it is useful to gauge their substantive impact. A one standard deviation difference in the hospital interest variable yields a small 3 percent difference in retaining a CON, other variables held equal. A larger effect of about 20 percent is generated by a similar calculation for the party makeup of each of the state legislative bodies. Thus differences in state legislative party makeup are more important, substantively, than state differences in interest group power.

Discussion

Retention of state CON regulation after federal support was withdrawn is partly explained by regulatory capture by hospital interests, but this theory does not provide a complete picture. The politics behind the maintenance or deregulation of CONs is more complex and interesting. Congruent with their general ideology, state legislative Democrats must believe that CON regulations lower hospital costs or that their constituents support the retention of CONs. This belief is bolstered by the result that states with relative higher hospital costs are also more likely to retain CON regulation. Independently, states with better-educated and wealthier consumers also are more likely to retain CONs.

Table 8-1. *Retention of Hospital CON Regulations, 1982–96*[a]

Explanatory factors	Coefficient
Hospital interests	0.81***
	(0.043)
Uninsured citizens	−0.032
	(0.021)
Physicians (per 100,000 population)	−0.0051***
	(0.0017)
State house party control	0.055***
	(0.013)
State senate party control	0.036***
	(0.012)
Citizens' education	0.041***
	(0.015)
Citizens' income	0.129***
	(0.032)
Average per diem hospital charges	0.0011***
	(0.0002)
Constant	−9.7642
	(1.56)

Summary statistics
Pseudo R^2 = .326
Log likelihood = 602.6***
Cases correctly predicted (percentage) = 84
N = 750

*Significant at .1 level; **significant at .05 level; ***significant at .01 level.
a. Standard errors are in parentheses.

These results suggest a "Baptists and bootleggers" type of coalition of "true believers" and self-interested groups behind the maintenance of state CON regulation (Yandle 1983, 2001). State hospital interests want to retain the barrier to entry against competition that CON regulations seem to provide, but Democratic Party politicians believe that CON regulations will be helpful to their constituents by lowering costs. Together, this coalition has been powerful enough to keep CON regulation in place in two-thirds of the U.S. states for more than fifteen years (while data here only cover through 1996, other sources of data suggest that not many states have dropped CONs since 1996).

An alternative, and more direct, possibility to consider is that Democratic politicians are captured by hospital industry campaign contributions. The hospital and health services industry is the second largest lobbying group in state capitals. Some state Democratic politicians no doubt receive significant financial and other support from hospital interests.

Across the nation, however, according to the Federal Election Commission, health care interests overall provide about 60 percent of their political action committee (PAC) contributions to Republican candidates, suggesting that the Democratic state legislative response is based more on an ideological perspective of consumer protection than it is on capture by interest group campaign contributions.

Despite the strength of this coalition, since the federal government has not required CON regulations for fifteen years, and since empirical studies are mixed on whether CONs actually lower costs, it is surprising that so many states have retained them and have not deregulated. Another part of the explanation may be that there are no strong countervailing interest groups pushing to eliminate state CON regulations, a problem that was faced by those interested in deregulating state trucking in the 1980s (Teske, Best, and Mintrom 1995).

These findings raise the intriguing general question of whether states tend to be more or less resistant to deregulatory initiatives than the federal government. As firms in many industries can vote with their feet, competitive economic pressure could force states to adopt deregulation more readily than the federal government, or at least quickly after other states act, in a race to the bottom (and after all, complete deregulation is the bottom). A mobility threat is less credible from entrenched or new hospitals, however, which are largely bound to their consumers by state geography.

Since studies have not verified that hospital CON regulation is clearly a costly policy for states, the more complex state political mixture of interest groups, institutions, and ideas evident in these quantitative results predicts state responses better than a single, simple causal explanation.

PART FOUR

Occupational Regulation

The states regulate occupations and professions with no significant, direct role for the federal government. In theory, such regulation can serve the public interest by helping to solve an information asymmetry market failure in which professionals know far more about their own competence than do their customers. In practice, most occupational regulation provides restrictions on entry into the profession, so it bears some similarities to monopoly and competition regulation. Thus to some degree, occupational regulation reflects a combination of these two market failure concepts. An important question is whether occupational regulation usually serves the purposes of improving quality or whether it usually limits competition, raises prices, and protects producers instead.

In recent years, rather than focusing on the information asymmetry issue, scholars generally link occupational licensing to political capture by the regulated interest groups, a political form of an "unnatural monopoly" (Friedman 1962; Stigler 1971). In addition to higher prices, Friedman (1962) argues that the limits on innovation resulting from the reduction of competition actually lower the standards of professional practice. Friedman further maintains that the domination of licensing boards by professional associations leads to leniency in disciplining incompetent professionals (1962, p. 157), so that consumers are actually harmed and misled about quality rather than helped by this form of regulation. Whether private or public interests are primarily served, the U.S. states have chosen to regulate many different occupations and professions. Kleiner (2000) notes that at least one of the states regulates one of eight hundred different occupations or professions. Occupational regulation covers 18 percent of the American work force, so how states regulate, and the effects of such regulation, are important policy issues.

This section analyzes the regulation of lawyers and doctors. In each state, lawyers must be licensed to practice, new lawyers must pay bar exam fees, and most lawyers must take some continuing legal education courses. Using cross-sectional data from 1994, Robert Howard and I find that various measures of the strength of lawyers or legal interest groups in a state are associated with higher entry barriers for new attorneys. Only the continuing legal education component does not fit the capture model, suggesting some room for professional regulation that serves the public interest rather than the private interests of lawyers.

Friedman (1962) argued explicitly against the licensure of medical doctors since it seems like the hardest case for free market advocates, as very few observers would initially support Friedman's idea of a completely open market for medical services. Using three fifty-state panels of data from 1986, 1989, and 1992, Andreas Broscheid and I find that state regulation of doctors creates more strict licensing, or higher entry barriers, in states where medical interest group associations are more powerful, as per Chicago School capture expectations. We also find that, contrary to expectations, a licensing board that is not independent is associated with licensing requirements that are less strict than the requirements in a state with an independent board, as are boards with fewer public members.

Thus these quantitative studies of state occupational regulation of the two most important professions in the United States demonstrate that the stronger the groups are that support restrictive regulation to raise their incomes, the more states actually regulate in that manner. This does fit the classic Chicago School model. Given the very high political profile and salience of these two occupations, and the fact that consumer and other public interest groups might monitor their behavior more than the eight hundred other occupations that are regulated in some states, like barbers, fortune-tellers and rainmakers, this provides strong support for the capture argument.

If capture is a dominant political pattern for occupational regulation, we need to understand how and why. The Council of State Governments defines licensure as "the granting by some competent authority of a right or permission to carry on a business or do an act which otherwise would be illegal. The essential elements of licensing involve the stipulation of circumstances under which permission to perform an otherwise prohibited activity may be granted—largely a legislative function; and the actual granting of the permission in specific cases—generally an administrative responsibility" (cited in Gross 1984, p. 8). With professional entry requirements, for example, while state legislation generally defines the broad education and entry standards required for licenses, the licensing board usually certifies qualifying educational and training programs. In some cases, to ease their administrative burdens, states apply national standards; for example, in medicine, all states now use a nationally unified licensing examination.

The role of administrative agencies in occupational regulation is changing. Historically, state legislatures granted most of these professions the right to essentially self-regulate, a professional role that is also incorporated into the authority of lawyers and doctors to dictate critical elements of legal and medical education requirements. Such self-regulation left a limited role—or even none—for the type of bureaucratic commissions and agencies that are influential independent sources of policy and implementation in the other areas of state regulation discussed in this book. And the boards, with most appointments usually made by governors based on nominations from the state professional associations, until recently were composed almost exclusively of members of the regulated profession. As a result, disciplinary action against professionals was quite rare, despite the fact that boards often hold impressive investigative, prosecutorial, adjudicatory, and punishment powers on paper. For example, with MDs, Ginsburg and Moy write (1992, p. 14): "The rate of disciplinary actions varies from state to state and is generally very low," ranging from two to thirty-two physicians for each thousand in a state—far lower than actions taken against incompetent physicians by their malpractice insurers.

But the composition and practices of these administrative boards may be important for how regulation is carried out in practice. For example, with more public members being placed on state medical boards, discipline cases are growing. New York had over six thousand disciplinary cases related to medical professionals in 2000, a 50 percent increase in just three years.

Historical Development

Occupational and professional licensure has long been the "poster child" for captured state regulation. The general argument against it goes back to Adam Smith, and many prominent modern economists believe it should be eliminated (Friedman 1962; Stigler 1971). Despite considerable professional mobility across the U.S. states, there is no parallel federal regulation of occupations, nor has there been any strong effort to experiment with any form of federal occupational regulation. This may change in 2004 if the federal government decides to intervene in state insurance broker licensing.

Starr (1982) illustrates in great detail how the medical profession emerged as a profession, and the history of regulation of MDs, which goes back to precolonial times, is discussed in more detail in chapter 10. Not surprisingly, interest groups like the American Medical Association (AMA) played a critical role in the expansion and institutionalization of professional requirements. Stigler (1971) and Zhou (1993) analyzed historical data on when particular professions were regulated by the states. Zhou examined thirty professions and found that there were about 35 state licensing acts, each covering one occupation in the 1880s, a number that peaked at over 110 in the 1910s and 1920s. Thus the idea of state occupational regulation spread quickly in the late 1800s and early 1900s in the American states. In the medical professions, for example, Texas first regulated MDs in 1873, and by 1925 licensing of MDs was required in every state. Other medical professions were regulated soon after MDs; for example, New York State first began regulating physicians in 1891, dentists and veterinarians in 1895, registered nurses in 1903, pharmacists in 1910, and podiatrists in 1912.

Using these historical examples, capture theorists argue that the most organized and powerful occupations lobby state legislators, and if their profession is politically powerful enough, then the legislature provides barriers to entry into that profession. These barriers, which often include education or other requirements for professionals to be licensed to practice, combined with prohibitions on professional practice by the nonlicensed, make it more difficult for others to get into this occupation, thus raising incomes for those already employed in the field. The fact that some eight hundred occupations are regulated by at least one state suggests that most occupations do indeed try to seek regulatory protection, and that many are successful, at least in some states.

The requirements to practice in these fields are often "marketed" by legislators to voters as necessary to protect consumers against low-quality occupational providers. And sometimes, though not always, consumer groups do indeed support such licensure, leading to "Baptist and bootlegger" type political coalitions (Yandle 1983, 2001). But often not even consumer groups care much about the professional requirements, and the rhetoric of quality is used more than the inclusion of actual consumer groups in coalitions pressing for licensure.

Rather than licensure that restricts entry, many economists argue that voluntary certification is a superior mechanism for sending consumers a signal about the quality of a provider without limiting market competition (Friedman 1962; Kleiner 2000). An example would be tax preparation, where consumers can employ any accountant or prepare their return themselves but might choose to hire a certified public accountant to ensure competence, especially for complicated returns. In this proposed solution, states could still require providers of particular services to register their practice, so that states could collect fees from them and so that they could contact them if a public health problem developed that required specific occupations to provide information about their experience.

In reality, state occupational licensure often seems to fly below the radar screen of any organized political opposition. The restrictions usually do not seem so onerous, and the costs are spread across such a wide body of consumers that outright opposition is minimal, despite the scholarly assault on these restrictions. How much these restrictions really matter, in terms of costs to consumers or restricted choices, is an empirical question that may vary in each state and especially for each profession.

There are good reasons to suspect that the costs of occupation restrictions are not trivial. Kleiner (2000) points out that about 18 percent of U.S. workers are regulated under occupational licensure, compared to only 10 percent who are affected by minimum wage laws or 15 percent who are labor union members. Given the scholarly and political attention paid to these other labor issues, it seems likely that licensure should have significant economic impacts. In one specific case, Kleiner (2000) finds that dental care costs may be 30 percent higher because of licensure. Related regulations on professional advertising also can raises prices; Benham (1972) found that states with restrictions on optometrists' advertising had prices 25 percent higher.

Licensure rules also influence consumers' access to services. Declercq and others (1998) demonstrate that consumer access to certified nurse-midwives is largely a function of state regulations. In 2002 New Mexico became the first state to allow psychologists to prescribe drugs, which has been opposed by psychiatrists, because of a concern that a shortage of psychiatrists to dispense medication was contributing to a high suicide rate in the state.

While the creation of entry barriers is the usual story told by political economists about state occupational regulation—to the point of becoming a myth that is often believed without explicit empirical evidence—some scholars have noted that there is at least the theoretical possibility of appropriate regulation of these professions (Akerlof 1970; Arrow 1963). Licensure may provide a quality signal to help bridge the information asymmetry gap between professionals and consumers of their services. Many consumers interact with professionals like lawyers and medical doctors rarely, only in times of extreme crises, in which they may have difficulties making the informed, rational choices that we associate with consumers in free markets for goods and services they purchase often. This naive public interest perspective is no longer given much credence in the serious political economy literature. It may help explain some continuing education requirements, which are not entry barriers, but which force incumbent professionals to upgrade their skills and knowledge in the service of consumers.

An approach that mixes these two perspectives would suggest that some aspects of professional licensure regulation are clearly a form of protective capture that does not help consumers pick better-quality service provides, while others, such as continuing education requirements, may improve the quality of professionals to the benefit of consumers without creating significant barriers to entry and price hikes. This approach recognizes that licensure incorporates multiple elements. Gross (1984) distinguishes between input, process, and output regulation. *Input regulation* is control of professional activity by controlling entry into the profession. Depending on the profession, for specific candidates entry requirements might include qualifications such as educational credentials and demonstration of professional competence. Some states impose additional qualifications for applicants, such as minimum age requirements or reference letters assuring "good moral character."

Related to entry, accreditation of professional schools, law schools, medical schools, or hospitals as training institutions is another form of input regulation that allows professionals to control gatekeeping institutions. A type of backdoor entry licensure is the so-called institutional licensure, which extends the licensure of an institution (for example, a hospital) to perform certain activities to the personnel employed by the institution. As Friedman (1962, pp. 150–51) notes, the requirements for educational credentials from accredited institutions can be used to limit entry by accrediting fewer institutions or by pressuring institutions whose accreditation has to be renewed to accept fewer students.

In contrast, *process regulation* is control of the professional activity itself, while *output regulation* involves influence over outcomes. Continuing education requirements are an example of process regulation, while malpractice suits are one example of output regulation.

Evidence from Other Occupations

There is scant empirical evidence on the effects of occupational regulation, though scholars have performed more studies of health professions. Young (1987), for example, provided a comprehensive argument regarding the anticompetitive nature of much occupational regulation, relying on work by other scholars to conclude that occupational regulation restricts entry, creates maldistributions in supply, and increases costs for the consumer. For example, Begun, Crowe, and Feldman (1981) used a multivariate model to find that the greater economic power of optometrists led to greater regulation of their profession. Brazier and others (1993) found strong anticompetitive self-regulation of the medical and legal professions in Great Britain. Gaumer (1984, p. 396) summarized other studies that find that specialist MD licensure tends to improve care quality, while general MD licensure does not. Kleiner (2000) has assessed this literature and finds that occupational regulation is severely underresearched compared to its importance. At the same time, licensure issues appear to be growing, especially in health professions. Recent professions seeking licensure in New York, for example, include genetic counselors, mental health therapists, and medical physicists.

In another example of the growth of licensure issues, in 1982 only twelve states had licensing requirements for mortgage brokers or lenders. By 1997, however, as these actors became more important in initiating mortgages across the country, forty-four states established licensure or registration requirements. These regulations include net worth requirements, posting of surety bonds, establishing physical in-state offices, fingerprinting, and examinations. Part of this may be attempts to deal with competition, or questionable practices, provided by Internet-based mortgage brokers, especially the physical office requirement. Notes Lotstein (1997, p. 69): "Because each state has its own laundry list of requirements for licensure, licensing requirements can present a formidable obstacle for entities seeking to expand their businesses in multiple jurisdictions."

Licensure of insurance agents has also become an issue of national attention. The federal 1999 Gramm-Leach-Bliley financial service reform act requires twenty-nine states to coordinate their procedures on insurance agent licensure by 2004 or they will face federal preemptions. It is questionable whether states will meet this deadline.

Chapter 9 adds to the evidence on state professional regulation with a fifty-state cross-section of state regulation of lawyers in 1994 and chapter 10 with a three-time panel across the fifty states of the regulation of MDs in the late 1980s and early 1990s.

CHAPTER NINE

OCCUPATIONAL REGULATION

Attorneys

with

ROBERT HOWARD

The law is among the most important, well-paid, and prestigious professions in the United States. Lawyers are the gatekeepers in the judicial policymaking process, and they often develop legal ideas and concepts that later become part of law and policy. At some point in their lives, almost all Americans will need to employ a lawyer. The law is thus an influential profession, its practitioners possessing power and wealth beyond most other occupations. For example, in most state legislatures, they represent the single largest occupation bloc.

History of State Role

There was little regulation of lawyers from the colonial era through the 1870s. Only nine of the thirty-nine states had any admission standards at all to practice law, usually the simple requirement of an oral exam administered by state judges. Discipline was restricted to occasional disbarment proceedings, instituted by groups of lawyers through a civil lawsuit, against a lawyer who had committed a crime or "outrageous behavior," with a high burden of evidence required.

This changed when lawyers formed the American Bar Association (ABA) in 1878 and most state bar associations at about the same time. In terms of self-regulation, the Alabama Bar Association created a code of conduct in 1877, and ten other state bar organizations soon enacted their own codes, with the ABA following suit in 1908. Reflecting this trend toward greater professionalization, by 1890 half of the states required some formal legal training before bar admission, by 1920 three-fourths of the states had such requirements, and by 1940 all the states had admission standards that required lawyers to have some formal legal education and to pass a statewide competency exam. New York in 1914 was the first state to formally authorize a committee to prevent those not admitted to the bar from practicing law, but by 1938 over four hundred state and local bar associations had authorized such committees. In part this was related to concerns about competition in the 1930s, especially from title insurance companies and trust companies, a competition issue from nonlawyers that has resurfaced in recent years.

These efforts did not resolve all concerns about lawyer conduct over time. Thus in 1970 U.S. Supreme Court justice Tom Clark led a commission on lawyer conduct that concluded the profession was in crisis due to the lack of lawyer discipline. The ABA responded by reworking its 1908 code into a comprehensive code of professional responsibility. Thus all states now regulate the process of becoming a lawyer and maintaining a law license. Each state requires lawyers to have some level of training or education and to pass a licensing exam, whether in the state of admission or in some other state or jurisdiction that has reciprocal privileges. The overall process typically involves obtaining a four-year college degree from an undergraduate institution, a three-year law degree from an accredited law school, and passing a statewide competency examination called the bar exam. Licensing is supposed to assure clients that the lawyers they retain possess the necessary degree of competence and skill to represent their interests. As the American Bar Association (1995, p. 3) explains its competency and moral character standard: "The public interest requires that the public be secure in its expectation that those who are admitted to the bar are worthy of the trust and confidence clients may reasonably place in their lawyers."

Despite this general coverage, states have developed different specific approaches to the regulation of lawyers. Some states do not require by statute a law degree for lawyers to practice. Others do not require any continuing legal education. Some admit lawyers from other states on motion, meaning that the incoming lawyers do not have to take the bar exam in the new state, they merely pay a fee to become admitted. Other states require that even a veteran lawyer admitted in another jurisdiction must take a bar examination to practice in their state. Some states admit lawyers from foreign countries; others require such graduates to attend an American law school. One state charges as little as $50 for the bar exam, while others charge as much as $1,200.

If the primary goal is to protect the public interest by ensuring competence, why do states take such different approaches? It seems unlikely that consumers of legal services in different states should require such varying levels of protection. As with other areas of occupational regulation, one must ask whether these differences serve legitimate elements of the public interest by reducing the information asymmetry with citizens and ensuring competence, or whether they are shaped by political power that ultimately harms the public interest by restricting entry, access, and competition.

Factors Likely to Influence Regulation

Historians, legal scholars, and even law school deans have made arguments parallel to the Chicago School economists (Friedman 1962; Stigler 1971) about the harmful effects of licensing lawyers in the United States. Auerbach (1976) and Abel (1991) have argued that wealthy lawyers use the bar associations to control educational qualifications and bar admissions and as a discriminatory tool against the urban poor, all to maintain their incomes and prestige. Lawrence Velvel, dean of the Massachusetts School of Law, sued the ABA, claiming that its law school requirements significantly increased the cost of a law school education and disadvantaged the poor (see Stumpf 1998). Rhode (1994) suggested that the organized bar itself precludes effective oversight of lawyer-client relations.

As is the case in other professions, current lawyers are likely to try to create and increase entry barriers to limit the supply of practitioners in their state. They can do this by making required education and training longer and more expensive, by raising fees and requirements for the right to practice, and by other limitations and restrictions. The general arguments about capture of professional regulation apply well to lawyers, especially given their strong power in and over state legislatures. But the economic and political power of lawyers, relative to other groups with political claims, may vary across states, and state bar associations may vary in the extent to which they are effective lobbying organizations for their members' interests.

While the capture theory is compelling and suggests that researchers should examine the influence of the political power of lawyers in states, other forces may exist whose push for regulation of lawyers is more likely to serve the public interest. Since lawyers have such a high profile in the media and elsewhere, it is not unreasonable to assume that some politicians have gained favor with constituents by championing regulations to improve quality that might not also be explicit entry barriers. For example, continuing legal education would upgrade the knowledge and skills of lawyers, and if all lawyers in a state are required to engage in such training on a regular basis, it is difficult to perceive that as an entry barrier or advantage of incumbents. Requirements such as continuing legal education courses may improve the quality of legal services to consumers, but they require practitioner time and money, an opportunity cost against their time to create billable hours. In that sense, it is actually cheaper for a relatively new lawyer, earning lower fees, to engage in continuing education than it is for a more experienced one. For example, states with higher average incomes may be willing to spend the time and effort to force more consumer-oriented regulations than others.

Measuring Regulation

Capture theory implies that the stronger the hold of lawyers over those who make the most important regulatory decisions (generally state legislators), the more regulation of entry we should see. Conversely, once lawyers have obtained a license, they have incentives to uphold the entry barriers to new competitors but to reduce any other requirements, like continuing education, that might limit their own incomes or freedom to practice. Several regulations offer an opportunity to test these expectations. For example, greater entry barriers, as defined by fees and educational requirements, make it more difficult to become a lawyer in the first place. Once a license is obtained, however, similar political forces may try to influence the burdens on admitted lawyers to maintain their license, in the form of continuing education requirements.

These concepts can be measured by combining several regulatory entry barriers into a scale and dichotomizing and summing these dummy variables.[1] The "entry barrier" scaled dependent variable is tested with data from a cross-section of the fifty states for the year 1994.[2] Specifically, this

1. The dichotomous elements composing the scale include (1) ABA-approved law school required; (2) admitted on motion; (3) foreign law students admitted; (4) admitted even if have felony conviction; (5) multistate professional responsibility exam required; (6) post–law school training required; and (7) pre–law school education required. These elements are sufficiently correlated to allow the use of a scale.
2. With a sample size of only fifty states, this is essentially just a snapshot of lawyer regulation in 1994; a pooled sample of the fifty states over several years

information on state admission and license maintenance requirements comes from the ABA's guide to legal education and admissions to the bar (American Bar Association 1995). Many state admission and ethics requirements are easy to classify into a yes or no variable, as the state either has a requirement or it does not, which are turned into zero or one dummy variables. For example, coded with a one are states that require law school graduates to come from ABA-approved law schools, while others were given a zero for that measure. These seven entry barrier regulations are then combined together in a scale that shows that all states have at least some entry barriers (minimum of 1.00), with most occupying the exact mid-range (3.55) on the restriction scale, which has a theoretical range of 0 to 7.

The measure of fees is straightforward. State bar examination fees vary considerably, from a low of $50 to a high of $1,200, with an average fee of slightly less than $370. The measure of continuing education is also simple. Once a lawyer earns a law degree and is admitted to practice in a state, many states require that lawyer to take continuing legal education (CLE). The mean yearly required time for CLE across the states is ten hours, with a range of none to a maximum of fifteen hours.

Explaining Regulation

Greater regulatory capture can be expected in states with more concentration of power and wealth in the regulated industry. Sometimes, of course, particularly skillful lobbying can make up for lack of overall wealth and concentration. Thus, states with a greater concentration of attorneys, more powerful attorneys, wealthier attorneys, and a more organized attorney lobbying organization should succeed in winning more regulations that create or enforce entry barriers.[3] Also expected is that states with a greater

---

would be better. Data limitations prevent such a sample. Small sample size often means that important predictor variables fail to show any statistical significance. The fact that several of the variables here do show significance suggests that this modeling approach is proper.

3. There is an argument that there is a potential simultaneity problem in any study examining entry barriers. The argument is that the profession erects entry barriers through regulation. The entry barriers, however, determine the members of the profession. Thus the two variables are potentially endogenous. Unless controlled, the use of endogenous variables can lead to biased estimates. In these studies, however, the entry barriers determining the members of the profession

concentration of attorneys, more powerful attorneys, wealthier attorneys, and a more organized attorney lobbying organization should be able to convince state legislatures to impose fewer requirements for license maintenance, to reduce the regulatory burden to attorneys that are already licensed and practicing.

One way of measuring lawyer power and influence is to examine the percentage of lawyers in that state relative to the rest of the work force. The greater percentage of lawyers in the state work force, the greater their expected economic and political power. Nationwide, lawyers compose less than 1 percent of the labor force, with certain states, such as New York and Massachusetts, having a higher percentage. Another way to measure political power is to examine the percentage of lawyers as members of the state legislature. The greater the percentage of lawyers, the more power and influence the lawyers presumably have passing laws in that state, especially related to regulation of their own profession. This varies from a low of about 2 percent to a high of nearly 40 percent, with the mean percentage of lawyers in the statehouses at 16 percent.

A measure of concentration is population per lawyer. The greater this is, the less concentrated the lawyers are in that particular state, and hence the less influential. Another way to measure concentration, particularly for institutions providing legal education, is the number of law degrees awarded per capita state resident.

I measure the wealth of lawyers in a given state by their per capita income. Lawyers' incomes averaged more than $94,000 in 1994. To account for the fact that wealthier states are more likely to support wealthier lawyers, the analyses include lawyer per capita income as a percentage of average state per capita income.

Finally, lobbying power can be crudely measured by membership in the national bar association. Bar associations mainly exist to lobby and promote benefits for their attorney members. The most important is the ABA which, more than any state bar association, regulates and monitors the performance and standards of law schools. ABA membership records are kept by state, and membership percentage varies from a low of 29 percent in Massachusetts to a high of 76 percent in Delaware, the home state of corporate chartering and the "Delaware effect." Nationwide, ABA membership averages less than half of all lawyers. The greater the percentage

---

and the members determining the entry barriers are not occurring simultaneously—there is a lag between the two. Because of this time lag, endogeneity does not cause a problem with the estimators.

of ABA members in a state, the greater should be the lobbying ability of lawyers in that state. While one might also examine state bar association membership as a measure of lobbying strength, this is difficult to obtain. In addition, its value is limited due to lack of variation; in many states, the membership rate is close to 100 percent because these states require lawyers to become members.

These data come from a variety of sources. State information, including population, per capita income, total labor force, lawyer percentage of labor force, and total income from legal services comes from the Census Bureau (1995). Data on income per lawyer and law degrees awarded per state derive from the Gale State Rankings (Alampi 1994) and the New England School of Law.[4] The number of lawyers per state and the percentage of ABA members per state are from the ABA's research department.

Despite some concerns about sample size in this fifty-state cross-section, the analyses employ OLS regressions, which are appropriate where the dependent variable, such as continuing legal education hours, is continuous. Where, however, the dependent variable is bounded, such as here, by a 1 to 7 scale, OLS regression can produce the problem of predicted out-of-range results (Greene 1997). To account for this, as is standard practice, the variables are transformed through a log of the odds ratio.[5]

In addition to the specific explanatory factors described above, we examine as a control variable the wealth of the state, on the assumption that higher levels will generate a greater demand for legal services.[6]

Results

The first column of table 9-1 tests the explanation of entry barriers. Two explanatory variables are statistically and substantively significant: average lawyer income in a state (a power variable) and degrees conferred (a

4. "Online Lawyer Income Statistical Report," 1994 (www.nesl.edu.faculty/table2.htm [September 2002]).

5. This variable is the log of the odds ratio of entry barriers. This was computed by dividing the total number of entry barriers (7) by the entry barriers less the actual entry barrier number, 7/(7 − barriers), then taking the log.

6. Since many of the independent variables are potentially linearly related, multicollinearity diagnostics were performed for each equation. The presence of multicollinearity could inflate the standard errors of the coefficients. Several tests are available for multicollinearity, including examining the eigenvalue for each equation and examining the variance inflation factor. An examination of these two multicollinearity indicators detected no severe multicollinearity, thus giving confidence in the estimated coefficients.

Table 9-1. *Regulation of Lawyers, 1994*[a]

Explanatory factors	Entry barriers	Bar exam fees	Continuing education
ABA membership (percentage)	.0016	−11.36*	−0.02
	(.008)	(5.57)	(.095)
Average lawyer income	43.88*	−244.67	.02
	(18.86)	(165.64)	(0.02)
Law degrees in population (%)	2.25**	−507.56	.176
	(0.61)	(394.74)	(7.19)
Lawyers in work force (%)	−1.8E-08	288.4*	−10.9*
	(5.1E-07)	(135.58)	(5.24)
Population per lawyer	−.001	.273	−.02**
	(.001)	(.782)	(0.009)
Lawyers in legislature (%)	−.008	10.3*	.06
	(.016)	(4.78)	(.09)
Per capita income	−.00037	−.05	−8E-08
	(4.21)	(.03)	(2E-07)
Constant	1.64	1079	1.79
	(1.02)	(573)	(5.61)
Summary statistics			
F	2.3*	2.7*	3.0**
AR^2	0.28	0.35	0.29
N = 50			

*Significant at .1 level; **significant at .05 level; ***significant at .01 level.
a. Standard errors are in parentheses.

concentration variable). Both had influence in the expected direction, with more power and concentration resulting in higher entry barriers in those states. The power variable has a strong substantive impact—an increase from the average income to 5 percent above the national mean results in a 92 percent probability of an increase in entry barriers. The results for the concentration variable suggest that for every 1 percent increase in degrees conferred per population, the result is an 84 percent probability of an increase in entry barriers. Though not statistically significant at high levels, nearly all of the other variables had effects in the expected directions.[7]

The second column of table 9-1 examines another entry variable, the dollar amounts of state bar exam fees.[8] Again, the results support the capture hypothesis. Three predictor variables demonstrate influence at a high level of statistical significance, all of which are political power or

7. As stated earlier, perhaps using pooled time-series data and thus increasing the sample size will yield more statistically significant results for the other coefficients.

8. Since bar exam fees are a continuous variable, the problems mentioned above do not apply here. One might argue that bar exam fees of even $1,200 are small

influence measures—lawyers as a percentage of the state legislature, lawyers as a percentage of the work force, and the ABA membership percentage. On average, for every 1 percent increase in the percentage of lawyers as part of the state work force, the bar exam fee increases by $288. On average, for every 1 percent increase in the percentage of lawyers in a state's legislature, bar exam fees increase by $10. The ABA percentage variable showed influence in the direction opposite from the expectation. On average, a 1 percent increase in membership resulted in a decrease of fees by $11. Perhaps by 1994 the ABA had become more sensitive to the claims of scholars and law school deans about opening up legal education to the economically disadvantaged.[9]

The final model, column 3 of table 9-1, explains variation in states' continuing legal education requirements. Recall here that lawyers generally do not favor extensive CLE requirements, as they create opportunity costs for practicing lawyers in time lost from business, and thus lost billable hours. The power variable of lawyers as a percentage of the work force shows high levels of statistical significance—as this factor increases by 1 percent, there is a decrease in continuing legal education required in that state by about eleven hours. Indeed, where lawyers constitute a percentage of the work force far in excess of the average, there is essentially no CLE requirement. States in which lawyers are not as powerful allow the imposition of CLE, perhaps at the behest of consumer interests, though these are not measured directly here.

Discussion

Taken together, these three analyses provide evidence that most regulation of attorneys has more to do with the power, wealth, and the concentration of the attorneys in a given state than it does with protecting the

---

in comparison to a potential annual average income of $200,000, and that therefore this is not really much of an entry barrier. Such reasoning ignores the financial condition of the average law school graduate. Many twenty-five- or twenty-six-year-old graduates of law school have been students for some seven straight years, and many have taken out loans during that time, loans that can exceed $50,000. Disposable income is tight if not nonexistent. In addition to the expense of the bar examination, in order to pass, many students need to take a bar review course, which can cost in excess of $1,000. Thus requiring a financially strapped, debt-ridden student to pay high bar examination fees can be quite a barrier to entry.

9. Once again, perhaps using pooled time-series data and thus increasing the sample size will yield more statistically significant results for the other coefficients.

public interest. For example, a strong predictor of anticompetitive regulation that benefits existing attorneys is the percentage of attorneys making up the total work force of a state. This attorney power variable was statistically and substantively significant in causing higher bar exam fees and in causing a lower requirement for CLE. In states where they make up a greater percentage of the work force than average, it appears that the attorneys are able to throw their collective economic weight around and stiffen the regulations that decrease potential competition while decreasing regulation that hurts practicing attorneys. The same is true of the influence of lawyer income on entry barriers. Where lawyers are wealthier relative to others in the work force, they are able to erect greater barriers to entry. Where there are more lawyers in the state as defined by law degree, states also erect greater entry barriers.

Thus even in a profession that seems to part of a national job market for new law school graduates, states regulate in different and important ways. State regulation is shaped heavily by the power and concentration of attorneys, who are able to limit entry into their profession and to limit maintenance requirements. Admittedly, the size of these barriers may not be so high as to limit entry by new lawyers who truly want to work in a given state. But at the margin they must have some influence. Otherwise, why would lawyers bother to lobby for these regulations in the first place, and why would state legislatures go to the trouble of imposing them?

While we do not have good measures for state propensity to regulate as reflected by culture, urbanity, or public opinion, if these factors influenced lawyer regulation, we would expect to see consistent influence. That is, states that want greater professionalism in all aspects of legal services should require it in both entry barriers and in maintenance requirements. Based on these studies, this consistency is not apparent. States with greater entry barriers are often the same states with *fewer* continuing legal education requirements. This is consistent with the capture hypotheses presented here but inconsistent with the notion of different state cultures influencing lawyer regulation.

Important to highlight is the fact that the maximum state CLE requirement imposed on lawyers in any state is fifteen hours. For an average attorney earning $94,000 in 1994, this translates into $705 in lost income (or less than 1 percent of $94,000) each year, assuming that the CLE takes away from otherwise billable work hours. While this is not a huge expenditure, it is comparable to the differences in state bar exam fees, which seem to be designed as entry barriers.

CHAPTER TEN

OCCUPATIONAL REGULATION

Medical Doctors

with

ANDREAS BROSCHEID

More than 13 percent of the U.S. gross national product goes to pay for health care, and medical doctors are the most critical players in that business. This percentage will likely increase as the baby-boom generation retires, and the elderly portion of our society increases in both absolute and relative numbers.

MDs may also be the profession for which it seems easiest to justify government licensing. While most people might be as amused as Milton Friedman that barbers once had to be instructed in "hygiene, bacteriology, histology of the hair, skin, nails, muscles and nerves, structure of the head, face and neck" (Friedman 1962, p. 142), many will not agree with Friedman that anyone should be allowed to offer medical services to the public. If licensing improves the quality of medical services, the value of services increases, search costs decrease, and externalities due to low-quality consumption by other market participants decrease (Arrow 1963; Leffler 1978). Still, despite Friedman's provocation, scholars have attempted few empirical investigations of the effects of medical licensure, in part because there are few examples of nonregulated health care markets against which to estimate the impact of licensure.

Though all U.S. states regulate medical doctors to some degree, here Broscheid and I examine the political forces that seem to be associated with various specific forms of state medical licensure, some of which may clearly create entry barriers, while others may be legitimate efforts to ensure a high average quality of physicians. As with other forms of occupational and professional licensure, there is no federal role here; the states are the only regulators of medical professionals (although the federal government sometimes does play an indirect role, by determining what kinds of medical practitioners, including possible competitors to MDs, can be reimbursed by federal health funds).

History of State Role

The current system of U.S. medical licensure is the second attempt at state regulation. The first states introducing licensure requirements for physicians were still British colonies: Virginia in 1639, Massachusetts in 1649, and New York in 1665. Entrance into the medical profession in this era was dominated by the apprenticeship system, which lasted well into the eighteenth century. At that time, the first medical schools were founded, and their standards were included in the system of medical licensure.

Medical consumers challenged this early form of apprenticeship licensure in the 1840s, resulting in a change to complete deregulation by the time of the Civil War. Gross (1984, p. 55) summarizes the popular rhetoric surrounding this deregulatory policy, explicitly noting its "modern sound": "It included complaints that the professions (1) made things so complicated that intelligent persons who ordinarily could be expected to take responsibility for themselves could not argue in a court of law or obtain the information to properly take care of their health, (2) were monopolies in restraint of trade, (3) maintained a subordinated class system that hoarded privileges and blocked the entry of the lower classes, and (4) retarded developments and blocked talent in nonorthodox realms of practice."

Scholarly accounts of this deregulatory era come to contradictory conclusions. According to one side, pointing to the growth in the number of medical schools and practitioners, deregulation had positive results, raising innovativeness and medical standards (Tabachnik 1976). The other perspective is that deregulation promoted quackery and deterioration of standards (Shryock 1967). There are few definitive medical statistics from that era to be confident in the results of this deregulatory policy. In any case, medical professions did not stay unregulated for long: Texas passed the first modern medical practice act in 1873, California followed suit in 1875, and by 1925 physicians were again licensed in every state.[1]

---

1. Similar developments took place with respect to other professions in the health sector—for example, nurses.

Starting with the founding of the American Medical Association (AMA) in 1847, professional associations were behind this new licensing. The AMA's 1910 Flexner report introduced criteria of modern natural science into medical licensure, based on research on germ theory and modern hospital accreditation. The AMA's Council on Medical Education incorporated the recommendations of the Flexner report into its hospital accreditation program, which raised standards for medical schools, leading to a 40 percent decline in their number over the next few decades, and creating an educational entry barrier for new MDs.

These new entry restrictions were not merely aimed at increasing the quality of U.S. medical education, which at the time was relatively low compared with European standards. There was explicit discriminatory intent; the Flexner report itself concluded that "an essentially untrained negro wearing an MD degree is dangerous. . . . the practice of the negro doctor will be limited to his own race" (quoted in Stewart and Thomas 1996, p. 50). Stewart and Thomas report that five of the seven existing medical schools serving black students were closed by these tighter regulations. In addition, the proportion of female physicians dropped drastically after the implementation of the Flexner report. Another example of discriminatory provisions promulgated by the AMA was the requirement of American citizenship for licensure. Only in 1973 did the Supreme Court outlaw state requirements of citizenship in order to attain a medical license.[2]

Today, regulation of physicians has become institutionalized in all states. Medical licensing statutes create expert boards that are supposed to administer the requirements of the law. These boards have similar status in most states, with some variation in whether they are subordinated under an administrative agency—an institutional difference that evidence suggests does not restrict the boards' independence (Graddy and Nichol 1990).[3] With members usually appointed by the governor, licensing boards consist mostly of "experienced practitioners," often nominated by their state medical association (Rubin 1980, p. 36).

2. Otherwise, the Supreme Court was generally supportive of medical licensure, despite its "substantive due process" doctrine, which prohibited interference into the freedom of economic contracts until the 1930s. In *Dent v. West Virginia* (1888), the Court allowed professional licensure if it was necessary to protect "the health, welfare, or safety of citizens" (Gross 1984, p. 57).

3. Graddy and Nichol find some evidence that centralization of boards influences disciplinary actions.

The state licensing statutes define the required education and entry standards. Licensing boards specify which educational and training programs qualify to produced licensable MDs. Further, the boards administer examinations required for licensure; monitor codes of conduct; and have investigative, prosecution, adjudication, and punishment powers required for professional discipline. All states now use a nationally unified licensing examination (FLEX) as the official medical licensing examination. The most extreme punishment boards have for violations of codes of conduct is revocation of the medical license.

States vary in their precise requirements and in how they implement these requirements. An example is endorsement of out-of-state medical licenses; in addition to requiring specified FLEX scores, many states require a further oral examination or an interview from out-of-state applicants.

Factors Likely to Influence Regulation

Past research does not provide evidence on the factors behind or effects of medical licensure, in part because of a limited number of cases. Much of the literature focuses on the effect of physician licensure on related medical professionals (see Gaumer 1984 for a summary of earlier work). Begun, Crowe, and Feldman (1981) find that the size of the optometrist profession relative to its competitor profession (MD ophthalmologists) leads to stricter regulation. They also find that the state legislature matters—legislative interparty competition has a negative effect on regulation in their model, and legislative turnover has a positive impact.

The most complete analysis of regulation of related professions is Graddy's (1991) multinomial logit analysis of licensure of dietitians, nurse-midwives, occupational therapists, physician assistants, psychologists, and social workers. Graddy finds that the size of competitive occupations has a positive impact on the probability of certification, but not on the probability of licensure once the profession is certified. The presence of institutional health consumers, rather than just individual consumers, also reduced the probability of licensure versus certification.

For studies of physicians, Benham, Maurizi, and Reder (1968) determined that states with higher incomes for physicians also had stricter licensing standards. Somewhat paradoxically, high income attracts a higher proportion of physicians to a state, which may result in the potentially "negative" effect of attracting more physicians to a state by stricter licensure. In terms of medical care quality, Gaumer (1984, p. 396) summarizes other studies that suggest that specialist licensure tends to improve quality, while general licensure does not. Leffler (1978) finds that poor states and states with a higher population of elderly residents have less strict MD licensure standards, perhaps because they favor lower prices.

Turning to institutional studies, Graddy and Nichol (1990) conclude that centralization of investigative activity and the size of the investigative staff of a board increase the disciplinary actions taken by licensing boards. They find that the presence of public members on the board has no impact. In a recent paper, Svorny and Toma (1998) find that the autonomy of board funding from the legislature is significantly related to the overall restrictiveness of medical licensing.

Most studies of medical licensure do not focus on physicians because states do not vary tremendously in the licensure requirements, in part because the AMA has pressed state legislatures for a degree of uniformity. But there is some variation across states and over time, so to fill this research gap, the focus here, as with regulation of lawyers, is on MD licensure and entry restrictions versus seemingly more consumer-oriented regulations.

As with other forms of professional licensure, capture theory seems compelling. Historical evidence demonstrates that medical associations were clearly dominant in the formation of regulation, and the consumer or broader public interest was not organized into interest groups. Public opinion usually seemed swayed by the AMA's arguments. The only interests really competing with MDs are substitute professions like osteopathy or chiropractors, trying to achieve licensure for themselves, or other licensed medical professions like nurses, trying to obtain the rights to perform activities often reserved for physicians. However, these interests have not challenged medical associations directly about physician licensure.

As in other areas of regulation, the major problem with capture theory is that it does not incorporate institutional factors. Weingast (1980) proposed an alternative perspective based on his observation that while medical licensure produces rents for physicians, it does not maximize them because entry restriction is primarily achieved by making professional qualification contingent on costly academic education. Weingast suggests that state legislators are dependent not only on campaign contributions from interest groups like medical associations, but also on votes, meaning that consumer interests will have at least some influence on the winning coalition's policy, often specified in terms of continuing education requirements for physicians.

Thus this study examines the mechanisms that states use to license physicians. Since MDs tend to dominate their licensing boards (they form the majority of members on all boards in the sample), consumer representation may influence the type of licensing requirements rather than the overall level of licensing.[4] As the relative strength of consumer representation on licensing boards increases, the incidence of licensing requirements that are difficult to justify with quality-control arguments should decrease and the incidence of quality-related licensing requirements should increase. Boards with more public members should be more likely to impose stricter educational requirements and less likely to support entry barrier regulations like interviews and character certification requirements. We test these expectations using data on state medical licensing requirements in 1986, 1989, and 1992.

Measuring Regulation

Of the seven measures of MD regulation examined, three represent requirements reflecting educational standards and four relate to other issues. The licensing requirements data come from the 1986, 1990, and 1993 issues of *The Exchange,* a publication of the Federation of State Medical Boards.

The first educational requirement is the number of years of postgraduate training needed before U.S. or Canadian graduates may take the nationally uniform licensing examination, FLEX. On average, candidates need about 8.5 months of postgraduate training before they are eligible to take the licensing exam, although some states require no postgraduate training and others up to three years. Postgraduate education is probably perceived as a quality-related licensing requirement to address the problem of low-quality services due to lack of experience.

The second educational licensing, or entry, requirement analyzed is the difference between years of postgraduate training required from foreigners and years of postgraduate training required from U.S. or Canadian graduates for FLEX eligibility. Although this measure may be related to quality of education, the purpose of this requirement may also be the re-

4. This is further supported by the fact that consumer representatives on licensing boards tend to be of a relatively high social status, which implies a relatively high demand for quality services.

striction of entry for foreign graduates.[5] In order to ensure the quality of foreign graduates, medical boards already employ additional examinations. Although most of the states, over most of the time covered by the sample, did not require additional postgraduate training from foreign graduates, the number of states requiring more has grown, with some requiring three additional years of training.

The third educational variable is the number of hours of continuing medical education (CME) needed for the reregistration of licenses. The amount of continuing education is averaged per year. Compared to continuing legal education, states vary more in requiring continuing medical education. About three-fifths of all states did not require any continuing education for license renewals. In contrast, about one-fifth of the states required as much as fifty hours of continuing education. The mean value for the entire sample is thirteen hours per year, similar to the CLE requirements for lawyers discussed in chapter 9. CME is aimed at improving service quality, but it creates costs for physicians who have already received their license.

The first noneducational measure of regulation is the fees that MDs must pay to obtain a medical license. These fees consist of a variety of amounts that have to be paid for FLEX examinations, the license itself, and license renewal after some years. Since the period varies after which licenses in the different states have to be renewed, calculated here is the total amount in fees that has to be paid during the first six years of a physician's practice in a state. The variable ranges from $350 to $2,171, with a mean of $792, not too different from the level and range of fees required for lawyers to practice in a state.

The remaining noneducational measures are three binary variables that add time-consuming requirements to the licensing process without an obvious relationship to quality control: the requirements for letters of recommendation, personal interviews, and fingerprints. All elements are coded such that the additional licensing requirement is coded as 1 and having no requirement is coded as 0.

Explaining Regulation

First to be tested are factors that directly measure the strength of medical and consumer interests. The strength of medical interests is measured by

5. American citizenship requirements, another type of provision that more openly discriminated against foreign graduates, were outlawed by the Supreme Court in 1973.

the amount of political campaign contributions made by state medical associations (divided by the size of the state's population) in the relevant election cycles. The organizational and lobbying strength of medical interests should be reflected in their ability to provide funds for political purposes. These data come from Federal Election Commission reports.[6] The percentage of state residents older than sixty-five years measures the size of the elderly population stratum, which has a particularly high demand for medical services: a high percentage should strengthen consumer interests in a state.

Information about the institutionalized strength of competing medical and public interests can also be gleaned by examining state medical boards, the central government regulatory institution that implements licensing laws. In many states, legislative standards for medical licensure are so general that medical boards actually determine most of the specific licensing requirements. In states in which legislative standards are more specific, because of their technical expertise medical boards are probably still influential in establishing the licensing standards passed by the legislature, as well as in implementing them. To gauge the relative strengths of medical and nonmedical interests in a state, we use the proportion of public members on medical boards, who are appointed to represent consumer interests.[7] In the overall sample, less than 10 percent of the states (and less than 16 percent in 1986) had established medical boards without any public members. The maximum proportion of public members was 46 percent (on the Rhode Island board).

Despite the presence of public members, all states still have a majority of physicians on the licensing boards: their numbers, combined with their substantial information advantages, mean that MDs are likely to dominate the boards. Therefore, controlling for the impact of public board members, medical boards that are more independent from the legislature should be more likely to support medical interests. While board independence can have several dimensions, such as integration into executive departments, the strongest type of independence should be related to the

6. Federal Election Commission, *Campaign Expenditures in the United States, 1987–1988,* Freedom of Information Act data, 2d release (Washington, 1990).

7. See, for example, section 25-22.5-2-1 of the Indiana Code: "The membership of the board shall consist of the following: . . . (3) One (1) member to serve a term of four (4) years who: (A) will represent the general public; (B) is a resident of this state; and (C) is in no way associated with the medical profession other than as a consumer."

budget. Somewhat more than a quarter of all licensing boards in the sample had complete budgetary independence; the rest were dependent on legislative appropriations. Svorny and Toma (1998) show that the autonomy of board funding is significantly related to the overall restrictiveness of medical licensing (measured in terms of the physician-population ratio in a state).[8]

Board funding autonomy and the proportion of public members are related to interest representation in two ways. First, both measures are indicators of the differential strength of public and medical interests: States with strong consumer interest representation should be more likely to have public members on medical boards, whereas states with strong medical interest representation should be more likely to have independent licensing boards (Moe 1989). Second, those two variables measure the political resources of medical and public interests: budgetary control is an effective means of legislative control, which implies that budgetary independence largely removes boards from one important form of democratic control. On the other hand, the presence of public members on medical boards can strengthen consumer interests and legislative control through the implementation of police-patrol type oversight (McCubbins and Schwartz 1984).

The theoretical expectations about the measure of regulatory policy are that states with relatively strong consumer interests (that is, where medical interests are relatively weak), should require a lower level of noneducational licensing requirements, and vice versa. Therefore, in the analyses using fees, letters, interviews, and fingerprints as measures of regulation, we expect a negative influence for the explanatory variables public members and elderly and a positive influence for funding source and medical interests. States in which consumer interests are relatively strong should require a higher level of educational licensing requirements based on quality concerns. Therefore, in the examinations of postgraduate training and CME as measures of regulation, we expect a positive relationship for the measures of public members and negative influence from funding source and medical interests.

A few additional control variables are included: the median income in each state, the region to which the state belongs, and period (year) dum-

---

8. This measure for board funding autonomy differs from Svorny and Toma's because it codes boards as dependent if their budgets are paid by board funds but are subject to appropriation. However, the difference does not substantively influence the results.

mies.[9] Except for the last three analyses, we use ordinary least squares regression analysis to analyze the relationships between the variables. Since all the measures of regulation, except for the fees category, have a very limited range and are only approximately continuous, there are concerns about heteroscedasticity, which are addressed by using Huber/White robust standard errors.[10] Logit models are used to examine the three ancillary (0,1) licensing requirements.

Results

The results for the analyses of postgraduate training and CME are provided in table 10-1.[11] As predicted, the strength of medical interests in a state is significantly and negatively related to regulation concerning postgraduate training for domestic and Canadian applicants for FLEX. On average, a per capita increase in $10 of state medical association campaign spending is associated with a reduction of almost five months in postgraduate education required for FLEX eligibility. The coefficients for the variables measuring consumer interests are not significant.[12]

While the results of the postgraduate training regression provide some support for our hypotheses, the evidence from the regression of CME is stronger: First, in states with medical boards that have funding autonomy, there is a highly significant average ten-hour reduction in continuing education. Second, states with a higher proportion of public board members tend to require more hours of continuing education. An increase in the proportion of public board members of 0.1, on average, adds about 5.5 hours of continuing education for MDs. The coefficient for medical inter-

9. We use the binary distinction between the South and non-South, being aware of the fact that this distinction does not completely capture the diversity of the regional cross-section. However, reducing the number of dummy variables included in the analysis helps avoid a multicollinearity problem. For the same reason, we center the median income variable.

10. The condition index for all OLS regressions is below twenty, which indicates that there is no serious problem of multicollinearity.

11. The seven different measures of regulation are presented in two separate tables to make them more readable.

12. The impact of median income, though significant, is not substantively large. On average, a median income increase of $10,000 is associated with a 2.4-month increase in postgraduate education needed for FLEX.

Table 10-1. *Educational Requirements for MDs, 1986–92*[a]

Explanatory factors	Postgraduate training	Postgraduate training for foreigners	Continuing education
Medical interests	−0.039**	0.003	0.146
	(0.014)	(0.022)	(0.408)
Elderly	0.031	−0.061*	0.690
	(0.022)	(0.028)	(0.620)
Public members	0.863	−2.136*	55.485**
	(0.607)	(1.050)	(13.505)
Funding source	−0.027	0.209	−10.233**
	(0.095)	(0.154)	(2.794)
Median income	0.00002**	−0.0000	0.0004
	(0.00000)	(0.0000)	(0.0004)
South	−0.016	0.040	−3.768
	(0.109)	(0.183)	(2.897)
1990 dummy	−0.107	0.374*	0.597
	(0.117)	(0.179)	(3.623)
1992 dummy	−0.156	0.375*	1.964
	(0.118)	(0.182)	(3.482)
Constant	0.356	1.426***	0.444
	(0.277)	(0.424)	(7.799)
Summary statistics			
F	4.54**	2.50*	9.34**
AR^2	0.17	0.14	0.32
N	150	150	137

*Significant at .1 level; **significant at .05 level; ***significant at .01 level.
a. Standard errors are in parentheses.

ests is not statistically significant. The results for CME are of particular importance because the theoretical argument that physicians and consumers have different preferences over licensing requirements is particularly strong in this case. After all, continuing education takes place after a physician has received his or her initial license, and therefore imposes higher costs on physician members of the board than all other licensing requirements.

The results of the analysis of postgraduate training for foreigners further supports expectations, as they show that the proportion of public board members significantly and negatively influences the additional training required from foreign graduates before they are eligible to take FLEX. On average, if the percentage of public members is increased by ten points, the predicted additional postgraduate education required from foreign graduates who want to take FLEX decreases by about 2.4 months. Also, states with a larger percentage of elderly people tend to require less additional postgraduate education from foreigners: a ten-point increase in the percentage of elderly people reduces the additional postgraduate training by more than seven months.

Moving to the analyses in table 10-2, the results for fees do not support expectations. Both measures of medical interest representation do not significantly influence the size of licensing fees, and the direction of the public interest coefficients are either statistically insignificant or they are in the wrong direction. The only factor that explains licensing fees is the time trend of increasing fees. A likely explanation for the lack of results regarding licensing fees is the possibility that they do not constitute a strong entry restriction, especially for well-paid MDs. Although licensing fees could be a straightforward and easy mechanism to restrict entry at high levels, they may also be too transparent in political terms (Stigler 1971).

The analyses of the three binary variables that represent other noneducational licensing requirements lends some support for the overall argument. The proportion of public members on licensing boards significantly reduces the probability of interview requirements; the proportion of elderly people in a state is significantly related to a reduction in fingerprint requirements, whereas states with stronger medical interests are more likely to require fingerprints.[13] These statistically significant effects also have strong substantive impacts on state regulatory requirements.[14]

13. The only factors that significantly influence the probability that states require letters of reference from licensees are regional and period effects.

14. To get a clearer sense of the substantive impact of these factors, we compare the predicted probabilities due to different values of the independent variable under investigation. As a baseline, we fix all continuous independent variables at their respective means, assume board financial autonomy, and set the other dummy variables to zero. The logit model then predicts that such a hypothetical state has an interview requirement with about 0.33 probability, and that it requires fingerprints from licensees with approximately 0.17 probability. If, for example, the proportion of public members is increased from 0.18 (the mean) to 0.28, the probability of an interview requirement decreases to approximately 0.21. If the percentage of elderly is increased by about 5 points, the probability of a fingerprint requirement is reduced to about 0.06. Finally, if the per capita campaign contributions of state medical PACs is increased by five dollars, the predicted probability of a fingerprint requirement is increased from 0.17 to about 0.35. These predicted changes are all substantively important and would affect a large number of states.

Table 10-2. *Noneducational Requirements for MDs, 1986–92*[a]

Explanatory factors	Fees	Letters	Interviews	Fingerprints
Medical interests	2.663	−0.108)	0.030	0.190*
	(6.703)	(0.069)	(0.067)	(0.078)
Elderly	−9.187	0.199	0.137	−0.246*
	(14.473)	(0.106)	(0.098)	(0.106)
Public members	1131.36**	1.775	−5.99**	−1.74
	(334.10)	(2.394)	(2.33)	(2.73)
Funding source	68.416	0.286	−0.603	0.825
	(56.113)	(0.414)	(0.391)	(0.480)
Median income	0.007	−0.00	−0.00	−0.00
	(0.006)	(0.00)	(0.00)	(0.00)
South	79.918	1.793**	0.758	0.379
	(59.214)	(0.546)	(0.42)	(0.49)
1990 dummy	118.94*	−0.70	−0.004	0.54
	(57.03)	(0.505)	(0.444)	(0.55)
1992 dummy	236.5**	−1.33**	0.089	0.51
	(59.8)	(0.51)	(0.449)	(0.56)
Constant	522.464**	−1.727	−0.754	0.613
	(174.981)	(1.382)	(1.237)	(1.323)
Summary statistics				
F	3.93**	. . .	. . .	. . .
R^2	0.24	. . .	. . .	. . .
Wald Chi^2	. . .	24.01**	24.01**	16.55*
N	144	150	150	148
Cases correctly predicted (%)	. . .	71	59	75

*Significant at .1 level; **significant at .05 level; ***significant at .01 level.
a. Standard errors are in parentheses.

Discussion

The analyses support several of the expected relationships, particularly the general notions that strong state consumer interests increase education-related licensing requirements, whereas professional interests are associated with licensing requirements whose purpose does not seem to go beyond entry restriction. These results parallel closely the results for state legal regulation presented in chapter 9.

The amount of political contributions made by state medical associations was significantly and negatively related to the years of postgraduate education required from U.S. and Canadian graduates to be eligible to take the licensing examination, but positively related to the requirement of fingerprints. The percentage of elderly people in a state was shown to reduce additional postgraduate education required from foreign graduates and the probability of fingerprint requirements.

The presence of public members on medical boards is associated with an increase in the hours of continuing education required for license renewal. Also, public members are associated with a decrease in additional postgraduate training required from foreign graduates and a reduction in the use of interview requirements. Similarly, medical boards with budgetary independence, which implies a stronger representation of the medical profession, implemented fewer continuing education requirements.

While a simple capture explanation of state occupation regulation can seem compelling, it is not complete. In reality, different interests and patterns of interest representation are behind the specific forms of licensure and other regulations. Consumer interests matter, if only in influencing continuing education requirements that the professionals oppose, and consumers seem to influence the budgetary independence and membership form that legislatures give to state medical licensing boards, which then provide more regulations.

Considering both lawyers and MD regulation, it is true that the overall size of their entry restrictions are not overwhelming obstacles for determined professionals, who are likely to become well paid. The state-imposed continuing education requirements are also not very large. But these regulations do vary systematically with the power of different interests in a state. In the end, if capture by the lawyers and the ABA, and by MDs and the AMA, is a pattern for state regulation of these prestigious professions, one might suspect that capture is even more likely for less well-analyzed occupations, which are likely to use state regulation as a form of protection.

PART FIVE

Environmental
Regulation

The final area of regulation this book examines is justified by the problem of externalities. Externalities are market inefficiencies that arise when a transaction between two parties affects third parties who do not want to be involved. In historical progression, externalities were the last category of market failures to be addressed by U.S. government regulation. Like other market failures, externalities alter market efficiency and can sometimes be addressed effectively by government regulatory policies.

The classic negative externality is pollution. The direct and indirect affects of accumulated pollution from the industrial era gave rise to environmental regulation. States often implement important federal policies, but increasingly they also generate policies of their own, following the devolution pattern. In terms of costs and benefits, environmental regulations are an overwhelmingly large component of all U.S. regulations. Indeed, federal government estimates of the benefits of regulation vary widely, largely depending on one's evaluation of the benefits of environmental regulation. Estimates vary widely because environmental benefits are notoriously hard to quantify in dollar terms, as most of these benefits are not traded in markets.

People living near a source of pollution are affected negatively. Over time, ecologists have recognized that some forms of pollution can cause problems much further away in geographic space, including modern concerns about ozone, greenhouse gases, and global warming. Free-market advocates stress that there is a market solution to such problems, requiring no more regulation than the establishment of property rights. If there are few people affected, they might be able to bargain, in a marketlike way, with the polluters to get them to stop or reduce such pollution in return for a payment, if they do not have an established "property right" to clean air or water (see Coase 1960). If the nearby residents do manage to establish a property right to clean air, than polluters may have to pay them to accept the pollution. However, when many people are affected, as with modern air and water pollution that can travel great distances, the transactions costs become very high and a government regulatory policy may be more efficient than attempts to bargain with large numbers of participants.

At first, American government environmental policies were largely "command and control," in which government dictated pollution reduction targets, dates, and sometimes even specific technologies for noncomplying firms. Over time, a more cooperative regulatory approach has been tested—sometimes called "reg-neg," or regulatory negotiation—in which regulators show greater flexibility and allow state and local actors to strike bargains that might reduce pollution as much as a command and control mechanism, but in a more efficient manner. The success of these approaches may depend in part on the trust built up by participants. Newer approaches to environmental regulation have also tried to incorporate market trading of the right to pollute, up to a specified level in a region, so that firms can control better how much to pay for their own reduction of pollution.

State and local governments are critical actors in the implementation of environmental regulatory policy in large part because, over time, federal officials delegated a number of critical policy tasks to them. That delegation is significant because of state variation in both the desire and the ability to regulate effectively. Proponents of a vigorous state role in the U.S. system of regulatory federalism argue that local actors and interests are better situated to assess local policy needs, allowing a more responsive and adaptive policymaking system. On the other hand, Rabe (1986) notes the potential for significant administrative fragmentation in the conduct of environmental regulatory policy by state and local governments. Opponents of decentralization also argue that significant policymaking authority located at the state level potentially creates incentives for lax environmental standards and enforcement (see Swire 1996; Engel 1997). Still, in recent years many states have developed greater capacity and more interest in becoming vigorous environmental regulators. This is even true when states implement federal programs, such as the hazardous waste Superfund.

In this section Brian Gerber and I examine state implementation plans for clean air in the 1990s, which are the detailed plans state must develop to reach federal standards, and which must be explicitly approved by the U.S. Environmental Protection Agency (EPA). Alka Sapat and I examine state leadership in the area of groundwater protection, which, in contrast to clean air policy, is an area where the federal government does not play a large role but leaves much discretion to the states. In both cases state legislative ideology plays an important role in how quickly and to what degree states address these pollution problems. For groundwater protection, states also demonstrate a responsive politics, regulating in response to the size of their pollution problems, but this is not the case for clean air regulations.

Historical Development

Compared to the other areas analyzed in this book, environmental protection is a relatively recent area of regulation. Although the federal government has provided funds for wastewater treatment and similar projects since the 1940s, only from the late 1960s has U.S. public policy addressed pollution with explicit regulations. Since pollution does not respect city or state boundaries, national (and sometime international) policies are presumed to be necessary for at least some kinds of pollution. Yet local or state implementation may be more efficient in dealing with more localized problems and in balancing the various interests that are affected by the policies "on the ground."

The largest state, California, with its history of smog based on rapid population growth and associated automobile emissions, has often acted earlier than the federal government, and with more strict regulation. The California legislature passed laws requiring reductions in pollutants from automobiles in 1969, pushing Congress to pass the U.S. Clean Air Act in 1970. The oft-cited "California effect" (Vogel 1995) is most prominent in air pollution. When California acted again in 2002 with new laws to reduce greenhouse gas pollutants from automobiles, a policy that Congress had rejected, this continued the trend of California moving earlier than the federal government. Since the market for automobiles is so large in California, its state regulations often force international automobile manufacturers to upgrade their technology to reduce emissions in all cars, since it is not practical for them to either ignore the California market or to produce two separate sets of cars. As Christopher Preuss, a General Motors spokesman, noted: "This is rooted in the fact that California is the center of the environmental regulatory universe. Whether it's feasible, reasonable, or in the best interest of the citizens often takes a back seat to the environmental agenda."[1] Still, the recent legislation includes a long lead time for implementation, and the automotive industry has already challenged it in court, part of a growing legalization of regulation, which is discussed further in chapter 15.

Thus the United States has developed a hybrid national-state environmental regulatory program. Typically, except for the California effect, Congress sets national standards and deadlines in a general way. From the beginning of environmental regulation, as with the Clean Air Act in 1970, Congress was concerned that without national standards, the states might pursue a negative race to the bottom, with lax environmental regulations based on their concerns about economic development and the mobility of firms. Congress delegated authority to the EPA to define more specific goals for various pollutants. Then, in delegated turn, the states have some flexibility in how to meet these standards. States can implement and enforce pollution regulation using their own state agency and approved plan, or they can let the EPA implement the regulations directly. For environmental issues that are not addressed explicitly in federal policy, states can decide to regulate or not, based on their own political and policy calculations.

Despite some concerns about regulatory laxity in the states due to economic competition, environmental groups have pressed the states to pass—and to implement—tight regulations, with varying success. "State battles are more difficult to fight but in a way more essential," asserts Andy Gussert, national director of the State Environmental Resource Center. "Major activity at the state level has significantly increased in the last 10 to 15 years" (quoted in Penniman 2002, p. 13). A number of states besides California have tried to move aggressively to deal with pollution problems, viewing federal policymaking as increasingly in a condition of policy gridlock.

The analyses in this section address different degrees of the impositions of federal standards on the states. In the SIP clean air permitting process, the federal government required action but did not specify exactly what policies were necessary, leaving it to the states to come up with acceptable plans. States had to comply eventually, and they faced some negative sanc-

1. Quoted in Danny Hakim, "At the Front on Pollution: California Is Moving to Guide U.S. Policy," *New York Times,* July 3, 2002, p. A1.

tions from the federal government, such as reduced highway funding and still higher environmental standards, if they did not move fairly quickly to satisfy the EPA. The groundwater regulation chapter examines an area of pollution that tends to be more localized in its impacts than air pollution and in which the states have more discretion about whether to regulate. In both cases state officials need to balance the concerns of environmental interests and of firms that want to keep their production costs down, though they are much more constrained by federal standards in clean air regulation than groundwater.

Other State-Regulated Environmental Areas

In both cases examined in this section, the internal political balancing act of state regulators is complicated by their location in a larger game of interstate economic development rivalry. This influences all areas of environmental regulation. Some manufacturing firms with high costs to reduce their pollution are relatively mobile and might want to relocate in states that offer less costly environmental regulations, fueling a race to the bottom. On the other hand, there is some evidence that some states in addition to California are willing to provide "leadership" or innovation in environmental policy, going beyond federal minimum standards (Lowry 1992). Indeed, Potoski (2001) demonstrates that this leadership is best explained by the environmental attitudes of citizens of those states.

There are a number of other environmental problems that states address, acting within varying relationships with the federal government. For example, the federal Superfund is supposed to address toxic waste sites but has been mired in problems doing so (see Kline 2003). But not all sites with hazardous waste problems have been deemed to be Superfund cleanup sites. States are free to designate their own additional sites and address those problems. Many states have pursued aggressive policies in this area, often reclaiming "brownfield" sites for better uses. States also deal with a range of other air and water pollution problems beyond those analyzed in these chapters.

CHAPTER ELEVEN

ENVIRONMENTAL REGULATION

Clean Air Plans

with

BRIAN GERBER

Part of the concept of devolution is that it gives states more flexibility to meet federal target goals. But, as a natural consequence of such flexibility, programs are not implemented automatically or in exactly the same manner by the states. The state role in regulating air quality is characterized by some unevenness in state willingness and capacity to address federal policy goals. States can choose to act as good-faith implementers of federal standards or even to try to go beyond them, as in California, or they can demonstrate recalcitrance—perhaps most often the reality is something in between these extremes.

This chapter examines state performance in developing an operating permits program under Title V of the Clean Air Act (CAA) amendments of 1990. The CAA was a central reform in the U.S. air quality regulatory regime. We assess how effective states are in meeting their administrative obligations under Title V. In operational terms, this means how quickly states secured EPA approval of their state implementation plans (SIPs).

One key question is whether states race to the bottom in trying to attract or retain industry by delaying or diminishing air quality standards relative to states with which they are competitive. Lowry's (1992) explanatory framework of state environmental policy leadership in a federal system focuses in part on such competition. Also examined is the extent to which state environmental regulatory commitment is explained by neighboring state behavior and by partisan political competition within the state.

History of State Role

Air quality regulation in the United States involves the federal establishment of air pollution control policies, which are then implemented and enforced largely at the state and local level. Different air pollution regulations have been developed based on the two main sources of the pollution: stationary sources, such as utilities, refineries, and other industrial works; and mobile sources, which are largely on- and off-road automobiles and other vehicles.

Before 1970 the federal government was not greatly involved in air pollution control issues. The CAA of 1970 created the overarching framework for air quality regulation, establishing several key principles that largely remain intact. First, Congress sets air quality goals and rules at the national level, but state and local governments bear the primary responsibility for implementation and enforcement. The 1970 act identified six criterion pollutants for ambient air quality (nitrogen dioxide, sulfur dioxide, ozone, carbon monoxide, particulate matter, and lead) and mandated that the EPA set concentration levels, referred to as national ambient air quality standards (NAAQS).[1] The EPA is supposed to review those standards at least every five years. The 1990 amendments to the CAA added some other pollutants and issues to this agenda.

Second, the CAA established that the critical mechanism states must use to meet their implementation and enforcement obligations is a SIP, essentially a master plan for how a state will meet federally established regulatory goals. The SIP establishes requirements for sources in an implementation area, spelling out how implementation, attainment, maintenance, and enforcement measures will ensure compliance with national standards. While SIPs are subject to federal approval through the EPA, the states maintain a great deal of flexibility in how they will meet federal goals.[2]

Third, the CAA draws an important distinction between stationary source pollution and mobile source pollution. Mobile source pollution is the easier of the two to define, with emissions and fuel requirements established as applicable to both on- and off-road individual vehicles. Iden-

---

1. More specifically, the Clean Air Act designates primary NAAQS, which pertain to human health, and secondary NAAQS, which pertain to broader ecological concerns.

2. This was guaranteed in the court case of *Train v. Natural Resources Defense Council*, 421 U.S. 60 (1975).

tifying stationary sources is more difficult; the statutory language includes "any building, structure, facility, or installation which emits or may emit any air pollutant."[3] The CAA clarifies that broad definition in more specific provisions, usually based on the amount of pollutants emitted from the source. The CAA also established the principle that states have significant autonomy in establishing rules for stationary source pollution, but the federal government holds greater authority in establishing rules for mobile sources, since automobiles and other vehicles are manufactured and marketed in national markets.

Allowing states to be the primary implementing agents of air pollution control introduces tensions and conflicting incentives. Clean air regulation has created significant financial concerns for the states, because the federal program requirements were imposed without necessarily being coupled with the provision of adequate funding. Further, the air quality regime has in some cases imposed federal preemption of state laws, especially in the area of restrictions on motor vehicles and motor vehicle fuels. Moreover, while automakers and fuel producers prefer national regulatory uniformity, stationary sources have just the opposite interest. Given that stationary sources generally operate under the purview of state regulatory control, they have little interest in establishing broad national standards but instead prefer minimal regulation from their local jurisdictional authority, creating incentives for a state race to the bottom. As a consequence, there are really two separate regulatory tracks or incentive structures, one for mobile source regulation and another for stationary source regulation.

Twenty years after the initial CAA, Congress took up these issues again. While maintaining the basic core principles, the 1990 CAA amendments considerably broadened the scope of the air quality regulatory regime, addressing acid rain, air toxics, and stratospheric ozone protection. In the hearing for these amendments, Congress paid attention to the problem of nonattainment of the NAAQS, strengthened enforcement authority and judicial review, and established an operating permits program to facilitate stationary source compliance as part of the SIPs.

The EPA advocated the operating permits program over some congressional opposition on behalf of organized industrial interests. Three factors drove the establishment of an operating permits program. First, permits are probably the most important tool state governments have for

3. CAA § 111 (a)(3), 42 U.S.C.

regulating pollution sources. Second, before the 1990 amendments, firms faced an incredibly complex set of requirements for any single stationary source pollution site. A permit program offered the possibility for consolidating all such requirements into a single permit document, making both firm compliance and agency enforcement more manageable. Firms benefit from flexibility, as permitted facilities can make changes to their operations and give notice to the state (often under a short notice period of one week); they can change their emissions output *without* having the state go through the process of issuing a newly modified rule—an adjustment to the SIP—as was previously necessary. Third, the permit program does not add more administrative costs, as the program was structured to charge a fee to permitted source firms, generating self-supporting revenue to sufficiently fund each state's program.

Operating permits augment the traditional state SIP and spell out the sources that require permits, including (1) power plants covered under the acid rain program; (2) large sources defined as having the potential to emit a hundred tons or more of a criterion pollutant; (3) sources of hazardous air pollutants covered under the air toxics program; (4) new or modified sources that are subject to prevention of significant deterioration; (5) new source performance standards for new or modified sources in nonattainment areas; and (6) any other source that the EPA says needs a permit.

After the 1990 act, states initially faced a November 1993 deadline for submitting their operating permit SIPs, after which Congress gave the EPA one year to review them. The EPA could then grant full approval, give interim approval, or disapprove the SIP. If disapproved, a state had 180 days to make revisions; for interim approvals, a state had two years to correct the SIP deficiencies noted by the EPA. Sanctions for state failure to respond to submission deadlines included the withholding of federal highway funds and the possible direct establishment by the EPA of even tougher emissions standards for that state.

EPA review requirements for the operating permits program included three categories of requirements for the states. First, states had to meet procedural requirements, such as showing timely determination on permit applications and giving opportunity for public comment on and judicial review of permit actions. Second, states had to satisfy substantive requirements that included clarifying monitoring and reporting requirements, duration of permits, emission limits specified in the permits, compliance certification, and allowance for source production modifications.

Third, the EPA required states to establish an annual emission fees requirement to help cover state direct and indirect administrative costs.

To illustrate more clearly how the SIP approval process evolved, consider three state examples. Though the EPA noted a few flaws, Mississippi received full approval of its operating permits program SIP in December 1994. The EPA disapproved Virginia's SIP twice, in 1994 and in 1995, because it did not include adequate standing provisions for citizens to challenge permit decisions as required by the CAA's section 502.[4] Montana received interim approval in 1995 but then took five additional years to achieve full approval status. Obviously, there was great variation across the states, and the initial deadlines were not met in many cases. Montana's experience is probably the most representative of these states. It received interim approval, but had a number of deficiencies in the submission, such as setting an unacceptably high threshold of fifteen tons a year for any nonhazardous pollutants as "insignificant emissions units." In correcting this target to gain EPA approval, Montana eventually had to lower this threshold to five tons per year.

Factors Likely to Influence Regulation

Why do states vary greatly in the approval time for their SIPs? Lowry (1992) demonstrated that state environmental regulation varies both across policy domains and in terms of leadership. He notes that the incentive structure for state government varies according to two key intergovernmental dimensions—the policy's susceptibility to horizontal competition between states, or likely race to the bottom, and the degree of federal control in the issue area, which Lowry calls vertical involvement. Lowry's vertical dimension refers primarily to the degree of federal government involvement with state implementation. This dimension can vary along a continuum of complete federal autonomy or authority, with no state or local government involvement, to complete state government autonomy, where policy authority is the exclusive purview of state and local governments, with no federal involvement.

The horizontal dimension Lowry identifies refers primarily to the competition between states over economic resources held by regulated firms.

4. The EPA's ruling on this case was upheld in *Virginia v. Browner*, 95-1052 (4th Cir. 1996).

Pollution control policies are one of the best policy examples with a high degree of horizontal competition, as the imposition of tough regulations in one state will impose higher costs for economic activities than in other states. The literature on relocation takes either a strong form of the mobility threat—business can and will move in response to regulatory burdens—or a softer form: important constraints on relocation exist; but states may modify their policies in anticipation of potential business relocation decisions (Bartik 1991).

Placing a policy area along these two dimensions yields expectations about probable state behavior. In general, Lowry hypothesizes that as horizontal competition between states is lower, the likelihood of state leadership increases, which he defines as state regulatory stringency that exceeds federal regulations. As states are in competition with each other to attract businesses and jobs, they are less likely to create negative incentives, such as regulation more stringent than federal regulation. In terms of federalism's vertical dimension, he asserts that the higher a policy is located on the vertical dimension, the greater the likelihood state leadership efforts are coordinated with other states. That is, the federal government can virtually "force" states to adopt policy innovations by writing them into federal requirements.

In this case, given flexible state responses, we expect that states may not react directly to the level of air pollution in their state. Specifically, states with major problems with nonattainment for the NAAQS from stationary source emissions may not be more likely to seek quicker SIP approval. Instead, using Lowry's logic, political factors within the state are more likely to be influential. The percentage of Democrats in the state legislature, a proxy measure for greater preference for regulatory activism, should be positively associated with faster approval of the operating permit SIP.

At the same time, because interstate competition is presumed to be so important in this policy area, the effect of neighboring states should be significantly related to SIP approval time. While the states are mandated to adopt the operating permit program, Lowry's argument suggests that states are reluctant to do so readily and might drag their feet on compliance. On the other hand, one can find the opposite argument in the state innovation literature, which suggests that innovation in proximate states might have a positive effect on a state's policy behavior (Berry and Berry 1992). Thus there is an open theoretical question about the effects of neighboring states.

CLEAN AIR PLANS   177

Measuring Regulation

The goal is to provide an understanding and explanation of why some states have been able to get their 1990 CAA Title V SIPs approved earlier than others. Trying to get a SIP approved earlier is a measure of a state commitment to clean air, as the guidelines for likely EPA approval are clear, and all states had some prior experience with permit programs. Approval time is a reasonable basis on which to compare states, and it measures how well states respond in developing a mandated framework for regulating stationary source pollution.

Another possible way to examine clean air policy choices would be an outcome measure—NAAQS attainment. But whether or not an NAAQS is in attainment is influenced by many other factors besides state commitment and SIP approval, including population density, topography, and climate. California, for instance, is regarded as a state strongly committed to air pollution control, but because of density and topography, the state struggles to meet NAAQS goals. Thus getting rapid EPA approval of a Title V SIP, rather than actually meeting NAAQS goals, is more reflective of state environmental regulatory politics.

Making rapid compliance and approval less likely is the fact that SIP permits will impose costs on firms with stationary source pollutants that they would prefer to avoid and are likely to actively oppose. There is also a history of noncompliance; states are well aware that the EPA historically has been reluctant to impose sanctions for missing statutory deadlines, so the threatened sanctions they hold are not necessarily strong threats.[5] The unclear nature of immediate sanctions also suggests that using SIP approval as a dependent variable in the analysis is a reasonable indication of a state's willingness to be proactive in regulating stationary sources, given this mix of incentives.

Finally, section 503(e) of the 1990 act provides for ample public notification of permit applications, compliance plans, and other elements, including notification between states when the air quality of one is affected by a pollution source in another. This policy makes regulatory information abundant, which may affect the degree of competition between states with regard to stringency of regulatory standards. This further enhances the negative incentive for strong state action as interested parties, includ-

5. For a similar case of such incentives and lack of strong federal disincentives, see Weissert and Hill's (2001) treatment of state welfare policies.

ing mobile firms, would be made readily aware of which states are the most aggressive regulators of stationary source pollution.

An event history analysis is the appropriate technique for examining how quickly states gain approval for the operating permit program SIP. That is, the length of time it takes to gain EPA approval of the SIP is the indicator of how strongly a state is committed to regulation of stationary source pollution sources. This analysis examines the yearly operating permit program SIP approval from 1994 to 1997. The starting year is appropriate, as states were given a specific SIP mandate in this area at the end of the 1993 calendar year. It is worth noting that the EPA was under a Democratic president for this entire period, which might have suggested to states that the EPA was more likely to follow up on sanctions for noncompliance than it had in the past.

The dependent variable here can take two values based on whether a state's operating permit program received at least interim approval by the EPA. As noted above, the EPA had three choices given a state submission: full approval, interim approval, or disapproval. Since interim approval has often been extended by the EPA for several years, it is treated as part of approval (= 1) in the model, essentially combining the first two categories into one. This is measured in the year in which the EPA publishes a final action in the *Federal Register,* usually several months after a comment period on the EPA's proposal for action on a SIP.

There are a few other factors to note about this measure of regulation. Several states have counties that submit their own SIPs (for example, thirty-four counties in California). Because data are not available for all of the explanatory measures at the county level, the study uses the modal county ruling for such states. For a few states there was a state SIP, but some additional counties were also required to submit SIPs (for example, Nebraska); the actual state SIP ruling is used for such states. Alaska and Hawaii are excluded since they do not have adjacent states and have very different environmental concerns and problems than the continental states.

Explaining Regulation

The model incorporates several factors that should help explain state actions. To assess the political power of the most important interest groups on this issue, manufacturing firms, we use an economic measure, the ratio of manufacturing employment to overall state employment for 1994–97, which comes from the *Almanac of the 50 States* (1999).

To measure the legislatures' amenability to stricter environmental regulation, we use the percentage of Democratic seats held in the state legislature for the years following the 1994 election cycle. With more Democrats in a state legislature, the state should have a greater willingness to devote political and bureaucratic resources to produce an acceptable SIP.

To control for a state's bureaucratic capacity (as distinct from its ideological commitment to regulation), the study tests the overall budget of a state's environmental quality department or agency and its specific spending on air quality issues to produce a ratio of air quality spending to overall environmental program spending from 1994.[6]

A measure of the degree of stationary source emissions controls for the need to address air pollution problems in a state. Politics aside, do states respond in proportion to the problem they face? The best measure of stationary source pollution from among the criterion pollutants is the amount of sulfur dioxide emissions in a state, because the bulk of emissions come from utilities and manufacturing processes, unlike other pollutants that have a much larger share of their emissions coming from automobiles. As a result, an operating permit program necessarily will have to deal with major sources of sulfur dioxide emissions. The variable is measured in thousands of short tons for 1994–97.[7]

A proportion of adjacent states that had received EPA approval for their SIP at the time of a state's approval accounts for the impact of neighboring policies. As noted above, economic competition with other states, particularly for manufacturing jobs, should provide a disincentive for states to be aggressive regulators—as the ratio increases, there may be a smaller likelihood that a state will submit an acceptable SIP. But other studies of state innovation diffusion have argued, and often found, that adjacent state actions stimulate more rapid policy change (Berry and Berry 1990, 1992).

Finally, to control for time maturation effects, yearly dummy variables for each year are added to the model.

Results

The analysis here models a dichotomous dependent variable (coded as one when a state's SIP is approved and zero otherwise) from 1994 to 1997.

---

6. The budget figures come from *The Book of the States* (Council of State Governments 1989–97).

7. This variable comes from the U.S. Environmental Protection Agency (1998).

In event history analysis, the hazard rate is the probability that a given state will receive SIP approval in a given year if the state has not received SIP approval before that time (see Berry and Berry 1990).[8] The risk set incorporates the idea that competition from neighboring states has an effect on the SIP approval performance of a state. As a state's SIP receives approval, it is no longer at risk of receiving approval and is thus removed from the analysis. The other states—those that had not received approval—remain in the risk set until they did. For example, three states out of forty-eight, Mississippi, Oregon, and Washington, had their SIPs approved in 1994, for a hazard rate of 0.063. Twenty-six states had their SIPs approved in 1995, for a hazard rate of 0.578, while fifteen were approved in 1996 and another four in 1997. All states received at least interim approval by 1997.

Table 11-1 reports the results of the quantitative model. As Lowry hypothesized, there is not a significant relationship between the actual air pollution problem in a state and how rapidly a state's SIP is approved by the EPA. The two variables expected to produce significant effects on SIP approval—effects of nearby states and the party strength of Democrats in the state legislature—are both significant. However, the neighboring state ratio is positive, not negative, suggesting an innovation diffusion effect rather than Lowry's economic development competition hypothesis. The other key explanatory variable is statistically significant in the appropriate direction: states with legislatures with more Democrats move more quickly to get their operating permit SIP approved by the EPA. This supports several other studies in this book that find a role for legislative ideology.

Discussion

States that are ideologically more committed to reducing air pollution, as measured by the partisan status of their legislatures, were more likely to get earlier approval for their SIPs. Legislative party control matters, and

8. The states with SIP approvals in 1995 were Alabama, Arkansas, California, Colorado, Delaware, Florida, Georgia, Illinois, Indiana, Iowa, Kentucky, Louisiana, Minnesota, Montana, Nebraska, Nevada, North Carolina, North Dakota, Ohio, South Carolina, Utah, Vermont, West Virginia, Wisconsin, and Wyoming. SIP approvals were granted in 1996 to Arizona, Idaho, Kansas, Maryland, Massachusetts, Missouri, New Hampshire, New Jersey, New Mexico, New York, Oklahoma, Pennsylvania, Rhode Island, Tennessee, and Texas. The final four states, approved in 1997, were Connecticut, Maine, Michigan, and Virginia.

Table 11-1. *Clean Air Implementation Plan Approvals, 1994–97*[a]

Explanatory factors	Coefficient
Manufacturing ratio	−1.204
	(4.11)
Sulfur dioxide emissions	.003
	(.002)
Democratic legislative seats (%)	2.423*
	(1.41)
Budget expenditures (%)	−34.858
	(49.33)
1995 time maturation dummy	−16.524***
	(1.138)
1996 time maturation dummy	−16.624***
	(1.709)
SIP approved in neighboring states	3.868***
	(1.50)
Constant	12.908***
	(.770)

Summary statistics
Pseudo R^2 = 0.442
Wald Chi^2 = 641.6***
Log likelihood = 43.7***
Cases correctly predicted (percentage) = 83.62
N = 116

*Significant at .1 level; **significant at .05 level; ***significant at .01 level.
a. Standard errors are in parentheses.

in the expected direction. Also, the activities of nearby states influence more rapid adoption rather than the reverse, which is interesting. The variable measuring bureaucratic resources devoted to the problem is not significant here.

The measure of manufacturing interest groups is also not significant in standard statistical terms. Perhaps the measure is flawed, since it focuses more on economic, rather than political, power. Still, the combination of the fact that adjacent state actions make a state more likely to get its SIP approved with the lack of significant influence from the most central interest group suggests that the race to the bottom is not a factor here. It may be that the relatively short time frame (three years) of this analysis, combined with threatened EPA sanctions, precludes a role for economic competition in developing SIPs.

CHAPTER TWELVE

ENVIRONMENTAL REGULATION

Groundwater Protection

with

ALKA SAPAT

The federal government has developed some programs and provided some funding for groundwater pollution regulation, but it has not established a core set of comprehensive regulations as it has for clean air policy. The states have considerable discretion to address these problems within their own boundaries. This is similar to other environmental areas, such as Superfund regulation of toxic sites, in which the federal government does regulate partially, but many sites do not meet federal standards, and some states have chosen on their own to regulate anyway. In a sense, this provides a more unconstrained test of states' willingness to address environmental problems at their own instigation—and their own cost.

Like clean air, clean groundwater is an essential resource. About half of the U.S. population relies on groundwater for drinking water, and in some areas groundwater provides almost all of the domestic water supply. The annual flow from groundwater is fifty times the volume of surface flows. Experts estimate that underground aquifers in the United States contain as much as sixteen times as much water as the Great Lakes (Hall and Kerr 1991, p. 32). Though groundwater was once perceived as a virtually unlimited natural resource that purified itself as it passed through sandy soil, scientific studies have revealed large amounts of contamination in groundwater supplies.

History of State Role

Groundwater regulation has traditionally been considered a state and local government responsibility. It was propelled onto the national policy agenda, however, with the highly publicized 1977 discovery of massive groundwater contamination at New York's Love Canal. The President's Council for Environmental Quality addressed groundwater resources in its 1979 report. Nonetheless, the federal government developed no comprehensive groundwater management program, and until 1992 approximately forty-five different federal programs influenced groundwater regulation at the state level. This chapter highlights the state role in the four most important federal laws relevant to groundwater regulation: the 1972 Clean Water Act (CWA), the 1974 Safe Drinking Water Act (SDWA), the 1976 Resource Conservation and Recovery Act (RCRA), and the 1987 Water Quality Act (WQA).

The 1972 CWA provided a set of ambitious deadlines to the EPA to grant permits to water pollution sources, issue effluent (wastewater) guidelines, require sources to install water pollution control technology, and eliminate all discharges into the nation's waterways to make them fishable and swimmable. The CWA established the National Pollutant Discharge Elimination System (NPDES), which authorizes state and federal regulators to provide permits to all industrial and municipal facilities that discharge wastes into public waterways. States were allowed to implement their own NPDES programs if they are as stringent as federal efforts; by 1992, thirty-eight states set permit requirements and investigated facilities.

The 1974 SDWA authorized the EPA to set maximum contaminant levels. Later amendments in 1986 banned lead pipes and lead solder in public water systems and established a three-year timetable for the regulation of eighty-three other specific contaminants.

Laws governing solid and hazardous waste disposal also influence the regulation of groundwater contamination. Amendments in 1984 to the 1976 RCRA stipulated monitoring of groundwater at hazardous and solid waste dump sites and also prompted the states to adopt underground storage tank legislation, with some federal financial support.

Under the 1987 WQA, states must prepare a nonpoint source pollution assessment and an implementation plan using "best management practices" to control these sources (Ringquist 1993b, p. 57). The WQA also provided states with financial support and discretion to follow their own priorities when constructing wastewater treatment plants.

In short, a number of federal laws affect state groundwater regulation, but they still leave the states with considerable discretion over whether and how to regulate further. The focus here is on how states use that discretion and why. Several states have adopted groundwater regulatory policies that go beyond federal requirements. This analysis focuses on the factors contributing to three important policies aimed at critical problems: pesticide regulation, groundwater monitoring programs, and wellhead protection.

Factors Likely to Influence Regulation

As noted more specifically below, prior research on state environmental policy suggests that five sets of factors are likely to influence regulatory choices over pesticides, monitoring programs, and wellhead protection. As with most of the studies in this book, the first set includes the strength of the relevant interest groups that care about groundwater protection. Second are the institutional factors in each state, with a particular focus on the state's commitment to cleaning up groundwater pollution and the capacity of the state government to carry out that commitment. The third set of measures addresses the actual severity of the groundwater problem in a state, or the actual need for regulation. Public interest theory suggests that governments are generally responsive to needs in their jurisdiction. The fourth set of factors is contextual ones included as controls. The fifth set captures elements of regional diffusion processes across states, which are particularly relevant for environmental regulatory policies, where problems often slip beyond state boundaries and policymakers show concern about races to the bottom.

Measuring Regulation

States have implemented a number of regulatory policies to deal with groundwater pollution. Data about these legislative policy innovations come from a survey of state groundwater protection legislation (Morandi 1994). Legislatures in twenty-three states have adopted regulations addressing the application, sale, labeling, and disposal of pesticides and fertilizers. Such legislation often increases pesticide and fertilizer registration fees, partly to provide finances for monitoring groundwater and for the development of educational materials and voluntary or mandatory best management practices to curb excessive chemical use. Some legislation also requires submission of analytical data on what happens to pesticides in groundwater or establishes centers for sustainable agriculture. Most of this legislation is highly technical, and it often relies on more traditional command and control tools rather than newer incentive-based concepts.

A smaller number of states—only five—have enacted legislation designed specifically to authorize or require a state agency to establish a groundwater monitoring program to determine ambient groundwater quality, detect sources, and identify vulnerable areas. Industries fear such programs will lead to detailed standard setting and increased regulatory burdens, so they often oppose legislative efforts. The five states that have chosen this approach—Idaho, Nebraska, Montana, Missouri, and Washington—are clustered fairly closely geographically.

In 1986 rules the EPA encouraged wellhead protection, but this has remained a discretionary state program. The thirteen states that have adopted wellhead protection legislation generally authorize a state agency to determine state and local responsibilities in developing and implementing a wellhead protection program, define the wellhead protection area, identify potential sources of contamination, provide technical assistance to local governments, and develop regulatory measures. This legislation tends to provide a favorable political environment for groundwater management by local governments and municipalities, using "carrots," or incentives, as well as "sticks" to protect groundwater.

These three categories of groundwater regulation vary in approach and stringency. They also vary greatly in the number of states that had adopted them in the early 1990s. Pesticide regulation is detailed, which may require more professional legislatures to adopt. Groundwater monitoring programs are more general in nature. Wellhead protection provides a stronger role for local governments in implementation. All three sets of legislative regulations create conflict with interest groups but are not, for the most part, widely salient issues except during crisis events, so they are most likely to face opposition from directly affected interest groups rather than the mass public.

Explaining Regulation

As noted above, the analysis models the choice of states to adopt these three regulatory policies as a function of five sets of factors: (1) the strength of relevant interest groups; (2) institutional factors (the commitment and capacity of state governments); (3) actual severity of the groundwater problem; (4) contextual factors; and (5) regional diffusion.

In groundwater regulations, three major interests have traditionally been affected negatively: manufacturing, mining, and agribusiness. Manufacturing and mining industries are major sources of groundwater pollution. Except for pesticide regulation, which they sometimes favor because it helps groundwater and affects agribusiness, these firms generally oppose the regulations analyzed here because they impose costs on them. Since agribusiness is chemical-intensive, it is estimated to be the single largest source of nonpoint source pollution in the United States. However, agribusinesses are also some of the largest users of groundwater, consuming almost 34 percent of the nation's groundwater. Thus agricultural interests have developed a somewhat complicated political strategy; typically, they tend to support wellhead monitoring programs but oppose pesticide controls. The strength of these three interest groups in each state is measured by their percentage of gross state product.[1] Agricultural interests are measured by the combination of farms, forestry, and fisheries.[2]

In addition, state environmental interest groups have been shown to have significant influence on state water quality regulations (Ringquist 1993b, p. 163). Thus stronger environmental groups should lead to a greater likelihood of a state passing these groundwater regulations. The specific measure is the number of Sierra Club, Greenpeace, and National Wildlife Federation members for each thousand persons in each state in 1990.[3]

Institutional factors are the second set of explanatory factors to consider. Theory suggests that four measures should be important: (1) environmental attitudes; (2) commitment of institutional actors; (3) institutional ability to develop regulations (legislative professionalism); and (4) state capacity or wealth, all measured from 1988 to 1993.[4]

The attitudes of institutional elites are important factors in shaping policy outcomes, affecting the way elites process information in a constrained environment and their subjective interpretations of the decision

1. For this analysis, data from the percentage of gross state product contributed by the mining industry for each state in 1986 are being used. This variable was logged to correct for skewness.

2. These variables were logged to correct for skewness. However, these measures are extremely crude in their present form. For instance, a refined measure of manufacturing industry strength would be the percentage of gross state product attributed to only those manufacturing industries that constituted significant sources of groundwater pollution. Also, not all manufacturing industries would affect the adoption of each of the three legislative provisions equally. The current measure being used is hence a crude proxy measure.

3. Data for environmental group strength for each year are not easily available. Hence data from the Green Index (Hall and Kerr 1991) are being used as a proxy for the years 1988–91.

4. All the policy innovations in groundwater were first adopted in 1988.

problem. Legislators who hold attitudes favorable to environmental protection should be more motivated to adopt these regulations.[5] Since there
are no data available on the environmental ideology of state legislators,
the ideology of state legislators is measured by the average League of Conservation Voters (LCV) scores for each state for the period 1985 to 1990.
The score that each state receives by the LCV is equal to the average percent of pro-environmental votes its congressional delegation cast from
1985 to 1990. This variable is a proxy variable for the pro-environmental
attitude of state legislators.

A second variable measures the motivation of institutional actors to
adopt these regulations—the past commitment legislators made toward
protecting the environment. One of the clearest indicators of legislative
commitment to the environment is economic—the funds spent on environmental protection.[6] Thus state commitment is measured by using the
percentage of state expenditures spent on environment/natural resource
programs, lagged by one year.[7]

The next set of independent predictor variables deal with the capacity
of state political institutions to initiate and enforce regulatory policies.
States with greater institutional capacity, as measured by legislative professionalism, should be better able to adopt these environmental policy
innovations. In the past three decades, state legislatures have increased
their institutional capacity considerably, from rural-dominated backwa-
ters to more representative and modern bodies. Although there is enormous variation across states, on average legislators now spend more time
on the job, both in and out of session, and they have more staff to help
them evaluate policies. These resources should enable them to be more

5. Party identification could also be a clue to the motivation or the propensity to
regulate stringently, with Democrats being presumably more pro-environmental
protection. However, party identification can be misleading given that environ-
mentalism has become to a large extent a bipartisan issue.

6. Commitment expressed in terms of funding can hence be related to pro-
environmental legislative attitudes and can perhaps be seen as the formal expres-
sion of those attitudes. In other words, legislators might "lock into" a position by
committing certain resources for protection.

7. Before proceeding further, a caveat is in order. The percentage of a state's
budget spent on environmental protection is also an indicator of the ability or the
capacity of state political institutions to protect the environment. Larger budgets
may mean that more resources are spent on environmental protection. Thus this
variable will be interpreted as an indicator of the commitment and capability of
state political institutions to adopt environmental policy innovations in groundwater protection.

likely to pass new regulations.[8] The measure of legislative professionalism is composed of factor scores from a set of variables capturing several of these elements.[9]

While political-institutional capacity is important, economic wealth is another form of capacity. The conventional hypothesis is that the greater per capita personal income available to a state, the more likely it is that the state can afford to undertake more stringent regulations (Lowry 1992; Ringquist 1993a). However, it is worth noting that some groundwater regulatory policies involve direct charges on businesses, such as registration fees, which might be more likely in states that have fewer economic resources, blunting the typical wealth effect.

As threats to groundwater quality emanate from a variety of sources including landfills, pesticides, wastewater disposal sites, and leaking gasoline storage tanks, there are three measures of problem severity in the model. The first addresses the need for safe groundwater, measured by groundwater consumption. States that consume more groundwater for irrigation, mining, industrial, or domestic drinking usage should be more likely to regulate to protect this resource. We examine the percentage of people within a state that are served by groundwater.[10]

A second, specific measure of need is the number of hazardous waste sites in each state for the years 1988 to 1992.[11] These sites include both

8. Some might argue that less professional legislators are indeed more responsive to issues like groundwater, since part-time legislators are attuned to local problems. The rationale is that these part-time legislators may themselves be a part of the agricultural community. However, for the analysis presented in this study, the interests of the agricultural community in issues concerning groundwater protection are already represented separately in the model as the strength of agricultural interests (see section on interest groups). This variable should account then for the representation of the interests of part-time legislators also, if they are a part of the agricultural community.

9. A single factor representing a general professionalism dimension was obtained from three variables for each year in the analyses: the length of the legislative session in days in each state, the number of bills introduced in the legislative session, and the level of compensation for state legislators (Council of State Governments 1989–97). These three variables are normally used in conjunction with a number of other variables to represent legislative professionalism.

10. For this variable, the data used are for the year 1988.

11. Since data were unavailable for 1990, the data from 1989 were used for this year. Since the variation across years is minimal, the use of the 1989 data is assumed to have an insignificant effect. Data are, however, being collected for the missing year.

proposed and final sites on the National Priorities List for the Superfund program as authorized by the Comprehensive Environmental Response, Compensation, and Liability Act of 1980 and the Superfund Amendments and Reauthorization Act of 1986. To control for state size, the analysis divides the number of waste sites by state population each year.[12]

The third measure comes from runoff water used for irrigation purposes that has been treated with fertilizers and pesticides to maximize crop production. Chemicals mix with rain or irrigation water and wash into streams or seep into groundwater, contaminating wells and reservoirs. In Nebraska, for example, 70 percent of wells are contaminated with pesticides, as Nebraska consumes almost one ton of fertilizer and pesticides for each person. The specific measure of this problem is the percentage of pesticides in the groundwater of a state.

While most of these measures so far have been specific to environmental policies, state policies also are likely to reflect the opinions and attitudes of their citizenry. A state with a more liberal electorate should be more likely to pass these groundwater regulations. Finally, prior studies have shown a regional diffusion pattern to new regulatory policies (Walker 1969; Berry and Berry 1990), which makes sense here given the nature of environmental problems. This is measured by the percentage of adjacent states that have previously adopted the groundwater regulation.

These explanatory variables are used in the models to predict whether a state legislature passed each of these three types of regulations in a given year from 1988 to 1992. Such a model calls for the use of event history techniques, the results of which are summarized in table 12-1.

Results

While several variables are significant in statistical terms, the overall pattern of results demonstrates the importance of institutional factors. Legislative commitment and to a lesser extent legislative capabilities increase the likelihood of state regulation of groundwater. The attitudes and ideological commitment of institutional actors are important determinants of state pesticide and wellhead regulation, but contrary to expectations, environmental attitudes are negatively related to state groundwater monitoring policies. This finding suggests that legislators may be influenced by

12. This variable was logged to correct for skewness.

Table 12-1. *Groundwater Protection Regulation, 1988–92*[a]

Explanatory factor	Pesticide regulation	Wellhead protection	Groundwater monitoring
Hazardous waste sites per capita	−0.31	0.46	1.48
	(0.42)	(0.34)	(1.14)
Pesticides in groundwater	0.06***	0.04	−0.01
	(0.02)	(0.03)	(0.09)
Population served by groundwater (%)	−0.02	−0.03	−.19**
	(0.02)	(0.03)	(0.09)
LCV scores	.08***	.10**	−.22**
	(0.02)	(0.04)	(0.10)
Budget expenditures (%)	.53***	0.39	−1.04
	(0.26)	(0.44)	(1.51)
State fiscal health	−0.00	0.00	−0.001
	(0.00)	(0.00)	(0.00)
Legislative professionalism	0.48)	−0.72*	0.91
	(0.28)	(0.49)	(1.07)
Manufacturing industry strength	−0.41	−0.40	−4.32
	(0.54)	(0.74)	(2.20)*
Mining industry strength	0.53	0.46	−2.83
	(0.26)	(0.34)	(1.31)**
Agricultural community strength	0.66	−0.29	0.74
	(0.10)	(0.23)	(0.35)**
Environmental group membership	−0.001	−0.17	0.27
	(0.12)	(0.15)	(0.49)
Liberal electorate	−0.05	−0.09	0.22
	(0.04)	(0.06)*	(0.16)
Innovation in neighboring states	0.47	−0.62	3.22
	(0.54)	(0.95)	(1.59)**
Constant	−6.11	−10.99	48.92
	(4.24)	(5.83)	(23.47)
Summary statistics			
Wald Chi^2	22.15**	19.8*	25.10*
N	180	207	226

*Significant at .1 level; **significant at .05 level; ***significant at .01 level.
a. Standard errors are in parentheses.

the strength of manufacturing and mining industries, which oppose these policies.

Budgetary commitment to environmental protection, which also measures state capability to some extent, is important in explaining state pesticide regulation. Since groundwater monitoring and wellhead protection programs do not require as much governmental spending, this variable is not significant in explaining them.

Legislative professionalism is the other significant institutional factor that explains pesticide regulation, which is more technical in nature than the other regulations. Legislatures that are more professionalized, and that possess a greater capacity to gather and absorb technical information, are more likely to adopt such measures. Thus despite some differences in the institutional determinants of these three regulatory policies, the overall results indicate that states with more committed and capable legislators are more likely to adopt innovative regulations to deal with groundwater pollution.

In contrast to the importance of institutional factors, variables reflecting the extent of actual environmental problems and groundwater need were less important predictors—need or problem severity was a significant explanatory variable only in the case of pesticide regulation and only for one measure: states with a high concentration of groundwater pesticides were more likely to adopt regulations. None of the problem severity variables are in the right direction as hypothesized in the two models for state wellhead protection and groundwater monitoring.

Regional diffusion is an important predictor of state groundwater monitoring programs. State legislators may be more willing and able to pass these regulations when neighboring states have already done so, as political uncertainty is reduced and legislators might also benefit from a "bandwagon effect."

It is a little surprising that interest groups are only important influences over state regulations for groundwater monitoring programs. Mining and manufacturing industries show significant opposition to state groundwater monitoring programs, while agricultural interests demonstrate significant support. Considering the relative explanatory power of each of these factors, as the strength of agricultural interests increases by one unit, holding other variables constant, the predicted hazard rate increases by 2.11. In contrast, unit changes in the values of the mining and manufacturing industries, ceteris paribus, only increase the predicted hazard rate by a factor of 0.01 and 0.05, respectively, demonstrating far greater relative influence by agricultural interests compared to these other interest groups. By way of comparison, when environmental attitudes, measured by LCV scores, increase by one unit, ceteris paribus, the odds of a state adopting a wellhead protection program increase by a factor of 1.11.[13] Taking this sensitivity analysis further, when LCV scores for wellhead pro-

13. The values of Exp(B) give the odds of an event occurring versus not occurring for a per-unit change in the independent variable, other things being equal (Liao 1994). If the beta coefficients are positive, this factor will be greater than

tection regulations are moved from the minimum to the maximum value, keeping the other variables at their means, the predicted hazard rates vary from 0.05 to 0.40, a fairly large substantive impact.

Discussion

More than half of our nation's population depends on groundwater as the principal source of drinking water. As a number of federal policies address groundwater only indirectly, state governments have the primary role in regulating groundwater, and since the mid-1980s a number of states have developed important new regulations. Adoption of state regulations, including pesticide regulation, wellhead protection, and groundwater monitoring, are supported most importantly by factors reflecting the ideological commitment of legislative actors and by a state's budgetary commitment to environmental regulation. Even when a state is addressing a specific problem, as when a high level of pesticide-contaminated groundwater has a positive influence on pesticide regulation, the influence of institutional factors is much more important than the actual severity of the problem in a state.

Surprisingly, interest groups do not appear to play a dominant role. Only in the case of groundwater monitoring programs do we find the three major industrial interests demonstrating strong and significant influence over policy decisions.

Thus in assessing the broad scope of state environmental regulation, both for clean air implementation, where federal mandates are strong, and for state groundwater regulations, which are without strong federal mandates, state legislative ideology is important and the actions of neighboring states also matter. While interest groups are involved and sometimes influential, they do not play a dominant role in shaping the regulations that states promulgate. These findings support the argument that states are not engaged in a destructive race to the bottom, at least in these specific areas of state regulation.

---

one, which means that the odds are increased; if the beta coefficient is negative, the factor will be less than one, which means that the odds are decreased. When the beta coefficient is zero, the factor equals one, which leaves the odds unchanged. This statistic is not a predicted probability but a ratio of predicted probabilities.

PART SIX

Conclusions

Even in a globalized, twenty-first-century economy, regulation of industries and professions by the states remains an important feature of the U.S. political economy. In fact, given the retreat by the federal government from some areas of regulation, the state role may now be more important, in relative terms, than it has been for many years. State regulation is not likely to disappear soon, even as a few more regulated industries become more competitive and ripe for further deregulation. And some new state regulatory efforts have been gathering steam, popping up their heads like sharks in an amusement park game, especially as the federal government has reduced its social regulatory enforcement efforts.

This section addresses patterns and trends that cut across state regulation of specific industries, examining existing and proposed reforms of regulatory processes and institutions that might improve state regulatory outcomes. Chapter 13 analyzes the quantitative findings across the industries to pick out the common patterns and critical differences. Since all of these studies find an influential role for state officials, chapter 14 examines actual and proposed reforms of the regulatory process from the perspective of the critical state officials—legislature, governors, and bureaucratic agencies. Here, a number of states have been active in providing a greater role for oversight of bureaucratic agency regulations and the regulatory process more generally. Since capture by powerful interest groups is a particular concern of state regulation, I pay close attention to reforms that might ameliorate that problem by increasing the contestation of the state regulatory process by a broader set of actors and by increasing the autonomous ability of institutional actors to analyze, assess, and implement solutions.

In chapter 15 Scott Graves, Colin Provost, and I examine the emerging regulatory role of legal actors, as regulation increasingly is shaped by lawsuits and by court decisions that cut across a large number of regulatory arenas. This is an area of state regulation that other scholars have not yet analyzed in any detail. Finally, chapter 16 offers some broader conclusions about the present and future status of state regulation and its reform. This discussion is informed both by the direct studies presented in the empirical chapters and by the general knowledge of state regulation that I have gained from this research.

CHAPTER THIRTEEN

Synthesis of Results across Industries

While those who doubt the efficacy of the states as regulators expect to see most regulation captured by dominant interest groups, the quantitative studies in this book do not demonstrate that pattern of influence. Instead, in most industries and arenas, interest groups compete, leaving state government actors (both elected and appointed) with room to make decisions that fit with their own general ideologies and analyses of the appropriate regulatory solutions. Differences across states in legislative ideology and professionalism, bureaucratic selection mechanisms and resources, and other factors influence industry outputs and outcomes, such as entry restrictions for firms, prices for consumers, and the even the solvency of firms in regulated industries.

Although this book is organized by the type of market failure that motivates or justifies the regulation of the industries discussed in chapters 4–12, there is no simple relationship between market failures and patterns of political influence. Overall, far more cases demonstrate significant influence from institutional actors than a pattern of simple interest group capture, which is a favorable finding for those interested in a pluralist, effective, and capable state regulatory politics.

Still, since interest groups are actively involved in all phases of the regulatory process of each industry, it is not surprising that some measure of interest group power, usually representing the dominant regulated industry, is significantly influential in eight of the ten cases. The only cases in which regulated industry interest groups are not highly influential are electricity rate regulation and clean air approvals—where my hunch is that there are measurement problems with the specific variables rather than a real lack of influence. Interest groups matter in shaping regulatory policy, and it is difficult to imagine an environment in which they would not have a strong degree of influence. The amount and exclusivity of that influence are the key issues in assessing the question of capture of state regulators.

Capture is the dominant pattern, however, only when an interest group is the only major source of influence; one group wants protective regulation, and no other group is activated or involved enough to pressure politicians and regulators into providing a more balanced outcome. The extreme example here is occupational regulation. This is not surprising given the way some states regulate occupations; for example, in Georgia the elected secretary of state, who regulates professions, recently received $115,000 in campaign contributions directly from the professionals she regulates.[1]

But even the captured industries analyzed in these chapters do not demonstrate extremely egregious cases. Even though licensing of lawyers and MDs demonstrates entry barriers directly related to the state political power of these professionals, thousands of applicants do manage to overcome these (relatively modest) entry barriers created by state regulation. Few would argue we have a shortage of lawyers in the United States (though some would suggest that prices are too high). And even though these professions oppose onerous continuing education requirements, many states do impose at least modest requirements, presumably with improved professional quality and consumer interests in mind.

In a case I have analyzed in book-length detail elsewhere (Teske, Best, and Mintrom 1995), state economic trucking regulation looked like a classic case of capture, and indeed it was in a few extreme states such as Texas. But while partially captured, shipping groups also had influence over trucking regulation, opposing the incumbent truckers. Ultimately, pressured by powerful emerging trucking competitors UPS and Federal Express, Congress preempted all states, including the completely captured ones, in 1994. So apart from occupational regulation, where the federal government has never trodden, complete capture of state regulation is rare and usually limited in time.

A middle ground of studies here demonstrates some significant influence by interest groups, but not exclusive influence or outright capture;

1. "Report: Officials Get Large Contributions from Those They Regulate," *Athens Banner-Herald,* October 27, 2002.

institutional actors also provide strong influence over regulatory decisions. In some of these cases, the winning coalitions behind state policies resemble Yandle's (2001) "Baptists and bootleggers," in which ideological "true-believers" in a particular type of regulation form a coalition, sometimes explicit and sometimes not, with interests that benefit from it. For example, hospital interests are successful in retaining the entry barriers that CON regulation provides in most states, but CONs are also supported by Democratic legislatures in wealthy states with high hospital rates. And one-third of the states have chosen to discontinue CON regulations even in the face of this support from hospital interests. The outcomes of insurance solvency regulation are influenced by the political power of insurance firms in a state, but state insurance commissions that aggressively audit the finances of such firms seem to protect consumers by limiting insolvencies. State S&L regulation was clearly influenced greatly by the S&L industry—and the fees and jobs they generated for states—but apart from Texas, the states did no worse a job maintaining the health of firms, even in the face of this political and economic pressure, than did federal regulators. While new energy providers like Enron as well as incumbent firms that bargained to get their stranded costs included in customer rate bases affected the course of electricity deregulation, state choices were also influenced greatly by legislators and PUC regulators.

When a range of different interest groups provides input into the regulatory process, it is far less likely that one can dominate, and institutional actors have more room to make choices that will be supported by some group. This gives institutional actors the ability to mediate and assess interest group arguments, coming to their own decisions. For telecommunications, electricity regulation and deregulation, clean air approvals, and groundwater protection, the structure and ideological makeup of the legislatures are highly influential, always in the expected direction—Democratic or liberal state legislatures are more likely to regulate or generate policies that favor consumer interests. Often the structure and resources of the bureaucratic agencies that actually regulate day-to-day also influence policy choices. Thus while these cases demonstrate some significant influence from all three nodes of the traditional "iron triangle," the econometric evidence suggests independent authority and action by these state institutions rather than the triangular capture pattern by interest groups.

Which institutional actors are the most important in state regulatory decisions? The evidence suggests that a combination of legislatures and bureaucratic agencies is most influential. Although states are unlikely to professionalize their legislatures or alter their ideology in order to change regulatory policies, it is instructive that these differences in state legislatures are associated with different policies in eight of the ten cases examined. Clearly, state legislatures are important; collectively they pass seventy-five times more legislation than Congress. Still, given their low average levels of professionalism and the fact that they have created some fairly insulated bureaucratic structures to make regulatory decisions, like PUCs and insurance commissions, we would not necessarily expect to find legislative influence in an "average" state (which is what the regression analyses look for). That legislative ideology influences policy can be viewed as a positive finding for democratic accountability because it suggests an impressive degree of electoral responsiveness by legislators. Since many other studies of state regulation also find a significant role for legislatures (see the review in Gerber and Teske 2000), we need more analysis of the representational role of state legislatures and of their relationship to broad state public opinion (see Erikson, Wright, and McIver 1993).

Legislatures play an important role when they are directly making regulatory policy themselves or when they are overseeing regulatory policies that are largely developed (via rule making) and implemented by state bureaucratic agencies. Several of the studies here involve regulatory policy outputs that are directly shaped by legislative actions—in particular, state electricity deregulation was passed, or ratified after PUC study, by state legislatures (see Andrews 2000 for a breakdown of legislative and bureaucratic decisionmaking on this issue), CON regulations are repealed directly by the legislature, occupational regulation is created by legislatures, and groundwater regulations are promulgated directly by the legislature. Not surprisingly, most of these regulations show influence from the state legislature in the quantitative studies. However, for bureaucratic rule-making decisions or implementation, like PUC rate ratios in telecommunications and electricity, firm solvency in the insurance and S&L industries, and clean air SIPs, state legislatures also show substantial influence. Thus state legislatures are clearly engaging in some forms of bureaucratic oversight or influence in these cases. We need more fine-grained research on how this happens, as regulators either read signals from legislators or are influenced by more direct actions that have not been measured here, such as oversight hearings (see Maestas, Gerber, and Dometrius 2003 for a promising approach to this issue).

Bureaucratic agency makeup and the resources provided to agencies are critical to differing state regulatory decisions and implementation actions. Since the PUC regulatory process is the most developed and well established, this is the example of state regulation developing the greatest capacity to counterbalance the power of the regulated firms with professional staffs and wide input (see also Gormley 1983; Berry 1984). The findings here that elected commissioners in telecommunications, electricity, and insurance regulation are more likely to favor consumer interests, given their desire for reelection, was often hypothesized but had shown only mixed results in prior studies (Teske 1990). When measures are available for even more specific aspects of bureaucracies, such as their power and authority (especially in telecommunications), their resources, and their inputs into the process (for example, insurance financial audits), these usually shape different policy choices in the expected directions.

Regulatory agencies, like state PUCs, operate in an environment that is slow moving, technical, and precedent-bound. Nevertheless, their decisions are shaped by political factors as well as by notions of good policy. This is probably what Americans want from their regulators—a fair balancing of technical and other inputs and a balance of political responsiveness and autonomy in their decisions. While some observers have criticized state regulators in these areas for being overly cautious and slow in making decisions, the decisions they have faced in the past twenty years in industries like telecommunications and energy have been enormously complex. Federal decisions have also been fraught with complications and compromise—as well as with continuing litigation—as with recent FCC decisions sharing telecommunications pricing authority with the states and with media deregulation.[2] State regulators have steered a useful course in allowing these industries to advance in technological and competitive terms while also guarding the interests of their most vulnerable consumers.

There is also current resonance from the findings for regulatory oversight of insurance and S&L firms, which suggest that bureaucratic accountability relationships and resources are important for regulating corporate fraud and abuse of lenient regulations in a deregulatory environment. In the recent environment of Enron, WorldCom, Global Crossing, and wider corporate accounting scandals, these findings suggest that the regulatory oversight mechanisms are particularly important when industries are partially or fully deregulated—at any level of government. Although it is likely that the provision of regulatory authority and resources to agencies is not entirely independent of the larger political

2. Christopher Stern and Jonathan Krim, "States to Keep Local Phone Service Regulatory Role," *Washington Post*, February 20, 2003, p. A3.

processes in a state, as the Chicago School theorists argue, neither is it likely that current state political battles completely determine the makeup of regulatory agencies that were established decades earlier.

Mainly because of measurement problems, I was not able to test for the influence of governors directly in most of these studies. More research needs to be done on specifying and measuring gubernatorial power and influence over state regulation and over state public policy more generally. In a recent study, Ferguson (2003) finds that the legislative success of governors is more a function of legislative professionalism than of the institutional powers of the governor, which reinforces the legislative role even as we study governors. Chapter 14 analyzes several cross-cutting regulatory reforms that governors have employed to centralize their power over regulatory bureaucracies.

The other variables tested in some of these studies vary in whether they demonstrate significant influence over regulations. Sometimes, though not always, the current price or fees charged in a regulated industry influence policy; sometimes, but again not always, the level of need, as in the degree of environment pollution, influences policy. Measures of broad economic differences, like unemployment and average income, sometimes influence policy, but often they do not. Generally, this suggests that nonpolitical factors are sometimes important but less consistently influential than the range of interest group, electoral, and bureaucratic factors noted above. Again, this supports the idea that the choices states make about how to set up their institutions have an influence on regulatory outcomes. How states regulate affects policy outputs and outcomes beyond the impact of state economics and demographics, the external pressures of federal mandates, interstate competition, and possible races to the bottom. Simple capture by one dominant group is not the common pattern of most state regulation anymore, if it ever was.

CHAPTER FOURTEEN

CONCLUSIONS

Reform by Legislatures, Governors, and Agencies

A s the evidence in this book indicates, many areas of state regulation are operating fairly well, particularly with agencies that have a long history and an established process, such as PUCs, even if the process sometimes seems slow. Industries that had demonstrated a more captured pattern of regulation have now often been deregulated, either by federal preemption or by state actions, so this is less of a glaring problem than in the past. But capture remains a major concern for state regulation, more of a potential problem than it is for federal regulation. This pattern is somewhat apparent in hospital CON regulations, in financial regulation, and especially in occupational regulation. Capture is more problematic in state capitals than in Washington, D.C., partly because state interest group lobbying environments, although becoming more pluralistic, are still less varied than at the federal level, because mobile firms may have more political influence over individual states looking for economic development and because some states still do not have adequate legislative and bureaucratic staff to provide an independent source of analysis and implementation capacity.

To minimize capture, an overarching set of reforms should attempt to bring more players into the regulatory process and provide the important institutions with more resources to develop the capacity for independent analysis and implementation. At times this may slow down the regulatory process by adding players, but the benefits are worth the costs. Generally, these reforms can lead to a more contested regulatory environment, with multiple points of access and entry, which I believe is better than a less contested, backroom process that is more easily captured. The federal environment of regulation has become much more contested in recent years, as presidents have paid more attention and centralized their powers, Congress has intervened more and overseen agencies better, and courts have been brought into the process more often. While dealing with all of these actors more can no doubt be frustrating for regulators in agencies, for society as a whole it seems preferable to the alternative.

State Legislature Reform

As noted in chapter 13, the quantitative studies demonstrate a clear and strong role for state legislatures in influencing regulation. Sometimes this role is direct, as legislatures pass laws that immediately shape regulatory policy, as with the removal of hospital CON regulations or the initiation of electricity deregulation. Other times the legislative influence is less direct: for example, legislatures pass administrative procedures acts that shape the regulatory process, they establish new or reformed regulatory bodies, they oversee the regulatory activities and budgets of regulatory agencies, or they veto regulations. All of these roles can make them influential even when they do not pass direct regulatory legislation in a particular domain.

Parallel to a large literature at the federal level sometimes known as "congressional dominance," state legislatures are clearly influential, even when measured in the most simple terms: usually either party dominance or control, or legislative professionalism. More liberal or Democratic state legislatures favor and influence more social regulation and more consumer-friendly regulation, and more conservative or Republican legislatures are more supportive of business and of less social regulation, which is probably a very positive sign for democratic accountability. To some extent, with their admittedly "blunt instrument," voters can get the regulatory policy they expect by electing the appropriate state representatives.

In terms of professionalism, it would be easy, but naive, to suggest as a reform that more states professionalize their legislatures. There may be good reasons to do that, related to the increased role of state policy generally and the increased role of interest group pressure in state capitals. Still, a number of states have long maintained the concept of a part-time citizen legislature and will not easily abandon that idea. So, to get better state regulatory policy, what else can state legislatures do? I address three broad areas—interest group pressure, administrative oversight, and legislative regulatory reviews.

Interest Groups

State legislatures are busy places, despite the quite sleepy feel in some state capitals at some times of the year. As a whole, state legislatures pass seventy-five times more legislation than Congress. Of course, not all of these bills are about regulation, but many of them are. In 2002 states considered 150,000 bills, and they passed about 25 percent of them as law.

It is worth considering what a professionalized legislature really means. Across the fifty states, only seven state legislatures operate full-time, in six states the legislature convenes only every other year, and in thirty-eight states legislators have no paid staffers (though most have access to some committee staffers). So while state legislatures in Sacramento and Albany may resemble mini U.S. Congresses, those in Montpelier and Austin do not. It is hard to conceive of part-time legislators who rarely meet having the time and resources to carefully develop and oversee the kinds of complex regulatory policies discussed in this book.

Even though many state legislatures are not professionalized, the stakes in state policy are high enough that they are now inundated with requests from interest groups to develop favorable public policies. From extensive data collection, Dunbar and Rush find that on average there are five registered state lobbyists for every state legislator.[1] This means that there are 37,000 registered lobbying organizations at the state level, and collectively they spent more than $1 billion in the states in 2000, attempting to influence policy decisions. There is some regional pattern; Hedge (1998, p. 69) notes that the states with particularly dominant interest groups tend to be in the southern and western regions of the United States, with greater contestation in the northern and eastern states.

It is clear that regulated industries are well represented among the most powerful interests in state capitals. For example, Hedge (1998, p. 73) compiled data from Thomas and Hrebenar (1999) that show that experts report fourteen interest groups as being "moderately" or "most" effective in more than half the states—of these fourteen, the role of nine were studied in the empirical chapters in this book. These are utilities (in third place),

1. John Dunbar and Meleah Rush, "The Fourth Branch: Study Finds $570 Million Spent on Lobbying in the States in 2000," Center for Public Integrity, 2002 (www.publicintegrity.org/dtaweb/index.asp).

lawyers (fourth), physicians (sixth), insurance firms (seventh), manufacturers (eighth), health care organizations (ninth), bankers (tenth), farm organizations (thirteenth), and environmentalists (fourteenth).

Common sense seems to suggest a link between these lobbying efforts and regulatory policy outputs, but the political science literature (mostly based on federal studies) is mixed, finding clearer evidence of interest groups buying access to legislators rather than actual votes. Still, it seems clear that state legislators, especially busy ones who do not work full-time and have little staff, are likely to have their views influenced by such expenditures. To address this concern, in the mid-1990s over half the states enacted tighter restrictions on lobbying. Still, weak enforcement efforts have limited the practical effectiveness of state agencies meant to monitor lobbying abuses. One recent example is Enron, which spent a considerable amount on lobbying at the state level to obtain favorable electricity deregulatory policies. Enron officials contributed nearly $2 million to state legislators in the 1998 and 2000 election cycles, with more than half of this amount spent in four key states then considering electricity deregulation—Texas, California, Oregon, and Florida.

Some observers argue that state interest group activity is so intense that legislators have too little time and not enough staff to assess all the input and information they receive. Bernie Horn, policy director for the Center for Policy Alternatives, a liberal think tank that works on state issues, argues: "State legislators are underpaid, understaffed and overwhelmed with work. Their lack of resources makes them vulnerable. . . . They're susceptible to influence even when they're well meaning."[2]

One proposed reform is to devote more resources to legislative professionalism. Dunbar and Rush quote former Indiana senator Greg Server: "To make us more effective, we've got to have more staff . . . to decrease the influence of lobbyists. We need to have people who can help us do research."[3] Ironically, another important recent trend in several states—term limits—may act in the other direction. Some political scientists believe that lobbyists may become even more powerful in the future as term limits force out experienced legislators and replace them with newer legislators without the same political experience and savvy.

Even though the policy stakes are high for interest groups, lobbying can be expensive and difficult if they have to reproduce efforts across fifty

2. Ibid., p. 2.
3. Ibid., p. 3.

states. To become more efficient, some lobbying groups have coordinated their multistate efforts. Though his report is highly partisan, Penniman (2002) documents how the American Legislative Exchange Council (ALEC), which bills itself as "a bipartisan, individual membership association of state legislators" is actually a conservative corporate group trying to shape state legislative agendas in favor of business interests. ALEC uses informational conferences and forums and actually drafts model legislation for state legislatures (see also Greenblatt 2003b). It has become quite powerful; one-third of all state legislators—65 percent Republican and 35 percent Democratic—are members of ALEC. In 1999 and 2000, ALEC claims, states collectively adopted 450 of its model laws. Some liberal policy groups are emerging to act as counterweights to ALEC's pressure, most notably the Center for Policy Alternatives.

Campaign finance reform is obviously one area that could help to reduce interest group pressure, though it is highly controversial. More states are also requiring further information from lobbyists about their expenditures and activities. At a minimum, that promotes "transparency" by allowing interested observers to see which groups are spending their money on what kinds of activities. Some states have also passed more restrictive laws on when former state officials can work for interested parties in order to reduce one aspect of the "revolving door" concern, a reform demonstrated to have significant influence over telecommunications price ratios in chapter 4.

Generally, however, it seems that interest group pressure is a fact of state regulatory life. And, of course, not all interest group input is negative or inequitable—lobbying produces information for legislatures and demonstrates a threshold level of concerns by interested parties. Still, in shaping state regulatory policy, a more pluralist interest group environment seems preferable to one dominated by a subset of strong interests.

Administrative Oversight

In 1946 the U.S. Congress passed the Administrative Procedures Act (APA) to provide general guidelines for most federal agencies regarding how to inform interested parties about changes in rules and regulations and about the procedures and processes necessary to develop new ones. Later most of the states followed suit with their own APAs or similar laws. These APAs are important for structuring the relationships between legislatures and regulatory agencies which, as the studies in this book demonstrate, can have important consequences for regulatory policies.

Research twenty years ago by Scholz (1981), which did not include data for all U.S. states, found that at least thirty-six states had adopted legislation based on the 1961 Model Administrative Procedures Act. Like the federal APA of 1946, these state laws standardized procedures for notifying the public, holding open rule-making hearings, receiving testimony, and issuing final regulations. Many state APAs go beyond federal requirements in insisting that proposed regulations be justified by the formal hearings record, and some require written justifications specifying the regulators' reasons and evidence supporting the proposal. As of 1981, on paper at least twenty-four states required cost analyses for major regulatory proposals. Some of the earliest states to pass APAs did so in the 1950s; most passed them in the 1960s and 1970s. Although considered a basic element of good government in most states, in a few APAs have been controversial—for example, a first attempt at codification of rules failed in 1943 in the Pennsylvania statehouse, another attempt succeeded in 1946 but was repealed in 1947, and Pennsylvania finally enacted an APA much later, in 1968. Today, nearly all states and the District of Columbia have some kind of APA.

State APAs often include the following elements: all proposed and adopted rules of every agency covered by the APA must be published somewhere, usually in a code and a register; proposed rules and final rules are filed with the secretary of state; and opportunities are created for legislative and judicial review of the regulations.[4] Some state legislatures, such as Alaska's, can veto administrative regulations directly. In Ohio, a concurrent resolution from the House of Representatives and the Senate may invalidate a proposed rule. The APA requirement for public hearings prior to passage of new regulations takes a variety of forms: hearings are mandatory in some states (such as Indiana, Kentucky, Nebraska), mandatory if a certain number of people or certain organizations request it (Arkansas, Maine, Wyoming—in New Jersey, a public hearing on a proposed rule is held "if sufficient public interest is shown"), up to the agencies themselves (California, Utah), or no hearings are definitely required (Missouri).

Some interest groups have gotten favorable treatment written directly into their state APAs. Small businesses, for example, are shielded explicitly from the adverse impacts of regulation in Florida and Ohio and face different compliance standards in New York.

4. Information on the specific elements of state APAs was gathered from various state websites.

Most APAs require agencies to prepare fiscal impact analyses of some sort, which can vary from simple descriptive assessments to detailed cost-benefit analyses. Generally, APAs require more rigorous analyses for more major regulations. In Indiana, for example, the APA requires that each agency submit a proposed rule with an estimated economic impact greater than $500,000 to the legislative service agency, which then prepares a fiscal analysis.

Many states have added "sunset" provisions to their APAs, so that inertia does not result in the addition of new rules and regulations while none are ever eliminated. By 1990 more than two-thirds of the states had some sunset provisions in place, often for regulatory agencies. For example, in Arizona, at least once in five years, each agency is supposed to review all of its rules to determine whether any should be repealed or amended. In Texas agencies are supposed to review a rule not later than the fourth anniversary of the effective date, and again every four years after that date. In Utah every agency rule that is in effect on February 28 of any calendar year expires on May 1 of that year (with some exceptions) unless it has been reauthorized by the legislature. Although these sunset provisions sound rigorous, in practice sunset approaches, like zero-based budgeting, have often not achieved many of their goals (Gormley 1989), though Lyons and Freeman (1984) find some evidence that sunset provisions do make both the legislative and executive branches more aware of the legislative oversight role.

While APAs generally stand as basic foundational statements of state rule-making procedures, states do alter them from time to time. For example, Minnesota realized that it had developed an increasingly complicated and rule-bound formal rule-making process, prompting the governor, legislature, and regulated communities to call for a review. In 2000 the Minnesota legislature created the Rules Reform Task Force, which proposed to extend the governor's veto authority, amend notice requirements to the legislature, reduce cases where state rules differ from federal requirements, and generally reduce regulatory burdens. Mississippi reformed its APA in 1999 to increase public access, as citizens previously had little realistic opportunity to comment before an agency. In an example of interest group pressure for change in procedures, North Carolina's largest business group, Citizens for Business and Industry, argued that the state APA fails to incorporate the principle that agencies have the burden of demonstrating that every rule adopted is needed and appropriate, no broader than necessary, and cost-effective. Among other reforms, the group argues for a stronger legislative review of regulations and improvement in the oversight and review of administrative decisions by independent third parties such as administrative law judges.

Regulatory Reviews

In addition to the procedural restrictions and analytic requirements of most state APAs, some state legislatures have held explicit formal reviews of their regulatory policies. Most state legislatures played some role in oversight of regulatory agencies in the 1990s. Ethridge (1984) provides some evidence that rather than being neutral in effect, regulatory rule review was employed by business groups as an opportunity to use legislative input to reverse state agency decisions they did not like. Maestas, Gerber, and Dometrius (2003) find in separate surveys of state agency heads that state legislatures with greater authority to review agency rules are more likely to be reported as influential over rule-making decisions.

Unlike at the federal level, scholars have not developed microlevel studies of individual state legislative committees and their oversight of agencies under their purview, so little is known about how that process operates. Probably such committees are engaging in some oversight in some states. The reviews discussed here have been broad in scope, and correspondingly expensive and time-consuming, which is probably why only a few states have undertaken them.

Hahn (2000) examines these cases. He notes that the Arizona legislature started a continuous regulatory review process in 1986, expanded in 1993, to ascertain whether economic benefits exceeded regulatory costs. Arizona found that about half of the nearly 1,400 rules reviewed in 1996 required some modification. The New York legislature instituted a one-time review starting in 1995, probably to counterbalance Governor Pataki's regulatory efforts (see below). Massachusetts reviewed about 1,600 regulations in 1996 and identified 19 percent for repeal and 44 percent for modification. In 1994 Virginia started a continuous review process, examining over 1,450 regulations and recommending that 30 percent be repealed and 41 percent modified. When one combines these legislative reviews with California's executive review, on average these states have repealed about 20–30 percent of the reviewed regulations completely, modified another 40 percent, and left about 30–40 percent untouched. At a minimum, then, more than half the regulations on the state books were eliminated or changed by these comprehensive analyses. This suggests that other states could streamline their regulations and perhaps reduce economic burdens with similar reviews.

In addition to their own legislative efforts, some state legislatures have worked with their governor to improve regulatory oversight. For example, in Michigan Governor Engler established the Governor's Office of Regulatory Reform by executive order in 1995, which the legislature then institutionalized and funded by statute in 2000.

Gubernatorial Reforms

The quantitative studies in this book and those by other scholars largely do not demonstrate clear evidence for the influence of state governors over regulation, though this is probably due to the lack of good measures of gubernatorial power and ideology. Simple party affiliation is often used, but it is not enough to discern different gubernatorial approaches. I do find some evidence about the role of divided government, when different parties control the legislature and the executive branch, which begins to bring in the governor's role relative to the legislatures, and there is substantial anecdotal evidence.

Governors are major players in state economic policy. Although the appointment powers of governors have not been greatly expanded in recent decades, on average governors stay in office twice as long as they did thirty years ago, and their office staffs have grown from an average of eleven to over fifty. Thus they have greater resources and time to influence policy decisions. Studies show that governors with more resources and more centralized authority generate more legislation (Gray and Lowery 1995), are more often cited as innovative (Hedge 1998, p. 107), and are more effective in shaping economic policies (Brace 1993).

Because regulation is a critical component of economic policy, several governors recently have established oversight offices to reduce regulation and to oversee the state agencies as they engage in the process of developing new regulations. To some extent the goals of these offices are ideological—to reduce regulations as much as possible. This is supported by the fact that conservative Republican governors established most of these offices. But these offices also usually provide review of regulations, ombudsmanlike services for frustrated businesses that seek rapid permitting, and they link their regulatory goals to state economic and job development. Such an agency can also coordinate regulatory activities across agencies and provide a single point of accountability that is often lacking in widespread agency decisions.

These state executive offices can be viewed as parallel to federal efforts over the past thirty years, especially presidential attempts to give the Office of Management and Budget (OMB) and within OMB the Office of Information and Regulatory Affairs (OIRA) greater oversight powers (see Waterman 1989). In some cases they also provide a state-level equivalent to the 1994 Republican Congress's Contract with America effort to increase cost-benefit analysis, oversee agency decisions, and reduce regulatory burdens, as partially codified in the 1996 Congressional Review Act.

Certainly, the timing of these gubernatorial offices shows influence from federal politics. For example, Arizona developed the first such gubernatorial office of regulatory reform in 1981, just one year after the federal government established OIRA in OMB under the Paperwork Reduction Act of 1980. A few other states followed quickly, such as Colorado and Pennsylvania. Then there was a long period without the establishment of new state offices. More recently, after the 1994 Contract with America, several other states, usually with Republican governors, established centralized offices. The Republican governors who instituted or expanded these oversight bodies include Pete Wilson in California, John Engler in Michigan, and George Pataki in New York.

Several states without explicit gubernatorial offices of regulation review nevertheless have given governors similar or related powers. For example, in Indiana the APA notes that the governor may disapprove a rule without cause and rescind an adopted rule by an executive order. The Louisiana APA provides that the governor may use an executive order to suspend or veto any rules or regulations. In Kentucky if a legislative administrative regulation review subcommittee finds problems, it transmits the regulation to the governor, who determines if it will be withdrawn or amended. Maryland has joint executive and legislative evaluation of regulations; if an agency disagrees with committee recommendation, the governor makes a final decision. In North Dakota an agency must issue a regulatory analysis if the governor requests it.

Arizona established an explicit governor's office by executive order in 1981: the Governor's Regulatory Review Council, which has six members, chaired by the director of the Department of Administration.[5] The council represents the final step in the rule-making process for most Arizona agencies. It is designed to ensure that the rules are necessary, not

5. Again, the specific details on these state gubernatorial offices come from state websites.

duplicative, and cause no adverse impact on the public. It also strives to achieve clear and concise regulations that are consistent with legislative intent and in which the benefits exceed the costs. If a rule does not meet these criteria, the council sends it back to an agency for reconsideration. The council takes public testimony before making a decision, even though the rule has already received public input earlier in the agency process.

Colorado and Pennsylvania established related offices soon after Arizona, although theirs are not explicitly part of the governor's office. Colorado established the Office of Regulatory Reform in 1981 to review rules and hold public hearings about them. It oversees the work of the Colorado Department of Regulatory Agencies. Pennsylvania established the Independent Regulatory Review Commission (IRRC) in 1982, which meets twice a month. The commission has five members who serve for three years and can be reappointed once. Each one of the caucus leaders of the Senate and House of Representatives appoints one commissioner and the governor appoints the fifth. The IRRC reviews all regulations established by nearly all Pennsylvania agencies based on whether the promulgating agency has the statutory authority to enact the regulations and whether the regulation is consistent with the intent of the legislature. If the proposed regulations meet these criteria, the IRRC then considers their economic impact, reasonableness, and clarity. The IRRC has no authority to enforce existing regulations and can only review current regulations once they have been in effect for at least three years.

More states moved toward some degree of centralization of regulatory review in the mid-1990s. (One of the more important organizations established to centralize and streamline regulatory decisionmaking was New York's Office of Regulatory Reform [GORR], examined in detail below.) Through executive order in 1995, Michigan governor John Engler created the Office of Regulatory Reform (ORR), an agency designed to review proposed rules, coordinate the processing of rules by state agencies, and work with agencies to streamline the rule-making process and to improve public access. A 2002 executive order transferred the ORR to the Department of Management and Budget, mimicking the relationship between the federal OMB and OIRA. Each agency is supposed to prepare an annual regulatory plan that reviews the agency's rules and to submit it to the ORR together with the list of new rules expected the next year. From 1995 through 2001, the ORR claims to have rescinded 4,979 rules, amended another 3,118, and coordinated the promulgation of 1,311 new ones. Since 2000 the ORR has produced the state's three administrative rule publications, the Michigan Register, the Michigan Administrative Code, and the Annual Administrative Code Supplement.

Also in 1995, in California Governor Pete Wilson issued an executive order requiring all state agencies to "develop a process for planning all regulations, regulatory policies, goals and objectives in a rulemaking calendar," which is supposed to help clarify their primary goal and show how regulation achieves the goal, consider alternatives, and estimate costs. An initial executive review identified nearly 4,000 regulations for repeal and 1,700 for modification (Hahn 2000). With oversight, the order also established a sunset review by 1999 to force all agencies to revisit and review existing regulations.

Washington was next with an executive order in 1997 creating the Governor's Subcabinet on Management Improvement and Results (GSMR). The goal was to ensure that state regulations are reviewed on an open and systematic basis and that they meet standards of need; reasonableness; effectiveness; clarity; fairness; stakeholder involvement; coordination among regulatory agencies; and consistency with the APA, legislative intent, and statutory authority. The GSMR is chaired by the governor's deputy chief of staff and is staffed by, and composed of, the heads of major agencies. The GSMR studies, recommends, and develops special pilot projects to make improvements in state regulation. In related activity, the governor's special assistant for business and regulatory reform created a coordinated system of permits and clear standards to promote state competitiveness while keeping in place important safeguards for citizen health and safety.

Virginia's governor acted next, with an executive order in 1998 (updating one from 1994) that established procedures for review of all new, revised, and existing agency regulations. This added a presumption in favor of the least burdensome and intrusive regulation. Under these procedures, before providing the registrar of regulation a proposed "notice of intended regulatory action," the agency head must submit a proposal to the appropriate governor's secretary and to the Department of Planning and Budget outlining the reasons to promulgate a new or revised regulation. The economic and regulatory analysis section of the Department of Planning and Budget reviews the proposal to determine whether it complies with all requirements and conducts an economic impact analysis within forty-five days, assessing cost and benefits and considering less intrusive alternatives, unintended consequences, and effects on employment, localities, and private property. Generally, the whole process of promulgating a new regulation in Virginia takes about eighteen months under these procedures. Under a sunset provision, regulations are not to be considered permanent and are subject to periodic reevaluations at specified dates.

Thus a number of states, usually under Republican governors, have moved to centralize regulatory review in the governor's office, following the federal pattern. Most of this activity has taken place in larger states with more staff and more professional government operations. It seems appropriate to foster centralized review of agency regulations in a governor's office. Voters increasingly hold governors more responsible for the performance of their state economies. By gaining greater control over regulatory policy, governors gain tools to achieve their goals, and voters gain an easier point of accountability for regulatory policy.

New York Governor's Office of Regulatory Reform

GORR was established in November 1995 by Executive Order 20. The office pulled together some predecessor organizations, going back to a permit assistance program from 1979 and the 1983 Office of Management Assistance established by Governor Cuomo. The 1995 impetus came largely from New York's loss of jobs from 1991 through 1995—a loss that newly elected Governor George Pataki attributed partly to excessive and unrealistic bureaucratic regulations. In his 1995 State of the State Address, Pataki noted: "The state bureaucracy has a reputation and a record of imposing rules and regulations that go far beyond what the Legislature intended. We want to stop that immediately, to make sure agencies remain true to the letter of the law and don't impose burdens that will be a drag on New York's ability to create and retain jobs." Under the order, newly proposed as well as existing regulations are subject to cost-benefit analysis, risk assessment, and peer review. As they assess regulations, GORR staff members confer with business groups, local governments, and not-for-profit organizations about their concerns. GORR claims to emphasize common sense, prudent science, and sound economics as it balances cost and benefits and assesses risk.

GORR is not a merely symbolic organization—it has forty full-time employees and a fiscal 2003 budget of $3.7 million. GORR is broken down into three teams: development, health and human services, and labor/workers' compensation, each with jurisdiction over several agencies. Each team includes a team leader, at least one attorney, and a research analyst. GORR also includes a specialized permit assistance team for business assistance.

There is not yet a thorough, independent evaluation of GORR, so one must rely on GORR's own information. The office claims that through 2002 it has generated one-time annual savings of more than $3 billion for New York State. It led a decline of more than 50 percent in the issuance of new state regulations. For these efforts, GORR won the Vision 2000 Award for Regulatory Reform from the U.S. Small Business Administration.

It is useful to consider specific accomplishments by each team. The development team claims a diverse range of successes, especially related to environmental issues. In 1995 GORR assisted the state Department of Environmental Conservation with improvements in the state SIP that led to $5.5 million in compliance savings. More specifically, in 1997 GORR's analysis helped delay the implementation (until 2000, when better rules, also acceptable to the federal EPA, could be developed) of a state "Clean Fuels Fleet" bill that would have cost $700 million in a ten-county downstate region for large truck and bus fleets, including school districts. The bill would have achieved only minimal reduction in targeted nitrous oxide emissions and was to be rendered obsolete by new, cleaner diesel engines. GORR's development team also convinced the Department of Environmental Conservation to eliminate special state standards for recycling labeling, substituting nationally accepted FTC standards, making it easier for businesses to market products in New York.

In an example that does not reduce social regulation but seeks to improve it, the GORR health and human services team was instrumental in developing a 1997 state regulation that allows New Yorkers to take an AIDS test in the privacy of their own home with FDA-approved kits; results are obtained directly from a lab using an anonymous numerical identification system. Previously, only doctors or other licensed medical professionals could order the test, discouraging testing.

The GORR labor team helped create a 1995 pilot project that encouraged alternative dispute resolution between construction industry employers and organized labor, which resulted in quicker resolution of cases, less litigation, and a more timely return to work, producing annual savings estimated at $63 million. In 1997 the labor team worked with the state public service commission to reform electric power plant construction rules, including a "one-stop" approval process for the siting of generation facilities, cutting existing regulatory procedures in half.

The GORR permit team handles more than 75,000 phone calls each year regarding state business permits. Its website provides specific information on 167 different business types, ranging from accounting to video stores to bed-and-breakfasts to residential general contractors and lawn and garden services. In terms of specific accomplishments, it cites its solution to a 1995 case in which an entrepreneur wanted to hire disabled workers to produce a special pillow designed to prevent Sudden Infant Death Syndrome (SIDS), but was blocked by the need for approval from the State Bedding Board, a state regulatory agency that existed on paper but had no inspectors and had not even met in ten years.

Since I have not performed or seen an independent evaluation of GORR, it is appropriate to be cautious in evaluating these claims of success. But clearly GORR aims to reduce business regulation, to accelerate new applications, and to coordinate across agencies. The AIDS and SIDS cases demonstrate some sensitivity to social regulatory concerns in addition to the broader goal of cutting back business regulations. GORR clearly has had an impact on the regulatory environment in New York State.

Agency Reform

As they do with their legislatures, states vary widely in the professionalism of their agencies. But this is one area where most observers agree that overall, the states have expanded their capacities and capabilities over time. In particular, a number of states were aggressive in the 1990s in their implementation of "reinventing government" reforms (Osborne and Gaebler 1992). And taking on new responsibilities can help foster greater capacity. Ferejohn and Weingast (1997, p. 162) write: "If the states take on more responsibilities, they will become more vigorous and vital political units; they will therefore attract public attention and support, along with high-quality officials."

Bureaucratic agencies are creatures of state legislatures and governors, and governors appoint most of the regulatory agency heads in most states. Thus while they have some scope for independent action and discretion, they are also constrained by current political overseers, or principals, as well as long-established procedures and principles, such as those incorporated in state APAs. For example, in their study of state bureaucratic "reinvention," Kellough and Selden (2003) find that legislative professionalism is the variable most positively associated with successful reinvention (with state labor unions as the strongest opponent to such changes).

As my studies demonstrate that the structures of state agencies influence their regulatory policy outputs, states might pay more attention to bureaucratic structures. The specific structures tend to last a long time, although states also periodically pursue waves of reform and reorganizations. The evidence now seems clear that elected regulatory commissioners are more likely than appointed ones to favor broader consumer interests in regulation and to constrain regulated businesses. If that is the balance states prefer, they should move toward more elected regulators, even though this is likely to reduce the overall power of governors, who presumably have more influence over the regulators they appoint.

Teaford (2002) emphasizes that the states were not able to develop their own administrative capacities until they had also developed stable and consistent revenue sources, such as income taxes and sales taxes. In some states these are relatively recent events. But compared to the administrative capacity that is required for education, welfare, and transportation programs, regulation is much cheaper, and regulatory agency budgets are often partly financed by fees paid by the regulated businesses. Thus further administrative professionalism of regulatory agencies is more a function of political will than of state treasuries.

In the specific area of bureaucratic monitoring of financial firms, the studies demonstrate that more state inspectors and inspections find more potentially insolvent firms sooner, likely reducing resolution costs in the long run. Clearly, greater budgetary investment in the oversight and enforcement arms of such agencies is an appropriate reform, particularly as greater industry deregulation takes place in infrastructure industries like electric power and telecommunications, to help reduce or prevent problems like Enron and WorldCom. Conservatives often fear that industry innovation will be reduced or frozen by greater bureaucratic monitoring; while this is a potential problem, it is a trade-off with effective oversight and perceived firm legitimacy.

Since capture is such a concern at the state level, and agency capture is one form of this, some reforms might address it. Above I noted some reforms related to two other nodes on the iron triangle of captured subgovernments: interest groups and legislatures. The remaining scope of this problem can be reduced at the third node by developing stronger and more resourceful bureaucratic agencies. The most egregious capture takes place in state occupational regulation, in which legislatures have often allowed effective "self-regulation" by interest groups. Though additional citizen members of licensing boards do not necessarily alter policy outputs, centralization of occupational regulation in one administrative body appears to reduce the likelihood of capture of a number of small, occupation-specific boards by opening the process to more actors and by making such an agency less beholden to any particular group. For example, the Wisconsin Department of Regulation and Licensing provides centralized administrative services to twenty-six regulatory boards with responsibilities for regulating over a hundred professions, occupations, and business establishments. The New York State Office of Professional Standards is an arm of the state education department and has a very high level of professionalism in regulating thirty-nine different professions. Of course, Wisconsin and New York have always been among the more progressive and innovative regulatory states, going back to their initial establishment of PUCs in 1907. Other states followed then, so this may be another appropriate regulatory experimental reform for other states to imitate.

CHAPTER FIFTEEN

Legal Actors in
the Regulatory Process

with

SCOTT GRAVES

COLIN PROVOST

Over the past twenty-five years, one clear trend in regulation and other areas of public policy is the increasing policy impact of courts, legal decisions, and legal actors. While it was not possible to measure and incorporate legal considerations into most of the empirical studies of state regulation, it is a cross-cutting phenomenon from which few regulatory arenas have escaped. Losers from legislative and bureaucratic decisions often challenge important regulatory decisions in court. This has been true in telecommunications and environmental regulation especially but also in electricity, insurance, financial regulation, and occupational restrictions. This allows interest groups another channel through which to try to influence regulatory policy.

Several developments supported this trend. One was the desire by some judges to play a more active role in public policy; originally the term *judicial activism* was aimed at liberal judges who decided in some cases to take over prisons or schools or to force zoning changes (Wilson 1989; Haar 1996), but now it is sometimes applied to conservative judges who seem to want to make new policy and reform the relationship between the federal government and the states (see Nivola 2001; Briffault 2003). A second contributing factor was that, especially in the 1970s (see Gormley 1989), Congress explicitly increased the standing of affected groups to encourage, and sometimes even financially supported, legal challenges to agency decisions. Groups that were previously not involved, such as environmental and consumer groups, developed expertise in the legal arena and, with some successes, found this route to be a fruitful one, especially when facing pro-business federal or state administrations. Third, as discussed in more detail below, the expansion of product liability and tort law gave consumers more rights in suing firms related to products and services, which has become a de facto form of regulation, especially as state attorneys general expanded their activities.

Thus public agencies, and particularly regulatory agencies, now operate in an environment in which legal challenges to their decisions are common. For example, Melnick (1983) noted that more than 75 percent of EPA rule makings are challenged in court by one party or another, even though courts side with the agency on a clear majority of these challenges (see also Wilson 1989). While environmental regulation may be a particularly salient area prone to legal challenges, other areas of regulation also face a more complicated and contentious legal environment.

In addition, state attorneys general (SAGs) have emerged, partly in response to a reduction in consumer regulatory protections from the federal government, to use legal strategies to regulate businesses. This chapter analyzes these trends—the growing role of state courts in regulation and the emergence of SAGs and "regulation by litigation." As with legislatures, governors, and bureaucracies, the role of legal actors cuts across several areas of state regulation.

State Courts

Scholars have paid considerable attention to the increased judicialization of regulatory policy at the federal level. Even as interested parties challenge agency decisions, scholars find that federal regulatory agencies often win their cases (Canon and Giles 1972; Humphries and Songer 1999). Agencies appear in court frequently and may benefit from the experience and familiarity that comes with regular practice. Songer and Sheehan (1992) found that the federal government is the most consistently successful litigant in the courts of appeals, in part because of its resources and expertise (see also Sheehan, Mishler, and Songer 1992). There is also some evidence that the federal government is a strategic litigator, appealing decisions only when the likelihood of victory is high (Zorn 2001).

Scholars have not generated nearly as much research at the state level, though the increasing availability of data is leading to more study of the policymaking role of state supreme courts (Glick 1999; Brace, Langer, and Hall 2000).[1] Such research is overdue, as state supreme courts are the courts of last resort in most cases and, parallel to collective state legislative activity as compared to congressional laws, their collective caseloads easily dwarf the number of cases decided by the Supreme Court. Furthermore, like the federal appellate courts, state supreme courts create rules of legal procedure that guide the administration of law for the lower state courts, which handle the bulk of litigation in the United States, and these rules can have substantial impacts on the outcome of cases. And, as they have with bureaucratic agencies, states have greatly improved the operation and professionalism of their court systems over time (see Teaford 2002).

There have been a few simple studies of judicial activism in state courts and the frequency of judicial review across issue areas (Glick 1991). In the early 1980s, for example, Emmert found that state supreme courts heard about 24 percent of the challenges to economic regulation legislation appealed to them, and they overturned legislation in 23 percent of those cases. In contrast, courts heard only 8 percent of civil liberties cases appealed but overturned legislation in 34 percent of those accepted for review (reported in Glick 1991), suggesting a greater desire of state judges to consider regulation challenges but greater deference to agency decisions in the outcomes.

Scholars have focused some attention on the institutional and political differences between state supreme courts to explain agenda and decision differences. Atkins and Glick (1976) found that courts in industrialized, politically competitive states handled a larger number of regulatory cases. More recent research has considered the influence of judicial selection mechanisms (Brace and Hall 1997; Langer 2002) and the structure of legal systems (Emmert 1992; Wenzel, Bowler, and Lanoue 1997). These scholars find that the political context of state supreme court justices—elected or appointed and under what system—affects how judges make decisions. Examining state PUCs, insurance commissions, and education agencies, Hanssen (2000) found that bureaucracies in states with more independent courts—that is, with appointed judges—are more likely to use more resources in developing actions that will be protected from judicial review.

---

1. Following other scholars, we use the terms *state supreme courts* and *state courts of last resort* interchangeably.

Although state supreme courts have a variety of ways to influence regulatory policy, the use of judicial review to reverse administrative decisions or overturn enforcements of regulation is the most visible method available and likely the courts' most effective tool. Our question here is whether state supreme courts are more or less likely to reverse state regulatory agency decisions than are the federal courts. To make this comparison, a parallel figure for the federal courts is needed. The data indicate that about 37 percent of regulatory actions are struck by the federal circuit courts of appeal.[2] This is similar to Humphries and Songer (1999), who found that federal administrative agencies' decisions were struck down in 42 percent of the cases over a similar time period (1969–88).[3] A parallel analysis for the U.S. Supreme Court shows a 39 percent overall reversal rate for all regulation cases, similar to the circuit court figure.[4]

Turning to state supreme courts, the data demonstrate reversal rates of about 36 percent, which are not much different from either federal appellate courts or the Supreme Court.[5] Thus state supreme courts support regulatory agency decisions most of the time, in about two-thirds of these cases, a rate quite similar to that of the important federal level courts. We do not find that state supreme courts are being overly "activist" in overturning regulations, but neither are they more deferential to state agency decisions than federal judges.

2. These data come from the Multi User Court of Appeals Database, Donald R. Songer, Principal Investigator, NSF # SES-8912678.

3. This relatively small difference can be explained by the fact that this sample includes private regulatory enforcement suits.

4. The data come from the Supreme Court Database, Harold J. Spaeth, Principal Investigator, NSF # SES-8313733, SES-8812935, SES-8842925, SES-9112755.

5. A regulation is reversed in 1,046 of the 2,682 cases in the data set. These data come from Paul Brace and Melinda Gann Hall, "The State Supreme Court Data Project," November 2001 (www.ruf.rice.edu/~pbrace/statecourt/ [January 2003]). The data set contains all cases decided by courts of last resort in each of the fifty states if the court in question decides fewer than or equal to two hundred cases and a random sample of two hundred cases from those issuing more than two hundred formal opinions (signed or per curiam) for the years 1995 and 1996. From this set of cases, we identified those falling into the civil government category and selected from those the decisions in which some government regulation was at issue. For most observations the dependent variable, whether the regulation at issue was reversed, could be discerned by outcome variables such as the winning party and whether the court had reversed an administrative action, but a few cases had to be eliminated due to ambiguities in the outcome.

Explaining Regulatory Reversals

To understand better why and when state supreme courts do reverse regulatory agency decisions in those 36 percent of cases (and not in others), the results of a probit analysis of regulatory reversals appear in table 15-1. Based on prior research largely done at the federal and state levels, the explanatory factors in this model come from three general categories: those relating to the litigation environment of the particular case, state court-related institutional factors, and state political conditions.

The litigation environment is captured with three variables. The first indicates whether there was an agency action preceding the court's decision. Governments are parties to all the cases in this study, but cases preceded by a procedure or action of a regulatory agency may garner more deference from judges due to the agency expertise presumably brought to bear, compared to cases without agency action. A second variable is whether it is a class action case, usually a more high-profile case affecting larger numbers of people. A third variable is whether interested parties filed amicus briefs, which provides some sense of case salience.

Institutional differences are measured by variables identifying whether the state has an intermediate appeals court, without which supreme courts are likely to hear many mandatory, but perhaps meritless, appeals, and by whether justices in the state are selected in competitive elections or appointed by the political branches.[6] These two categories of judicial selection leave merit selection and retention as the excluded, or baseline, category in the analysis.

Finally, to capture relevant political conditions, the analysis includes a variable measuring Democratic party control, indicating whether the Ranney interparty competition for control of government from 1995 to 1998 reflects advantage to the Democratic Party, a Ranney folded index that measures the degree of one-party dominance in the state,[7] regardless

6. States use five different methods to select justices for their highest courts: partisan elections, nonpartisan elections, gubernatorial appointment, legislative appointment, and merit selection. While most states require justices to be reappointed—sometimes in the same manner as their selection, sometimes in a different manner—a few states grant justices lifetime appointments. Partisan elections, according to advocates of judicial reform, should make judges more accountable and decrease their incentives for activism against prevailing political winds. However, the insulation of nonpartisan elections from partisan election politics is likely overstated.

7. The Ranney index is rescaled to a unit scale, such that perfectly competitive states, with no major party advantage, are coded zero, while perfect single party dominance registers a one.

of polarity, and an interaction term of these two variables, which captures the degree of Democratic Party dominance in the state.[8] Political competitiveness may influence judges, as legal scholars such as Eskridge (1988), Macey (1986), and Posner (1997) depict judicial interpretation and review as a monitoring mechanism to overcome deformities in the politically competitive market for statutes, urging judges to respond to the degree of public interest they detect in legislation. The table also includes a variable measuring the ideology of the state justices, which substantial research indicates is important on the U.S. Supreme Court (Segal and Spaeth 1993). Although state supreme court justices sit at the top of the judicial hierarchies of their states, they are still subject to some oversight from the federal court system. Furthermore, with the exception of those who hold life tenure, they face other political constraints. The measure of the ideology of the courts is from the party-adjusted justice ideology (PAJID) scores of Brace, Langer, and Hall (2000). For each case, the relevant variable is the median ideology of the justices who heard the case to represent the ideology of the court.

Results

Several explanatory factors are significant in statistical and substantive terms. Elected and appointed judges are both less likely to overturn regulations than judges who get their position by merit retention, deferring more to agencies. Merit retention may make judges more confident in their ability to counter the choices of other institutional actors in the regulatory process.

More liberal courts are less likely to overturn regulations. This makes sense and fits in well with results in earlier chapters about more liberal legislatures being more supportive of more regulation and more consumer-oriented regulation. Again, on average, judges provide outcomes that we would expect, given their ideologies. All else being equal, state supreme courts are more likely to reverse regulations in states with a stronger Democratic than Republican Party, though this finding varies with the strength of party control. Some state courts may be acting as brakes on what they perceive to be excessive regulation passed by Democratic legislatures.

When there has been an explicit agency action, courts are more likely to overturn a regulation. Courts are also somewhat more likely to overturn regulations faced with class action suits. On the other hand, the am-

---

8. The inclusion of this variable isolates the independent effects of Democratic Party control, Democratic Party dominance, and Republican Party dominance (measured by the Ranney folded index main effect).

Table 15-1. *State Supreme Court Overturns of Regulatory Decisions, 1995*[a]

Explanatory factors	Coefficient
Agency action	0.003**
	(0.0012)
Class action	0.426*
	(0.197)
Amicus filed	0.071
	(0.105)
Intermediate appeals court	0.042
	(0.075)
Justices elected	−1.39*
	(0.069)
Justices appointed	−0.304***
	(.115)
Democratic party control	−1.71**
	(0.677)
Ranney folded index	−0.325
	(0.289)
Democratic control/Ranney index	2.09***
	(0.748)
Median justice ideology	−0.0053*
	(0.0027)
Constant	−.192

Summary statistics
Wald Chi^2 = 29.56***
N = 2,592

*Significant at .1 level; **significant at .05 level; ***significant at .01 level.
a. Standard errors (robust, corrected for clustering on states) are in parentheses.

icus briefs by interest groups, often perceived to measure the salience of a case, and whether a state has intermediate courts are not significant at standard levels of statistical confidence.

Thus state supreme courts overturn state regulations at about the same rate that federal courts overturn regulations. They are not appreciably more or less activist in that sense. Factors relating to the litigation environment of the case, the state court institutions themselves, and the broader state political environment affect the rate of reversals. Still, state regulatory decisions go to court frequently, and by overturning more than one-third of regulatory decisions, state courts do play a significant role in shaping specific regulatory policies. As some of these conditions change through the adoption of merit selection plans, the continued use of class action suits to advance public policies, and changes in political competition in the states, the relative significance of state supreme courts in regulatory policy will also change over time.

Reforms

It is difficult to say what should be reformed about state courts and regulation without a broader discussion of the role of courts in U.S. society. Eskridge (1988) suggests that interest group pressures within the judicial branch are different, and less intense, than in legislative and administrative arenas, leaving judges qualified to correct the deficiencies and inequities of law- and rule-making in the political branches. Eskridge's ultimate justification for judges to assume this supplemental function is that common law can more easily ameliorate errors of neglect or favoritism endemic to regulations created by legislatures and agencies. In this view, a large amount of judicial oversight is appropriate. Other scholars and judicial analysts might prefer to see the courts be more deferential to the political processes that produced the regulations in the first place.

Although it is clear that state court decisions are important in influencing state regulation, another legal actor has been playing a critical role by bringing new legal challenges related to regulatory issues: the state attorneys general. While adding to the importance of court decisions, the very open and media-friendly approach of these SAGs has added public salience to many state regulatory issues that might otherwise have remained on the political back burners.

State Attorneys General

A very important actor emerged on the state regulatory scene in the last few decades, the state attorney general. In the 1980s as the Reagan administration scaled back federal regulatory enforcement, and as enforcement through litigation and courts became increasingly common in regulation, SAGs moved to center stage. Faced with a void in regulatory enforcement, SAGs expanded their operations into several areas of regulation, including environmental protection, antitrust regulation, and, most important, consumer protection.

The product liability movement was gaining momentum at the same time. Although there are many differences between regulatory enforcement by SAGs and product liability litigation, this new brand of lawsuits helped open the doors for SAGs to sue the tobacco companies and negotiate the largest government settlement in history. Since the final days of the tobacco settlement in 1998, some SAGs have exploited the precedent set in the tobacco lawsuits and have brought lawsuits against lead paint makers, HMOs, and handgun manufacturers.

The role of SAGs has been surrounded by controversy, as they have often sought publicity and future electoral gain from their efforts to zealously protect consumers and sue high-profile corporations such as Microsoft and the tobacco companies. Conservatives, in particular, have been frustrated by SAGs, as they expected the shift of greater regulatory authority to the states to result in less, not greater, enforcement. But the desire of SAGs to get reelected (they are elected in forty-three states and appointed in the other seven) and to move to higher office has motivated many to aggressively seek out market failures and corporate abuses and try to regulate them in the absence of federal activity.

Derthick (2001) illustrates these trends in tobacco litigation: "The more important development for politics and policymaking was [the tort lawyers'] union with a wholly new class of clients—the state attorneys general, who were elected officials of considerable vigor, dynamism, and political ambition. In news photographs they cluster in front of the camera, hair well groomed, jaws thrust forward, eyes intense, as if to pose for their next campaign poster." The list of well-known politicians who were SAGs includes Bill Clinton, Joseph Lieberman, George Deukmejian, Warren Rudman, Bruce Babbitt, and Walter Mondale as well as Senator Jeff Sessions from Alabama and New Jersey state supreme court member Peter Verneiro. Observers have dubbed the National Association of Attorneys General (NAAG), a coordinating group founded in 1907, the "National Association of Aspiring Governors." Provost (2003) finds that since 1980 over 40 percent of SAGs have run for gubernatorial office, though less than 20 percent have actually been elected.

SAGs have discovered that enforcement of consumer protection regulation is salient and highly visible to voters. Ambitious SAGs have tried to gain political credit by suing and regulating businesses, often with multistate lawsuits aimed at protecting consumers from illegal business practices, especially from deceptive or false advertising. One of the earlier examples was in 1988 when SAGs in all fifty states helped develop guidelines to regulate airline advertising in the wake of airline deregulation.[9] More recently, of the forty-one multistate lawsuits filed by SAGs between 1996

9. This action was overturned in 1992 when the Supreme Court ruled that states were preempted by the Airline Deregulation Act.

and 1999, twenty-four were directed at businesses that violated federal and state advertising regulations. This list includes major corporations like Compaq, Sears, Levitz, Honda, and Mitsubishi, but also large numbers of telemarketers, sweepstakes companies, and phony pyramid schemes. Given the prevalence of advertising claims in these industries—and their poor image in the eyes of many consumers—consumer complaints are quite frequent. For example, many SAGs have worked together recently to combat "slamming," a tactic of certain long-distance phone companies in which company representatives sign consumers up for a particular long-distance plan and later change it without notification. In 1997 EqualNet of Houston agreed to pay $225,000 to ten states to settle allegations of slamming. In 1998 a similar settlement was reached between eighteen states and Minimum Rate Pricing, a New Jersey–based long-distance service provider. These cases are attractive for SAGs because settlement money is often redistributed back to consumers. While SAGs are also heavily involved in antitrust, environmental, and utility regulation and criminal prosecutions, the benefits of these regulations to consumers are not as clear as with consumer protection regulation.

Several observers have noted the growing regulatory role of SAGs, but few scholars have presented analytic studies of their impact. Clayton (1994) offers descriptive evidence of their rise to prominence. Zimmerman (1998) got a low response rate to his survey of SAGs to gauge what motivates them to join multistate consumer enforcement actions. Gabel and Hager (2000) attempt to explain why each state joined the tobacco litigation when it did, using an event history model. Spill, Licari, and Ray (2001) demonstrate party differences in pursuing the tobacco litigation. It is clear that the successful emergence of SAGs in consumer protection litigation is partly related to a parallel trend in product liability law.

Product Liability Suits

The product liability movement set legal precedents that would eventually allow SAGs to sue large businesses, such as the tobacco companies. For many years product liability law operated under the general standard of "buyer beware," with the burden on consumers to prove malicious intent by producers, and with liability reduced further by warning labels. Over time tort law gradually overlapped with contract law, and consumers increasingly found themselves on the winning side of product liability litigation. Judges, juries, and policymakers recognized that consumers may suffer from defects in manufacturing, product design, or warnings. It became impossible to separate contract law from tort law because if a product had severe, potentially harmful manufacturing defects, a thorough warning label was not good enough if the probability of injury was sufficiently high. For example, automobile makers had long contended that car injuries were a matter of personal responsibility, but in the 1960s Ralph Nader shifted the frame of the debate by focusing on damage within the cars (secondary collisions) that could be reduced by producer actions (such as providing seatbelts). The 1960s controversy over the need for flame-retardant children's sleepwear also raised questions of personal responsibility versus product standards, resulting in federal action in 1967. Asbestos litigation in the 1970s and 1980s further accelerated the product liability movement, leading to numerous suits that are still in place today and also reinforcing the notion of manufacturers as the responsible party.

Product liability litigation may have reached its peak in the late 1980s, as it became clear that warning labels were not an adequate defense for producers. Numerous critics forecast disastrous economic consequences and the stifling of new product innovation, though Viscusi (2002) suggests that there was some exaggeration of the effects. Still, insurance rates increased greatly for some affected businesses, costs that were passed on to consumers.

Though insurance rates eventually peaked, the precedent for product liability litigation was set. Some lawyers transferred this concept to litigation against tobacco companies, which had previously won suits under the "buyer beware" regime and by outspending their opponents. A few decisions reflected a changed environment in the 1980s—in the 1986 case of *Nathan Henry Horton* v. *The American Tobacco Co.*, the jury awarded no damages, but found that American Tobacco was in fact liable for Horton's death. In 1988 the jury in *Cipollone* v. *Liggett Group, Inc.* ruled that "Liggett was negligent for its failure before 1966, the year the labeling law went into effect, to warn smokers adequately of the risks of smoking and for using advertising that could be interpreted as a warrant of safety" (Derthick 2001, p. 14).

With more scientific and industry insider information about the harm of nicotine, by 1994 tobacco firms were much more vulnerable, and tort lawyers and SAGs saw an opportunity. Using asbestos litigation as a precedent, Mike Moore, SAG of Mississippi, filed suit against tobacco firms in chancery court in 1994, with help from several different plaintiffs' lawyers. His suit was based on the argument that the tobacco companies had burdened the state with millions of dollars in Medicaid costs and that the state should be able to recoup those costs since it was merely a third party in the transaction between smokers and the tobacco companies. A few states made similar cases, and the Liggett group's decision to settle with the states in 1996 marked a major turning point, indicating as it did that tobacco firms were less sure of winning. Sensing vulnerability, by 1998 some forty SAGs filed suit against the tobacco companies. A settlement requires the firms to pay $246 billion to the state governments between 2000 and 2025 and sharply restricts advertising of tobacco products as well as political activity by tobacco firms.

Emboldened by this stunning success, some SAGs then pursued tobacco-style lawsuits against manufacturers of handguns, breast implants, and lead paint. Meanwhile, private tort lawyers continue to press the boundaries of product liability law with suits against HMOs and food manufacturers.

The rise of the product liability movement, culminating in the tobacco litigation, helped set the precedent for regulation through litigation, making regulation of business activity, especially social regulation, significantly different from thirty years earlier. It also fed the hunger of SAGs for attractive cases to pursue.

Recent Examples

In addition to tobacco litigation and crackdowns on telemarketing and telephone slamming, SAGs have been active in a number of regulatory areas. Indeed, before the tobacco cases, aggressive SAGs active in the food nutrition labeling battles of the 1980s were collectively referred to as the "chowhounds." Echoing that "terrier-like" intensity, James Tierney, who served as Maine's attorney general for ten years, notes: "Once the attorneys general have entered a field, they don't go out."[10]

As noted in chapter 1, Eliot Spitzer of New York is the recent SAG "cover boy" (literally, in the Sunday *New York Times Magazine* and *Governing* magazine, among others) for such regulatory activities. His aggressive, but still reasonable, efforts to curb Wall Street excesses garnered significant attention and respect. It revitalized a state role over financial regulation, "reenforcing" SEC and other federal inaction. Says Joseph Borg, director of the Alabama Securities Commission and president of the North American Securities Administrators Association: "State securities cops have

10. Quoted in James Traub, "The Attorney General Goes to War," *New York Times Magazine*, July 16, 2002, p. 40.

a duty to protect investors in their states, something they have been doing longer than the SEC's been around."[11] Traub summarizes: "It is . . . true that the regulation of the stock exchange has traditionally been left to the exchange itself and to the SEC. But Spitzer argued that the regulators had failed to pursue or even recognize the inherent conflict he had uncovered, and he seized on a state securities law, the Martin Act, that had been used in the past to pursue boiler-room operations and Ponzi schemes."[12]

There are many other recent examples. Six northeastern SAGs (including Spitzer) challenged in court the Bush administration's proposal to relax environmental standards for new plants or upgrades of industrial facilities, some twenty-nine SAGs sued Bristol-Myers in a December 2001 antitrust case over the issuance of a generic drug alternative to BuSpar, and eight states have suits against the U.S. Department of Energy over revisions to regulations on appliance energy efficiency. In 2003 ten SAGs pursued action against the consumer service and advertising of EchoStar, a satellite TV broadcaster, a move that was successfully timed to influence a federal regulatory decision about EchoStar's proposed purchase of the Hughes satellite TV operation.

SAG Power

Most generally, each SAG is charged with providing legal representation for his or her state, giving legal advice on public matters in the form of written opinions to other members of state government and in a general sense defending the public interests of the state. Authority to act on behalf of the state's public interests comes primarily from common-law powers and to a lesser extent from state constitutions or specific statutes. To derive power from common law essentially means that an attorney general has vast discretion to determine what is in the public's interest and what is not, and act accordingly. According to Ross (1990, p. 37), the importance of common-law authority was spelled out most clearly in the 1976 federal court decision of *State of Florida ex rel. Shevin* v. *Exxon Corporation*: "The court confirmed that the Attorney General was empowered by common law to institute litigation on his own initiative if he determined that the public interest so required."

---

11. Quoted in Gretchen Morgenson, "A Wall St. Push to Water Down Securities Law," *New York Times,* June 18, 2002, p. A1.
12. Traub, "Attorney General Goes to War," p. 41.

Although common law provides a solid source of authority for SAGs in most states, powers to act in the public interest vary across policy domains as well as across states. For example, in almost all fifty states, the attorney general is entirely responsible for enforcing consumer protection and antitrust regulations. However, authority is typically more limited in policy areas such as environmental protection and utility regulation because other agencies have primary responsibility in those areas. Thus instead of initiating lawsuits at the outset, SAGs often must wait for other agencies to bring complaints to them before they can act. This gives them less total authority in these other areas of regulation since there is a gatekeeping process that screens cases first. Mullen (2000, p. 9) summarizes the institutional structure well with an example from labor regulation: "In 1992, one state's attorney general's office had over 150 active cases brought under the state's wage and hour laws. In 1999 there were fewer than 15 active files under the same attorney general. Why? . . . A Republican governor replaced a Democratic governor and the new labor commissioner gave a much lower priority to wage and hour cases. As a result, the number of complaints dropped considerably."

Before the late 1970s and federal devolution, SAGs were mostly concerned with defending the state's legal interests and providing legal advice to state officials about policy matters. Their role was "merely as ministerial functionaries of the state administration"; they had little influence on the creation of policy (Morris 1987, p. 299). As that role changed, SAGs realized that they had several tools at their disposal to influence regulatory policy. First, they can bring lawsuits at the state or federal level to enforce state regulations. States often act alone in initiating lawsuits, but joint lawsuits and cooperative investigations across states have become increasingly common as the NAAG has helped SAGs share information, reduce costs, and pursue similar goals.

Second, as the chief legal officer of the state, SAGs issue advisory opinions to the governor and legislature. In fifteen states the SAG can draft bills to send to the legislature. Through NAAG, SAGs also lobby Congress to enact or amend specific regulations. For example, during the Reagan administration, SAGs lobbied Congress and the Supreme Court to compel the president to enforce regulatory laws. When this tactic proved unsuccessful, they often lobbied their own state legislatures to pass laws that mirrored the federal statutes.

Third, state attorneys general can file amicus curiae briefs in support of a particular position in federal court cases. A growing literature has documented the rise in amicus briefs as one of the most visible tools of cooperation among SAGs in enforcement of regulatory policy (Clayton 1994; Ross 1990; Zimmerman 1998). By filing an amicus brief in a regulatory case, state attorneys general can signal to the justices their own interest in a case and the importance they attach to it.

SAGs have a number of advantages in putting their issues at the front of the regulation agenda. First, as the head attorney of the state, the attorney general has common-law powers to initiate prosecutions in a very broad manner. The most basic and general duties of the state attorney general are to defend the state's laws and defend the state in court. They have broad authority to enforce those laws as they see fit. SAGs have authority to file civil lawsuits against businesses and take them to court. By taking the case straight to court, the attorney general can effectively bypass the governor as well as the state legislature. For example, when the governor of Mississippi, Kirk Fordice, sued his own SAG, Mike Moore, to prevent him from pursuing litigation against the tobacco companies, Moore was joined by thirty-eight other state attorneys general as amici curiae and Fordice's lawsuit was defeated.

As SAGs expanded their activities, they enhanced their resources by pursuing cases together, increasing the likelihood of victory. Such coordination also represents more effective policymaking because the new policies that arise from lawsuits are enforced in several states rather than just one. The cases against the tobacco companies and Microsoft are the most obvious and prominent examples of multistate litigation, but joint lawsuits have also proven enormously effective in consumer protection, including over telemarketers, sweepstakes publishers, and pyramid schemes. In addition to the Microsoft antitrust case, joint lawsuits have proven successful in several other antitrust cases, most notably in a 1998 case in which Cibavision and Johnson & Johnson were forced to settle a case after allegedly conspiring to inflate the price of contact lenses.

There is good reason to believe that SAGs have become more effective in court over time. Considerable research has demonstrated that the federal solicitor general typically wins most of his cases because of the resources available to him, his legal skills as one of the nation's top attorneys, and because of the respect bestowed on the office by the Supreme Court (Boucher and Segal 1995). Analyzing regulation cases at the state supreme court level, Provost (2003) finds that the state wins more often when a representative of the SAG's office argues the case. Thus state supreme courts might hold similar respect for the state's top legal officer as

U.S. Supreme Court justices do for the solicitor general. Such respect was not always evident. In the past SAGs did not have a good reputation in their arguments before the U.S. Supreme Court. In the 1990s the NAAG's Supreme Court Project explicitly assisted SAGs in improving the quality and presentation of their arguments.

Influences on SAG Activities

Provost (2003) has found that SAG partisanship does not influence the filing of amicus briefs and the joining of multistate enforcement actions. Though we might expect partisan differences, it is important to remember that these activities are a critical component of all SAGs' jobs. A majority of SAGs are Democrats, though of course Democratic attitudes toward business regulation vary somewhat across the country. Republican SAGs face a particularly difficult challenge in balancing their role in protecting consumers while adhering more closely to free-market principles that stress more relaxed regulation of businesses.

It is clear that state resources influence what SAGs can do. Having a larger budget allows the SAG to pursue more cases and to regulate more vigorously. SAGs also sometimes supplement their own legal staffs by employing private tort lawyers to assist them—Mississippi SAG Mike Moore did this in his tobacco suit.

Beyond these factors, we do not yet have much evidence about what drives particular SAGs to be more entrepreneurial in social regulation than others.

Reforms

Can and should SAG activism be limited? The increased regulatory activities of SAGs have come under attack from some conservatives, who argue that regulation by litigation usurps the democratic authority of the governor and state legislature, that it is based more on the depth of business pockets than sound analysis, that large cash settlements mainly benefit tort lawyers and SAG political aspirations, and that business advertisers can be punished for even bizarre and suspect interpretations of ads (Beales and Muris 1993; Derthick 2001). Some fear that the tobacco litigation set a dangerous precedent such that manufacturers of alcoholic beverages can be sued for drunk-driving damages and fast-food restaurant owners will next be targeted for suits from those who suffer from obesity or heart disease. Beales and Muris (1993, p. 134) argue that many SAGs employ a "fool's test" approach to consumer interpretations of advertising that the

Federal Trade Commission (FTC) rejected thirty years ago, stating: "Attorneys general are not experts in either antitrust or consumer protection."They are also concerned about "extrajurisdictional effects" like the "California effect," in which activist SAGs in large states like California, New York, and Texas can influence national advertising campaigns with their own concerns about businesses' health and environmental claims. More recently, Hahn argues that SAGs do not really understand the full implications of antitrust policy and that they should defer to experts at the U.S. Department of Justice on cases like Microsoft.[13] As a result, several policymakers and scholars argue that these activities of SAGs need to be limited.

Some compare SAG activism unfavorably to regulatory initiatives by the FTC. Unlike appointed FTC officials, most SAGs are elected, therefore facing incentives to appeal to voters for reelection and for election to higher offices, where name recognition is critical (Beales and Muris 1993). SAGs are most visible when they sue big business and when they reach settlements for large amounts of money. Moreover, FTC regulators include economists, lawyers, physicians, engineers, and other professionals, while SAG staffs are almost exclusively lawyers who tend to take the most litigious approach to problem solving.

The most common broad concern about SAG regulation through litigation is that it usurps traditional democratic authority from governors and state legislatures, especially during the tobacco litigation, as SAGs negotiated the settlements and the contingency lawyer fees with little input from other government actors. For example, after deciding to sue tobacco firms, Mississippi SAG Mike Moore surveyed Mississippi residents about the lawsuit and found public opinion opposed, relying on notions of personal responsibility. Moore therefore decided to file suit in a Mississippi chancery court, a court without a jury.

Still, this concern can be taken too far—forty-three of fifty SAGs are elected and are therefore directly accountable to voters. And if state politicians are truly concerned about SAGs, in most states the legislatures and governors can rein them in with specific statutes and budgetary limits. Despite SAG discretion to initiate lawsuits, "courts have determined that the legislature nevertheless may prescribe changes in the Attorney General's

13. Robert Hahn, "Antitrust Isn't the Concern of the States," AEI/Brookings Joint Center for Regulatory Studies, April 2002 (www.aei-brookings.org/policy [June 2002]).

common law powers" (Ross 1990, p. 22), and in many states this legislative power could be applied both to statutorily and constitutionally prescribed common-law powers. State legislatures could reduce SAG budgets, which might strain relations between branches but would likely reduce the number of cases SAGs could pursue. SAGs are not completely above the checks of separation of powers.

Concerned analysts have proposed other specific reforms. Debow (2001) suggests limiting, if not actually eliminating, contingency fee contracts between SAGs and private tort lawyers. He argues that such contracts are abused, as private lawyers provide collateral up front and then collect enormous fees from states' settlements: "If the state attorney general thinks the state has a valid claim under existing law, why should he not be willing to commit state-appropriated funds and personnel to it?" (p. 13). Four states have adopted measures limiting contingency contracts. While Debow makes a valuable point about private subsidization of government lawsuits, it comes mainly from the tobacco case and may not be representative. Most SAG enforcement activity remains government-financed, while private tort lawyers have been the only ones to file lawsuits against makers of breast implants, handguns, and junk food.

Another reform to reduce activism is for conservatives to support the election of more SAGs who are pro-business and less litigious. This started to happen in 2002 as business groups began to provide substantial funds for the election of Republican SAGs. Still, it only requires a few activist SAGs to bring actions against national firms, and Republican SAGs have been as pleased as Democrats to collect money from large settlements.

In any case, for now the public seems to support the "gap-filling" role of SAGs in our federalist system. Many SAGs will find it irresistible to continue to pursue high-profile cases, particularly if federal regulatory enforcement officials continue to exercise "hands-off" enforcement policies. Since SAGs' powers have not been curtailed substantially by state legislatures, state politicians may not agree with conservative analysts that SAG regulatory activism is a problem worth tackling.

CHAPTER SIXTEEN

The Future of State Regulation

S tate regulation has a very long history, longer—including colonial regulation—than that of the U.S. government itself. However, with surges in federal regulatory activity and some preemption of state responsibilities during the 1880s, 1910s, 1930s, and 1960s, some observers anticipated a greatly reduced role for state regulation. Some believed that perhaps it would eventually fade out completely. Even as devolution of powers back to the states advanced as a general public policy in the last quarter of the twentieth century, a more internationalized economy led many to question the relevance of state regulation for multinational firms.

Still, the states are not going away as regulators; to paraphrase Twain, rumors of their death have been greatly exaggerated. Those who see state regulation as a quaint anachronism in this modern global world will likely be disappointed by its continued life span. In fact, a good argument can be made that state regulation has become relatively more important compared to federal regulation, as the federal government has deregulated more and "de-enforced" in a number of areas. States have gained ground in relative terms, even as the larger arena of regulation has shrunk somewhat.

Conversely, observers such as Thierer (1998), who might expect a massive resurgence of state regulatory authority, one that reshapes the contours of domestic policy, are also likely to be disappointed. The federal government is not going to devolve most of its regulatory power to the states—and indeed, there are many good reasons why not (see, for example, Nivola 2001). And when states are given greater regulatory authority, they are not all going to use it to deregulate or reduce regulation, as some might hope would be a corollary to devolution. In fact, the states now seem to be acting as a partial counterweight to federal efforts to reduce social regulation, offering additional venues for activists to pursue.

Certainly, some forms of state regulation face specific threats from international agreements like those made by the WTO, NAFTA, the EU, and other similar organizations. The EU, for example, is playing a growing centralized role in consumer regulation, often taking more of a precautionary approach than U.S. regulators. NAFTA allows legal challenges to regulations; for example, the Canadian firm Methanex is suing California before a NAFTA dispute panel over methyl tertiary butyl ether gasoline additive restrictions. And WTO service industry agreements create a scenario in which, Walters (2001, p. 26) writes, "Under the new rules . . . it's not out of the question that states might lose control over licensing in a host of professional sectors, from the practice of law to the practice of medicine."

Still, for now state regulation is providing "balance" where some expected further "checks" in our federalist system. It seems reasonable to expect that a similar pattern will hold, even in the face of new supranational regulatory authority. Former governor Mike Leavitt of Utah argues: "This may be one of the great challenges to the American experiment: Can we adapt our version of federalism to accommodate rapidly changing technology and global business practices, and still protect the essence of local control and self-governance?" (quoted in Walters 2001, p. 26).

As state officials recognize these challenges and concerns, they may adopt more interstate compacts or agreements to coordinate their policies to deal with these threats to their authority. Such agreements can help provide the consistency and coordination that businesses prefer, but retain some state flexibility and authority. The National Association of Insurance Commissioners and the multistate work of SAGs provide two such examples. But there are limits to state cooperation as well, especially given real differences across the states in their regulatory goals and preferences and the simple difficulty in coordinating actions among fifty sets of legislatures, governors, bureaucratic agencies, and courts.

More Devolution, Preemption, or Venue Shopping?

The shape that state regulation will take partly depends on federal preemption choices and whether the federal government chooses to become a more, or less, active regulator over time. Will the twenty-five-year-old trends of deregulation and greater oversight over social regulatory enforcement continue, or will the pendulum begin to swing in the other direction? What direction would states go in, as a group, if the federal government returned to being a more active regulator?

For now there is a clear pattern of active states stimulating potential federal regulation that would otherwise not be the first choice of many federal officials and business interests. Another current example of this form of interaction between federal and state regulation, highlighted in chapter 1, is regulation of "predatory" lending. A few state legislatures have recently passed very strong laws prohibiting it, especially in Georgia.[1] This stimulated a strong lobbying push by the financial industry in favor of federal preemption. It remains to be seen if the federal government will become involved in this form of regulation.

In many of these recent cases in which state legislatures or SAGs provide policy leadership that then prompts federal action, business groups strongly support the federal response instead of multiple separate state actions. In the example of financial privacy, Jean Fox of the Consumer Federation of America notes: "As soon as state legislatures start considering bills to protect bank customer privacy, the private sector financial folks started saying maybe we ought to strengthen privacy language in federal law. But the price is that it preempts all state law" (quoted in Gurwitt 2001, p. 22).

In partisan political terms, this trend shows some interesting contradictions. Most generally, conservatives hoped that the combination of federal deregulation and devolution of powers to the states would lead to a greatly reduced regulatory role at both levels. Instead, federal deregulation and reduced social regulatory enforcement created a gap that some state actors have moved to fill. And while conservatives generally applaud the idea of different state and local jurisdictions pursuing different policy approaches, they get quite concerned when one or a few states or local jurisdictions are able to leverage their policies into, in effect, national policies.

On the other hand, from the historical lessons of segregation policies by the states, halted only by federal policy intervention, many liberals

1. According to the Center for Policy Alternatives' website, another seven states have outlawed predatory lending practices, while the national government has not yet actively taken a regulatory position.

retain strong skepticism about state policymaking even in an era when it often seems to their advantage, at least in regulatory policy. Can we expect to see pro-regulatory forces continue to succeed at the state level? In the present environment of economic uncertainty and skepticism, based on Enron, WorldCom, and other corporate accounting and information scandals, public confidence in corporations is at a historically low level. This should foster continued progressive regulatory efforts by at least some state legislatures and SAGs, especially if the federal government does not react strongly to quell public concerns.

It is also reasonable to expect continued state-level countermobilization efforts against these "enemies of business" (Wilson 1990, p. 6) by revitalized business interests. For most firms and industries, their preferred solution would have been to kill these bills in state capitals, prevent initiatives or provide heavy financing against them, or muzzle SAGs, but often these attempts failed. Despite lobbying power, money, and the threat of withdrawal from state economies, businesses cannot always win; this is often true even on regulatory issues where business is unified if other organized groups and the mass public (and hence politicians) also are aware and interested.

Given some continued failures to stop aggressive state regulatory actions, large national and international business will prefer federal intervention over the possibility of balkanized regulations across fifty different states or the possibility of a large and pro-regulatory state like California effectively dictating national standards, as with automobile emissions. This pressure is likely to keep federal regulation from falling below a certain threshold level, even as prominent federal elected officials themselves might favor an ideology of greatly reduced regulations. While not an optimal situation for them, in these circumstances business groups can at least claim a political victory compared to the potential negative situation they faced. At the same time, regulatory activists can also claim success, because they achieved some social regulation and enforcement in an unwelcoming federal climate. Ironically, while states collectively lose some power by forcing the federal government to act to preempt them, states are nevertheless the innovative government player in this interaction. Such leverage makes it more likely that states will continue to assert their initiatives on other regulatory issues.

What are these regulatory issues likely to be? A changing economy and society will force new regulatory questions onto the political agenda. New technologies, in particular, historically have generated new regulatory questions. What role, if any, will the states play in regulating biotechnology, genetically altered foods, cloning activities, Internet privacy, and identity theft? In some of these areas, the greater scientific expertise of the federal government might prove decisive, while in others, states' experiments will test the efficacy and impacts of new regulatory policies. For example, states are already playing a leading role in the protection of Internet privacy.

Unsolved social and economic problems also tend to generate pressure for new regulations in major industries. The FCC voted in mid-2002 to allow greater concentration of media ownership, which may alter the diversity of information many Americans receive, possibly causing a swing in the pendulum. It seems unlikely that the thorny problems of maximizing health care quality and access while containing costs will be solved, especially as the United States watches its aging baby boom population demand greater and more expensive health care interventions. Will these be viewed as national issues, or will the states take a lead in regulation?

The good news is that states continue to take up the role that Justice Brandeis famously ascribed to them: acting as experimental laboratories. This is especially true in social regulation but also in some remaining areas of economic regulation. These state innovations include both policy and institutional experiments. Examples of policy experiments include the case of Illinois, the only state to have no insurance price regulation, New Mexico's 2002 decision to allow psychologists to prescribe medication (which eleven other states are now considering), innovative state environmental implementation plans, North Carolina's pre-OSHA ergonomic repetitive-stress regulations, or several state PUCs' efforts to successfully deregulate electricity or to encourage greater local competition in telecommunications. Sometimes these experiments come more from political expediency than good regulatory policy, and they fail; for example, New Jersey's plan for buying and selling pollution rights was flawed and was abandoned in 2003. But, other times they succeed and are imitated by others. Even when they fail, they provide important information for other states and for national policy.

The presence of continued state institutional differences can be thought of as experiments of a different kind. It is not likely that the federal government is going to start electing regulatory commissioners, even if evidence shows that states with elected commissioners are more favorable to consumer interests. But other states might change their regulatory institutions (and many have done so) based on such evidence. As they are given responsibility to develop more policy solutions, there will be pressure for greater professionalization of state legislatures. And as we have seen, a patchwork of state regulatory choices often leads to pressure for new federal regulatory solutions.

References

Abel, Richard. 1991. *American Lawyers*. Oxford University Press.

Adams, James Ring. 1989. *The Big Fix: Inside the S&L Scandal*. New York: John Wiley and Sons.

Adiel, Ron. 1995. "Reinsurance and the Management of Regulatory Ratios and Taxes in the Property-Casualty Insurance Industry." Working Paper. MIT Sloan School of Management.

Akerlof, George. 1970. "The Market for 'Lemons': Quality Uncertainty and the Market Mechanism." *Quarterly Journal of Economics* 84:488–500.

Akridge, P. 1979. "The Politics of Energy Policy: Regulation of Electric Utility Rate Structure Design by the Public Service Commission of Wisconsin." Ph.D. dissertation, University of Wisconsin.

Alampi, Gary, ed. 1994. *Gale State Rankings*. Washington: Gale Research.

Allison, P. 1984. *Event History Analysis: Regression for Longitudinal Event Data*. Newbury Park, Calif.: Sage.

Almanac of the 50 States. 1999. Washington: Information Publishers.

Alt, James, and Robert Lowry. 1994. "Divided Governments, Fiscal Institutions, and Budget Deficits: Evidence from the States." *American Political Science Review* 88: 811–28.

Alt, James, and Charles Stewart. 1990. "Parties and the Deficit: Some Historical Evidence." Paper prepared for the National Bureau of Economic Research Conference on Political Economics. Boston, February 2–3.

Altman, J. 1997. "The Politics of Electric Utility Regulation: Explaining Energy Efficiency Policy in the States." Ph.D. dissertation, University of Tennessee.

American Bar Association. 1995. *Comprehensive Guide to Bar Admission Requirements, 1995–1996*. Chicago.

American Council of State Savings Supervisors. 1989. *A Profile of State Savings and Loan Supervisory Agencies*. Chicago: U.S. League of Savings Institutions.

Andrews, Clinton. 2000. "Diffusion Pathways for Electricity Deregulation." *Publius* 30:17–34.

Arrandale, Tom. 2002. "The Pollution Puzzle: The Federal Government Isn't Solving It—States Are Giving It a Shot." *Governing* (August): 15:22–26.

Arrow, Kenneth J. 1963. "Uncertainty and the Welfare Economics of Medical Care." *American Economic Review* 53: 941–73.

Atkins, Burton M., and Henry R. Glick. 1976. "Environmental and Structural Variables as Determinants of Issues in State Courts of Last Resort." *American Journal of Political Science* 20:97–115.

Auerbach, Jerold. 1976. *Unequal Justice: Lawyers and Social Change in Modern America*. Oxford University Press.

Bainbridge, Stephen. 2003. "The Creeping Federalization of Corporate Law." *Regulation: The Cato Review of Business and Government* 26 (Spring): 26–31.

Baron, David. 1995. "The Economics and Politics of Regulation: Perspectives, Agendas, and Approaches." In *Modern Political Economy*, edited by Jeffrey Banks and Eric Hanushek, 10–62. Cambridge University Press.

Barth, James. 1991. *The Great Savings and Loan Debacle*. Washington: American Enterprise Institute.

Barth, James, and Michael Bradley. 1988. "Thrift Deregulation and Federal Deposit Insurance." Federal Home Loan Bank Board, Office of Policy and Economic Research.

Bartik, Timothy J. 1991. *Who Benefits from State and Local Economic Development Policies?* Kalamazoo, Mich.: Upjohn Institute.

Baumgartner, Frank, and Bryan Jones. 1993. *Agendas and Instability in American Politics*. University of Chicago Press.

Beales, J. Howard, and Timothy Muris. 1993. *State and Federal Regulation of National Advertising*. Washington: American Enterprise Institute.

Beck, Nathaniel, and Jonathan Katz. 1995. "What to Do (and Not to Do) with Time-Series Cross-Section Data." *American Political Science Review* 89: 634–47.

———. 1996. "Nuisance vs. Substance: Specifying and Estimating Time-Series Cross-Section Models." *Political Analysis* 6: 1–36

Beck, Nathaniel, Jonathan Katz, and Robert Tucker. 1998. "Taking Time Seriously: Time-Series Cross-Section Analysis with a Binary Dependent Variable." *American Journal of Political Science* 42: 1260–88.

Becker, Gary. 1983. "A Theory of Competition among Pressure Groups for Political Influence." *Quarterly Journal of Economics* 96: 371–400.

Begun, James, Edward Crowe, and Roger Feldman. 1981. "Occupational Regulation in the States: A Causal Model." *Journal of Health Politics, Policy, and Law* 6: 229–54.

Bendor, Jonathan. 1988. "Review Article: Formal Models of Bureaucracy." *British Journal of Political Science* 18: 353–95.

Benham, Lee. 1972. "The Effect of Advertising on the Price of Eyeglasses." *Journal of Law and Economics* 15: 330–45.

Benham, Lee, A. Maurizi, and M. Reder. 1968. "Migration, Location, and Remuneration of Medical Personnel: Physicians and Dentists." *Review of Economics and Statistics* 50: 332–47.

Bernstein, Marver. 1955. *Regulating Business by Independent Commission.* Princeton University Press.

Berry, Frances Stokes, and William Berry. 1990. "State Lottery Adoption as Policy Innovation: An Event History Analysis." *American Political Science Review* 84:395–415.

———. 1992. "Tax Innovation in the States: Capitalizing on Political Opportunity." *American Journal of Political Science* 36: 715–42.

Berry, William. 1979. "Utility Regulation in the States: The Policy Effects of Professionalism and Salience to the Consumer." *American Journal of Political Science* 23: 263–77.

———. 1984. "An Alternative to the Capture Theory of Regulation: The Case of State Public Utility Commissions." *American Journal of Political Science* 28: 524–58.

Berry, William D., and others. 1998. "Measuring Citizens and Government Ideology in the American States, 1960–93." *American Journal of Political Science* 42: 327–48.

Besley, Timothy, and Stephen Coates. 2000. "Elected versus Appointed Regulators: Theory and Evidence." Working Paper 7579. Cambridge, Mass.: National Bureau of Economic Research.

Boucher, Robert, and Jeffrey Segal. 1995. "Supreme Court Justices as Strategic Decision Makers." *Journal of Politics* 57: 824–37.

Box-Steffensmeier, Janet, and Bradford Jones. 1997. "Time Is of the Essence: Event History Models in Political Science." *American Journal of Political Science* 41: 1414–61.

Boyes, W., and J. McDowell. 1989. "The Selection of Public Utility Commissioners: An Examination of the Importance of Institutional Setting." *Public Choice* 61: 1–13.

Brace, Paul. 1993. *State Government and Economic Performance.* Johns Hopkins University Press.

Brace, Paul, and Melinda Gann Hall. 1997. "The Interplay of Preferences, Case Facts, Context, and Rules in the Politics of Judicial Choice." *Journal of Politics* 59: 1206–31.

Brace, Paul, Laura Langer, and Melinda Gann Hall. 2000. "Measuring the Preferences of State Supreme Court Justices." *Journal of Politics* 62: 387–413.

Brazier, Margaret, and others. 1993. "Falling from a Tightrope: Doctors and Lawyers between the Market and the State." *Political Studies* 41: 197–213.

Brewton, Pete. 1992. *The Mafia, CIA, and George Bush: The Untold Story of America's Greatest Financial Debacle.* New York: SPI.

Briffault, Richard. 2003. "A Fickle Federalism: The Rehnquist Court Hobbles Congress—and the States, Too." *American Prospect* (June 12): A26–28.

Brock, Gerald. 1994. *Telecommunications Policy for the Information Age.* Harvard University Press.

Broscheid, Andreas, and Paul Teske. 2003. "Public Members on Medical Licensing Boards and the Choice of Entry Barriers." *Public Choice* 114: 445–59.

Brudney, J., and F. Hebert. 1987. "State Agencies and Their Enforcements: Examining the Influence of Important External Actors." *Journal of Politics* 49: 186–206.

Brumbaugh, R. Dan. 1988. *Thrifts under Siege: Restoring Order to American Banking.* Cambridge, Mass.: Ballinger.

Campbell, Heather. 1996. "The Politics of Requesting: Strategic Behavior and Public Utility Regulation." *Journal of Policy Analysis and Management* 15: 395–423.

Canon, Bradley C., and Michael Giles. 1972. "Recurring Litigants: Federal Agencies before the Supreme Court." *Western Political Quarterly* 25: 183–91.

Carpenter, Dan. 2001. *The Forging of Bureaucratic Autonomy.* Princeton University Press.

Cheit, Ross. 1993. "State Adoption of Model Insurance Codes: An Empirical Analysis." *Publius* 23: 49–70.

Chidambaram, N. K., Thomas Pugel, and Anthony Saunders. 1995. "Performance of the U.S. Property-Casualty Insurance Industry." Working Paper S-95-1-7. New York University, Salomon Center.

Clayton, Cornell. 1994. "Law, Politics, and the New Federalism: State Attorneys General as National Policymakers." *Review of Politics* 56: 525–53.

Clingermayer, James C., and B. Dan Wood. 1995. "Disentangling Patterns of State Debt Financing." *American Political Science Review* 89: 108–20.

Coase, Ronald. 1960. "The Problem of Social Cost." *Journal of Law and Economics* 3: 1–31.

Cohen, Jeffrey E. 1992. *The Politics of Telecommunication Regulation.* New York: M. E. Sharpe.

Cole, Barry, ed. 1991. *After the Breakup: Assessing the New Post-AT&T Divestiture Era.* Columbia University Press.

Conerly, Bill. 2003. "Allowing the States to Innovate." *Regulation: The Cato Review of Business and Government* 26 (Spring): 46–52.

Conover, Christopher, and Frank Sloan. 1998. "Does Removing the Certificate-of-Need Regulations Lead to a Surge in Health Care Spending?" *Journal of Health Politics, Policy, and Law* 23: 455–81.

Conradi, Melissa. 2003. "Ten Issues to Watch." *Governing* 16 (January): 32–33.

Cook, Brian. 1989. "Principal-Agent Models of Political Control of Bureaucracy." *American Political Science Review* 83:965–70.

Costello, Kenneth. 1984. "Electing Regulators." *Yale Journal on Regulation* 2: 83–105.

Council of State Governments. 1989–97. *The Book of the States.* Lexington, Ky.

Cummins, J. David, ed. 2002. *Deregulating Property-Liability Insurance: Restoring Competition and Increasing Market Efficiency.* AEI-Brookings Joint Center for Regulatory Studies.

Day, Kathleen. 1993. *S&L Hell: The People and the Politics behind the $1 Trillion Savings and Loan Scandal.* W. W. Norton.

Debow, Michael. 2001. "Restraining State Attorneys General." *Seton Hall Law Review* 31: 11–47.

Declercq, Eugene, and others. 1998. "State Regulation, Payment Policies, and Nurse-Midwife Services." Washington: People-to-People Health Foundation.

Derthick, Martha. 2001. *Up in Smoke: From Legislation to Litigation in Tobacco Politics.* Washington: CQ Press.

Derthick, Martha, and Paul Quirk. 1985. *The Politics of Deregulation.* Brookings.

Dingell, John D. 1990. *Failed Promises: Insurance Company Insolvencies.* Report by the Subcommittee on Oversight and Investigations of the Committee on Energy and Commerce, U.S. House of Representatives. Government Printing Office.

Dionne, Georges, and others. 1997. "Debt, Moral Hazard, and Airline Safety: Empirical Evidence." *Journal of Econometrics* 79: 379–402.

Doherty, Peter. 2001. "Certificates of Need: A Primer on a Program That Needs to Go." *Journal of the James Madison Institute* (Fall): 11–17.

Donahue, John. 1997. *DisUnited States.* Basic Books.

Ehrenhalt, Alan. 2002. "The Monkey or the Gorilla?" *Governing* 15 (June): 6–8.

Eichler, Ned. 1989. *The Thrift Debacle.* University of California Press.

Eisner, Marc. 1993. *Regulatory Politics in Transition.* Johns Hopkins University Press.

Eisner, Marc, and Kenneth Meier. 1990. "Presidential Control versus Bureaucratic Power: Explaining the Reagan Revolution in Antitrust." *American Journal of Political Science* 34: 269–87.

Eisner, Marc, Jeffrey Worsham, and Evan Ringquist. 2000. *Contemporary Regulatory Policy.* Boulder, Colo.: Lynne Rienner.

Emmert, Craig. 1992. "An Integrated Case-Related Model of Judicial Decisionmaking." *Journal of Politics* 54: 543–67.

Engel, Kirsten H. 1997. "State Environmental Standard Setting: Is There a Race and Is It to the Bottom?" *Hastings Law Journal* 48: 271–398.

Erikson, Robert, Gerald Wright, and John McIver. 1993. *Statehouse Democracy: Public Opinion and Policy in the American States.* Cambridge University Press.

Eskridge, William N. 1988. "Politics without Romance: Implications of Public Choice Theory for Statutory Interpretation." *Virginia Law Review* 74: 275–317.

Ethridge, Marcus. 1984. "Consequences of Legislative Review of Agency Regulations in Three U.S. States." *Legislative Studies Quarterly* 9: 161–78.

Fabritius, M. Manfred, and William Borges. 1989. *Saving the Savings and Loan: The U.S. Thrift Industry and the Texas Experience, 1950–1988.* Praeger.

Federation of State Medical Boards of the United States. 1986. *The Exchange 1986: FLEX and M.D. Licensing Requirements. Physician Licensing Boards and Physician Discipline.* Chicago.

———. 1990. *The Exchange 1989–90: FLEX and M.D. Licensing Requirements. Physician Licensing Boards and Physician Discipline.* Chicago.

——— 1993. *The Exchange 1992–3: FLEX and M.D. Licensing Requirements. Physician Licensing Boards and Physician Discipline.* Chicago.

Feldstein, Paul. 1988. *Health Care Economics.* New York: Wiley.

Ferejohn, John, and Barry Weingast. 1997. *The New Federalism: Can the States Be Trusted?* Stanford: Hoover Institute Press.

Ferguson, Margaret Robertson. 2003. "Chief Executive Success in the Legislative Arena." *State Policy and Policy Quarterly* 3 (Summer): 158–82.

Fiorina, Morris. 1992. *Divided Government.* Macmillan.

Ford, Jon M., and David L. Kaserman. 1993. "Certificate-of-Need Regulation and Entry: Evidence from the Dialysis Industry." *Southern Economic Journal* 59: 783–91.

Friedman, Milton. 1962. *Capitalism and Freedom.* University of Chicago Press.

Gabel, Matthew, and Gregory Hager. 2000. "Money for Nothing and Checks for Free: States, Attorneys General, and Tobacco Cases." Paper prepared for the Annual Meeting of the Midwest Political Science Association. Chicago, April 13–15.

Gaumer, Gary L. 1984. "Regulating Health Professionals: A Review of the Empirical Literature." *Health and Society* 62: 380–416.

Gerber, Brian, and Paul Teske. 2000. "Field Essay: Regulatory Policy-Making in the American States: A Review of Theories and Evidence." *Political Research Quarterly* 53: 849–86.

Gill, Jeff. 2001. "Whose Variance Is It, Anyway?" *State Politics and Policy Quarterly* 1: 318–38.

Ginsburg, Paul, and Ernest Moy. 1992. "Physician Licensure and the Quality of Care." *Regulation* 20: 12–24.

Glick, Henry R. 1991. "Policy Making and State Supreme Courts." In *The American Courts: A Critical Assessment,* edited by John B. Gates and Charles A. Johnson, 114–47. Washington: CQ Press.

Gormley, William. 1979. "A Test of Revolving Door Hypothesis at the FCC." *American Journal of Political Science* 23: 665–83.

———. 1981. "Nonelectoral Participation as a Response to Issue-Specific Conditions: The Case of Public Utility Regulation." *Social Science Quarterly* 62: 527–39.

———. 1983. *The Politics of Public Utility Regulation.* University of Pittsburgh Press.

———. 1986. "Regulatory Issue Networks in a Federal System." *Polity* 8: 595–620.

———. 1989. *Taming the Bureaucracy.* Princeton University Press.

Graddy, Elizabeth. 1991. "Interest Groups or the Public Interest—Why Do We Regulate Health Occupations?" *Journal of Health Politics, Policy, and Law* 16: 25–49.

Graddy, Elizabeth, and Michael Nichol. 1990. "Structural Reforms and Licensing Board Performance." *American Politics Quarterly* 18: 376–400.

Graves, Scott, and Paul Teske. 2003. "Perspectives: Explaining State Supreme Court Decisions to Overturn Regulations." *Albany Law Review* (April): 33–41.

Gray, Virginia, and David Lowery. 1995. "Interest Representation and Democratic Gridlock." *Legislative Studies Quarterly* 20: 531–52.

Gray, Virginia, and others. 2003. "Legislative Agendas and Mobilizers of Interest Advocacy: Understanding the Demand-Side of Lobbying in the American States." Paper prepared for the Third Annual Conference on State Politics and Policy. Tucson, March 9–11.

Greenblatt, Alan. 2002a. "Super-Activist: Expanding the Scope of Consumer Protection." *Governing* 16 (November): 22.

———. 2002b. "Where Campaign Money Flows." *Governing* 16 (November): 44–46.

———. 2003a. "The Avengers General." *Governing* 16 (May): 52–56.

———. 2003b. "What Makes ALEC Smart?" *Governing* 17 (October): 30–35.

Greene, William. 1997. *Econometric Analysis.* Englewood Cliffs, N.J.: Prentice-Hall.

Greenstein, Shane, Mercede Lizardo, and Pablo Spiller. 2002. "The Evolution of Large Scale Information Infrastructure in the United States." University of Illinois.

Gross, Stanley. 1984. *Of Foxes and Hen Houses. Licensing and the Health Professions.* Westport, Conn.: Quorum.

Gurwitt, Rob. 2001. "The Riskiest Business." *Governing* 15 (March): 18–24.

Haar, Charles. 1996. *Suburbs under Siege.* Princeton University Press.

Haase, Robert D. 1992. "Federal Regulation Revisited." *Journal of Insurance Regulation* 11 (1): 15–18.

Hagerman, R., and B. Ratchford. 1978. "Some Determinants of Allowed Rates of Return on Equity to Electric Utilities." *Bell Journal of Economics and Management Science* 9:46–55.

Hahn, Robert. 2000. *Reviving Regulatory Reform.* AEI-Brookings Joint Center for Regulatory Studies.

Hall, Bob, and Mary Lee Kerr. 1991. *The Green Index: A State by State Guide to the Nation's Environmental Health.* Washington: Island.

Hammond, Thomas, and Jack Knott. 1988. "The Deregulatory Snowball: Explaining Deregulation in the Financial Industry." *Journal of Politics* 50:3–30.

Hanson, Russell L. 1999. "Intergovernmental Relations." In *Politics in the American States: A Comparative Analysis,* 7th ed., edited by Virginia Gray, Russell L. Hanson, and Herbert Jacob, 32–65. Washington: CQ Press.

Hanssen, F. Andrew. 2000. "Independent Courts and Administrative Agencies: An Empirical Analysis of the States." *Journal of Law, Economics, and Organization* 16: 534–71.

Harrington, David. 2003. "Breathing Life into the Funeral Market." *Regulation* 26 (Spring): 14–18.

Harris, Malcolm, and Peter Navarro. 1983. "Does Electing Public Utility Commissions Bring Lower Electric Rates?" *Pubic Utilities Fortnightly* 112: 23–27.

Heclo, Hugh. 1979. "Issue Networks and the Executive Establishment." In *The New American Political System,* edited by Anthony King, 87–124. Washington: American Enterprise Institute.

Hedge, David. 1998. *Governance and the Changing American States.* Boulder, Colo.: Westview.

Hill, Edward. 1991. "The Savings and Loan Debacle and Erosion of the Dual System of Bank Regulation." *Publius* 21:27–42.

Hollman, Kenneth W., Robert D. Hayes, and E. James Burton. 1993. "Insurance Regulation: Where Do We Go from Here?" *Business Economics* 28 (4): 33–40.

Howard, Robert. 1998. "Attorney Regulation in the States." *Publius* 28:137–59.

Hrebener, Ronald, and Clive Thomas. 1993. *Interest Group Politics in the Northeastern States.* Pennsylvania State University Press.

Humphries, Martha Anne, and Donald R. Songer. 1999. "Law and Politics in Judicial Oversight of Federal Administrative Agencies." *Journal of Politics* 61: 207–20.

Huntington, Samuel. 1952. "The Marasmus of the ICC." *Yale Law Journal* 6: 487–509.

Jensen, Michael, and William Meckling. 1976. "Theory of the Firm: Managerial Behavior, Agency Costs, and Ownership Structure." *Journal of Financial Economics* 3: 305–60.

Jensen, Michael, and Jerold Warner. 1988. "The Distribution of Power among Corporate Managers, Shareholders, and Directors." *Journal of Financial Economics* 20: 3–24.

Joskow, Paul. 1972. "The Determination of the Allowed Rate of Return in a Formal Regulatory Hearing." *Bell Journal of Economics and Management Science* 3: 632–44.

———. 1973. "Cartels, Competition, and Regulation in the Property-Liability Insurance Industry." *Bell Journal of Economics and Management Science* 4: 375–427.

Joskow, Paul, and Roger Noll. 1981. "Regulation in Theory and Practice." In *Studies in Regulation,* edited by Gary Fromm, 1–65. MIT Press.

Ka, Sangjoon, and Paul Teske. 2002. "Ideology and Professionalism: Electricity Regulation over Time in the American States." *American Politics Research* 30: 323–43.

Kane, Edward. 1989. *The S&L Mess: How Did It Happen?* Washington: Urban Institute.

Kellough, J. Edward, and Sally Coleman Selden. 2003. "The Reinvention of Public Personnel Administration: An Analysis of the Diffusion of Personnel Management Reforms in the States." *Public Administration Review* 63: 165–76.

Kettl, Donald. 2002. "Sacramento Rules." *Governing* 16 (December): 14.

Khademian, Anne. 1996. *Checking on Banks.* Brookings.

King, Gary. 1989. "Variance Specification in Event Count Models: From Restrictive Assumptions to a Generalized Estimator." *American Journal of Political Science* 33: 762–84.

Klein, Robert W. 1995. "Insurance Regulation in Transition: Structural Change and Regulatory Response in the Insurance Industry." Working Paper. Kansas City: Mo.: National Association of Insurance Commissioners.

Klein, Robert, W. Nordman, and J. Fritz. 1993. "Market Conditions in Workers' Compensation Insurance." Interim report, NAIC Workers' Compensation (D) Task Force. Kansas City, Mo.

Kleiner, Morris. 2000. "Occupational Licensure." *Journal of Economic Perspectives* 14: 189–202.

Kline, Kurt. 2003. "Influences on Intergovernmental Implementation: The States and the Superfund." *State Politics and Policy Quarterly* 3: 66–83.

Kroszner, Randall, and Philip Strahan. 1999. "What Drives Deregulation?" *Quarterly Journal of Economics* 54: 1437–67.

Langer, Laura. 2002. *Judicial Review in State Supreme Courts: A Comparative Study.* State University of New York Press.

Laumann, Julie, and Paul Teske. 2003. "Principals, Agents, and Regulatory Federalism in the Savings and Loan Crisis of the 1980s." *State Politics and Policy Quarterly* 3: 139–57.

Leffler, Keith. 1978. "Physician Licensure: Competition and Monopoly in American Medicine." *Journal of Law and Economics* 21: 165–86.

Lester, James, and others. 1983. "Hazardous Waste Politics and Public Policy: A Comparative State Analysis." *Western Political Quarterly* 36: 258–85.

Lewis-Beck, Michael, and John Alford. 1980. "Can Government Regulate Safety? The Coal Mine Example." *American Political Science Review* 74: 745–56.

Litan, Robert. 1991. "Comment on Romer and Weingast's Political Foundations of the Thrift Debacle." In *Politics and Economics in the Eighties,* edited by Alberto Alesina and Geoffrey Carliner. University of Chicago Press.

Lotstein, Robert. 1997. "The Patchwork of State Regulation." *Mortgage Banking* (January): 69–76.

Lowry, William R. 1992. *The Dimensions of Federalism: State Governments and Pollution Control Policies.* Duke University Press.

Lowy, Martin. 1991. *High Rollers: Inside the Savings and Loan Debacle.* Praeger.

Lyons, William, and Patricia Freeman. 1984. "Sunset Legislation and the Legislative Process in Tennessee." *Legislative Studies Quarterly* 9: 151–59.

Macey, Jonathan R. 1986. "Promoting Public-Regarding Legislation through Statutory Interpretation: An Interest Group Model." *Columbia Law Review* 223: 599–629.

Maestas, Cherie, Brian Gerber, and Nelson Dometrius. 2003. "Assessing the Effects of LARRI: Legislative Authority to Review Rules as a "Flexible" Ex Ante Control over Agency Decision-Making." Paper prepared for the Third Annual Conference on State Politics and Policy. Tucson, March 9–11.

March, James, and Johan Olsen. 1989. *Rediscovering Institutions.* Free Press.

Marvel, Mary. 1982. "Implementation and Safety Regulation: Variations in Federal and State Administration under OSHA." *Administration and Society* 14: 15–33.

Mayer, Martin. 1996. *The Bankers: The Next Generation.* New York: Truman Talley.

Mayhew, David. 1991. *Divided We Govern: Party Control, Lawmaking, and Investigations, 1946–1990.* Yale University Press.

McCraw, Thomas. 1984. *Prophets of Regulation.* Harvard University Press.

McCubbins, Matthew, and Thomas Schwartz. 1984. "Congressional Oversight Overlooked: Police Patrols versus Fire Alarms." *American Journal of Political Science* 28: 165–79.

Meier, Kenneth. 1987. "The Political Economy of Consumer Protection: An Examination of State Legislation." *Western Political Quarterly* 40: 343–59.

———. 1988. *The Political Economy of Regulation: The Case of Insurance*. State University of New York Press.

Meier, Kenneth, Robert Wrinkle, and J. L. Polinard. 1995. "Politics, Bureaucracy, and Agricultural Policy: An Alternative View of Political Control." *American Politics Quarterly* 23 (4): 427–60.

Melnick, R. Shep. 1983. *Regulation and the Courts: The Case of the Clean Air Act*. Brookings.

Michener, Ron, and Carla Tighe. 1992. "A Poisson Regression Model of Highway Fatalities." *American Economic Association Papers and Proceedings* 82 (2): 452–56.

Miles, Robert, and Vinrod Bhambri. 1983. *The Regulatory Executives*. Beverly Hills: Sage.

Miller, Gary. 1992. *Managerial Dilemmas*. Cambridge University Press.

Mitnick, Barry. 1980. *The Political Economy of Regulation*. Columbia University Press.

Moe, Terry. 1982. "Regulatory Performance and Presidential Administration." *American Journal of Political Science* 26: 197–229.

———. 1984. "The New Economics of Organization." *American Journal of Political Science* 28: 739–77.

———. 1985. "Control and Feedback in Economic Regulation: The Case of the NLRB." *American Political Science Review* 79: 1094–116.

———. 1989. "The Politics of Bureaucratic Structure." In *Can the Government Govern?* edited by John Chubb and Paul Peterson, 267–329. Brookings.

Mooney, Chris. 1994. "Measuring U.S. State Legislative Professionalism: An Evaluation of Five Indices." *State and Local Government Review* 26: 70–78.

Mooney, Chris, and M. H. Lee. 1995. "Legislative Morality in the American States: The Case of Pre-Roe Abortion Regulation Reform." *American Journal of Political Science* 39: 599–627.

Morandi, Larry. 1994. "Groundwater Protection Legislation: Survey of State Actions, 1988–1992." Denver: National Conference of State Legislatures.

Morris, Thomas. 1987. "States before the U.S. Supreme Court." *Judicature* 70: 298–326.

Mueller, Milton. 1997. *Universal Service: Competition, Interconnection, and Monopoly in the Making of the American Telephone System*. MIT Press.

Mullen, Paul. 2000. "The Decision to Prosecute as a Policy Process: State Attorneys General and Organizational Politics." *Law and Courts* 15: 9–11.

Munch, Patricia, and Dennis Smallwood. 1980. "Solvency Regulation in the Property-Liability Insurance Industry: Empirical Evidence." *Bell Journal of Economics and Management Science* 9: 261–79.

Murphy, M. Maureen. 1989. "Powers of Federally Chartered Thrifts Compared with Those of the Various States." Congressional Research Service, Library of Congress.

Nathan, Richard. 1996. "The Role of the States in American Federalism." In *The State of the States*, 3d ed., edited by Carl Van Horn. Washington: CQ Press.

Nivola, Pietro S. 2001. "Does Federalism Have a Future?" *Public Interest* 142: 44–60.

Nordlinger, Eric. 1981. *On the Autonomy of the Democratic State.* Harvard University Press.

Nyman, John. 1994. "The Effects of Market Concentration and Excess Demand on the Price of Nursing Home Care." *Journal of Industrial Economics* 42 (2): 193–204.

Olson, Mancur. 1965. *The Logic of Collective Action.* Harvard University Press.

Osborne, David, and Ted Gaebler. 1992. *Reinventing Government.* Boston: Addison-Wesley.

Peltzman, Sam. 1976. "Toward a More General Theory of Regulation." *Journal of Law and Economics* 19: 211–40.

———. 1989. "The Economic Theory of Regulation after a Decade of Deregulation." *Brookings Papers on Microeconomics.*

Penniman, Nick. 2002. "Outing ALEC: The Most Powerful Lobby You've Never Heard Of." *American Prospect* (July 1): 12–13.

Pertschuk, Michael. 1982. *Revolt against Regulation: The Rise and Pause of the Consumer Movement.* University of California Press.

Petersen, John. 2002. "States and the Markets." *Governing* 15 (April): 58.

Peterson, Paul, and Mark Rom. 1990. *Welfare Magnets.* Brookings.

Pilzer, Paul Zane, and Robert Dietz. 1989. *Other People's Money: The Inside Story of the S&L Mess.* Simon and Schuster.

Pommeroy, Earl R. 1992. "State or Federal Regulation: Politics, Players, Prospects." *Journal of Insurance Regulation* 11 (1): 5–18.

Posner, Richard. 1997. "Legal Formalism, Legal Realism, and the Interpretation of Statutes and the Constitution." In *Public Choice and Public Law,* edited by Maxwell L. Sterns, 66–98. Cincinnati: Anderson.

Potoski, Matthew. 2001. "Clean Air Federalism: Do States Race to the Bottom?" *Public Administration Review* 61: 335–42.

Pratt, John, and Richard Zeckhauser. 1985. "Principals and Agents: An Overview." In *Principals and Agents: The Structure of Business,* edited by John Pratt and Richard Zeckhauser, 1–37. Harvard Business School Press.

Primeaux, Walter, and P. Mann. 1985. "Voter Power and Electricity Prices." *Public Choice* 47: 519–25.

Provost, Colin. 2003. "Litigation and the Electoral Connection: The Policy Making of Ambitious State Attorneys General." Ph.D. dissertation, Stony Brook University.

Rabe, Barry. 1986. *Fragmentation and Integration in State Environmental Management.* Washington: Conservation Foundation.

———. 2002. *Greenhouse and Statehouse: The Evolving State Role in Climate Change.* Arlington, Va.: Pew Center on Global Climate Change.

Rawls, John. 1971. *A Theory of Justice.* Harvard University Press.

Renzulli, Diane, and the Center for Public Integrity. 2002. *Capitol Offenders: How Private Interests Govern Our States.* Washington: Center for Public Integrity.

Rhode, Deborah. 1994. "Institutionalizing Ethics." *Case Western Reserve Law Review* (Winter): 665–76.

Ringquist, Evan. 1993a. "Does Regulation Matter? Evaluating the Effects of State Air Pollution Programs." *Journal of Politics* 55:1022–45.

———. 1993b. *Environmental Protection at the State Level: Politics and Progress in Controlling Pollution.* Armonk, N.Y.: M. E. Sharpe.

Ringquist, Evan, and James Garand. 1999. "Policy Change in the American States." In *American State and Local Politics,* edited by R. Weber and P. Brace, 268–99. New York: Chatham House.

Rom, Mark Carl. 1996. *Public Spirit in the Thrift Tragedy.* University of Pittsburgh Press.

Romano, Roberta. 1997. "State Competition for Corporate Charters." In *The New Federalism: Can the States Be Trusted?* edited by John Ferejohn and Barry Weingast, 129–56. Stanford: Hoover Institute Press.

Romer, Thomas, and Barry Weingast. 1991. "Political Foundations of the Thrift Debacle." In *Politics and Economics in the Eighties,* edited by Alberto Alesina and Geoffrey Carliner, 67–93. University of Chicago Press.

Rose, Nancy. 1989. "The Economic Theory of Regulation: Comments." *Brookings Papers on Microeconomics.*

Rosenthal, Alan. 1993. *The Third House: Lobbying and Lobbyists in the States.* Washington: CQ Press.

Ross, Lynn, ed. 1990. "State Attorneys General: Powers and Responsibilities." Washington: National Association of Attorneys General.

Rubin, Stephen. 1980. "The Legal Web of Professional Regulation." In *Regulating the Professions: A Public-Policy Symposium,* edited by Roger Blair and Stephen Rubin, 29–60. Lexington, Mass.: Lexington Books.

Ruhil, Ani, and Paul Teske. 2003. "Institutions, Bureaucratic Decisions, and Policy Outcomes: State Insurance Solvency Regulation." *Policy Studies Journal* 31: 353–71.

Sabatier, Paul, and Hank Jenkins-Smith, eds. 1993. *Policy Change and Learning: An Advocacy Coalitions Approach.* Boulder, Colo.: Westview.

Schneider, Mark, Paul E. Teske, and Michael Mintrom. 1995. *Public Entrepreneurs: Agents for Change in American Government.* Princeton University Press.

Scholz, John. 1981. "State Regulatory Reform and Federal Regulation." *Policy Studies Review* 1: 347–59.

Scholz, John, and Feng Heng Wei. 1986. "Regulatory Enforcement in a Federalist System." *American Political Science Review* 80: 1249–70.

Segal, Jeffrey A., and Harold J. Spaeth. 1993. *The Supreme Court and the Attitudinal Model.* Cambridge University Press.

Sheehan, Reginald S., William Mishler, and Donald R. Songer. 1992. "Ideology, Status, and the Differential Success of Direct Parties before the Supreme Court." *American Political Science Review* 86: 464–71.

Shepsle, Kenneth. 1979. "Institutional Arrangements and Equilibrium in Multidimensional Voting Models." *American Journal of Political Science* 23: 27–59.

———. 1982. "Review of Wilson's *Politics of Regulation.*" *Public Choice* 13: 80–83.

Shryock, Richard. 1967. *Medical Licensing in America, 1650–1965.* Johns Hopkins University Press.

Skalaban, Andrew. 1992. "Interstate Competition and State Strategies to Deregulate Interstate Banking, 1982–88." *Journal of Politics* 54: 793–809.

Sloan, Frank. 1981. "Regulation and the Rising Cost of Hospital Care." *Review of Economics and Statistics* 63: 479–87.

Smith, Mark. 2000. *American Business and Political Power.* University of Chicago Press.

Songer, Donald R., and Reginald S. Sheehan. 1992. "Who Wins on Appeal? Upperdogs and Underdogs in the United States Courts of Appeals." *American Journal of Political Science* 36: 235–58.

Spill, Rorie, Michael Licari, and Leonard Ray. 2001. "Taking on Tobacco: Policy Entrepreneurship and the Tobacco Litigation." *Political Research Quarterly* 54: 605–22.

Squire, Peverill. 1992. "Legislative Professionalization and Membership Diversity in State Legislatures." *Legislative Studies Quarterly* 17: 69–79.

Starr, Paul. 1982. *The Social Transformation of American Medicine.* Basic Books.

Stewart, Joseph, and Thomas Clark. 1996. "Regulating Occupations." In *Regulation and Consumer Protection,* edited by Kenneth Meier and E. Garman, 41–72. Houston: Dame.

Stigler, George. 1971. "The Theory of Economic Regulation." *Bell Journal of Economics and Management Science* 2: 3–21.

Stimson, James. 1985. "Regression in Space and Time: A Statistical Essay." *American Journal of Political Science* 29: 914–47.

———. 1991. *Public Opinion in America: Moods, Cycles, and Swings.* Boulder, Colo.: Westview.

Strunk, Norman, and Fred Case. 1988. *Where Deregulation Went Wrong: A Look at the Causes behind Savings and Loan Failures in the 1980s.* Chicago: United States League of Savings Institutions.

Stumpf, Harry. 1998. *American Judicial Politics.* Upper Saddle River, N.J.: Prentice-Hall.

Svorny, Shirley, and Eugenia Toma. 1998. "The Influence of Board Funding on Regulatory Outcomes." *Public Choice* 97: 93–106.

Swire, Peter. 1996. "The Race to Laxity and the Race to Undesirability: Explaining Failures in Competition among Jurisdictions in Environmental Law." *Yale Law and Policy Review/Yale Journal on Regulation* 16: 112–56.

Tabachnik, L. 1976. "Licensing in the Legal and Medical Professions, 1820–1860: A Historical Case Study." In *Professions for the People,* edited by J. Gerstl and G. Jacobs. New York: Schenkman.

Teaford, Jon. 2002. *The Rise of the States: Evolution of American State Government.* Johns Hopkins University Press.

Temin, Peter, and Louis Galambos. 1987. *The Fall of the Bell System.* Cambridge University Press.

Teske, Paul. 1990. *After Divestiture: The Political Economy of State Telecommunications Regulation.* State University of New York Press.

———. 1991. "Interests and Institutions in State Regulation." *American Journal of Political Science* 35:139–54.

———. 1995. *American Regulatory Federalism and Telecommunications Infrastructure.* Hillsdale, N.J.: Lawrence Erlbaum Associates.

Teske, Paul, Samuel Best, and Michael Mintrom. 1995. *Deregulating Freight Transportation: Delivering the Goods.* Washington: American Enterprise Institute.

Thierer, Adam. 1998. *The Delicate Balance: Federalism, Interstate Commerce, and Economic Freedom in the Information Age.* Washington: Heritage Foundation.

Thomas, Clive, and Ronald Hrebenar. 1999. "Interest Groups in the States." In *Politics in the American States: A Comparative Analysis,* 7th ed., edited by Virginia Gray, Russell L. Hanson, and Herbert Jacob. Washington: CQ Press.

Thompson, Frank, and Michael Scicchitano. 1985. "State Implementation Effort and Federal Regulatory Policy: The Case of Occupational Safety and Health." *Journal of Politics* 47: 686–703.

Tulloch, Gordon. 1980. "Efficient Rent Seeking." In *Toward a Theory of the Rent Seeking Society,* edited by James Buchanan, 39–59. Texas A&M University Press.

U.S. Bureau of the Census. 1995. *Money Income in the United States.* Government Printing Office.

U.S. Environmental Protection Agency. 1998. *National Air Quality and Emissions Trends Report.* Research Triangle Park, N.C.

Viscusi, W. Kip. 1993. *Product-Risk Labeling: A Federal Responsibility.* Washington: American Enterprise Institute.

———, ed. 2002. *Regulation through Litigation.* Brookings.

Vogel, David. 1995. *Trading Up: Consumer and Environmental Regulation and International Trade.* Basic Books.

Waldman, Michael. 1990. *Who Robbed America? A Citizen's Guide to the Savings and Loan Scandal.* Random House.

Walker, Jack. 1969. "The Diffusion of Innovations among the American States." *American Political Science Review* 63: 880–99.

Walters, Jonathan. 2001. "Save Us from the States." *Governing* 14 (June): 20–27.

———. 2002a. "Leaving It to the Court." *Governing* 15 (September): 14–16.

———. 2002b. "The Snoozing Watchdogs." *Governing* 15 (March): 10.

Waterman, Richard. 1989. *Presidential Influence and the Administrative State.* University of Tennessee Press.

Waterman, Richard, and Kenneth Meier. 1998. "Principal-Agent Models: An Expansion?" *Journal of Public Administration Research and Theory* 8: 173–202.

Weingast, Barry R. 1980. "Physicians, DNA Research Scientists, and the Market for Lemons." In *Regulating the Professions: A Public-Policy Symposium,* edited by Roger Blair and Stephen Rubin, 81–96. Lexington, Mass.: Lexington Books.

Weingast, Barry R., and Mark Moran. 1984. "Bureaucratic Discretion or Congressional Control." *Journal of Political Economy* 91: 765–800.

Weissert, Carol, and Jeffrey Hill. 2001. "Federal Influence over State Policy Decisions: Modeling State Responses to Welfare Reform Surpluses." Paper prepared for the State of the States Conference. Texas A&M University, March 2–3.

Weissert, Carol, and William Weissert. 1996. *Governing Health: The Politics of Health Policy.* Johns Hopkins University Press.

Wenzel, James, Shawn Bowler, and David Lanoue. 1997. "Legislating from the Bench." *American Politics Quarterly* 25: 363–79.

White, Lawrence. 1991. *The S&L Debacle.* Oxford University Press.

———. 1995. "The NAIC Model Investment Law: A Missed Opportunity." Working Paper S-95-18. New York University, Salomon Center.

Wilson, Graham. 1990. *Business and Government.* Chatham, N.J.: Chatham House.

Wilson, James Q. 1980. *The Politics of Regulation.* Basic Books.

———. 1989. *Bureaucracy: What Government Agencies Do and Why They Do It.* Basic Books.

Winston, Clifford, and Robert Crandall. 1994. "Explaining Regulatory Policy." *Brookings Papers on Microeconomics.*

Wood, B. Dan. 1989. "Principal-Agent Models of Political Control of Bureaucracy." *American Political Science Review* 83: 970–78.

Wood, B. Dan, and Richard W. Waterman. 1991. "The Dynamics of Political Control of Bureaucracy." *American Political Science Review* 85: 801–28.

———. 1993. "The Dynamics of Political Bureaucratic Adaptation." *American Journal of Political Science* 37: 497–528.

Woolley, John. 1993. "Conflict among Regulators and the Hypothesis of Congressional Dominance." *Journal of Politics* 55: 92–113.

Worsham, Jeff, Marc Eisner, and Evan Ringquist. 1997. "Assessing the Assumptions: A Critical Analysis of Agency Theory." *Administration and Society* 28: 419–40.

Yandle, Bruce. 1983. "Bootleggers and Baptists: The Education of a Regulatory Economist." *Regulation Journal* 7: 14–24.

———. 2001. "Bootleggers, Baptists, and Global Warming." In *The Greening of U.S. Foreign Policy,* edited by Terry L. Anderson and Henry Miller. Stanford: Hoover Institute Press.

Young, S. David. 1987. *The Rule of Experts.* Washington: Cato Institute.

Zhou, Xueguang. 1993. "Occupational Power, State Capabilities, and the Diffusion of Licensing in the American States: 1890 to 1950." *American Sociological Review* 58: 536–57.

Zimmerman, Joseph. 1998. "Interstate Cooperation: The Roles of the State Attorneys General." *Publius* 28: 71–89.

Zorn, Christopher. 2001. "A (Very) Simple Model of Government Appeals." Working Paper. Emory University.

Index

Printed in the USA
CPSIA information can be obtained
at www.ICGtesting.com
LVHW040828050124
768064LV00001B/94